The Crane Wife

'*The Crane Wife* is brilliantly idiosyncratic... ...beautiful and strange, full of seemingly random collections of cultural references and stories from Hauser's past – things that seem like they won't make sense together, until they do. The collection, written in Hauser's very immediate voice, traverses broad subject matter, including family, breakups and home ownership' *Independent*

'Hauser builds life's inventory out of deconstructed personal narratives, resulting in a reading experience that's rich like a complicated dessert – not for wolfing down but for savouring in small bites . . . A delightfully wide assortment of literary and cultural digressions enriches Hauser's musings, making their book a lot of fun in a brainy, melancholic way . . . An intellectually vigorous and emotionally resonant account of how a self gets created over time, *The Crane Wife* will satisfy and inspire anyone who has ever asked, "How did I get here, and what happens now?"' *New York Times Book Review*

'While it's always difficult to summarize an essay collection, what holds *The Crane Wife* together is Hauser's unpacking of emotional truths: who do we love, and why, and what happens when they're gone? When we're alone? When we forget what it was like to love them?' Lit Hub

'Hauser considers love in all its forms and how it shows up in families – both biological and logical – friendship, queerness and in fleeting moments between strangers. *The Crane Wife* will make you think, laugh, cry and keep turning the pages' *Red*

'In *The Crane Wife*, Hauser undertakes a new way to tell stories, playing with history and personal history, exploring the possible hidden truths in their family's past and their own. The result is like interconnected short stories but about their life, the person they are and were, maybe even the person they never knew themselves to be' Alexander Chee, author of *The Queen of the Night* and *How to Write an Autobiographical Novel*

'Thoughtful and fitfully funny . . . Across seventeen confessional essays, we find [CJ] furtively spreading their grandparents' ashes at their old house in Martha's Vineyard, reflecting on their relationships with a high-school boyfriend and a divorcee who is clearly still in love with his ex' *Guardian*, Best Memoirs of 2022

'A frank exploration of intimacy and romance that doesn't always lead to a "happily ever after". . . Hauser is a playful, energetic and always likeable writer . . . I kept thinking about all of the people in my life into whose hands I can't wait to put *The Crane Wife*' *Washington Post*

'Hauser is refreshingly candid and self-aware. They're unafraid to get into the hard stuff – and it's that vulnerability that makes their writing so accessible' *Time*, 100 Must-Read Books of 2022

'Funny and tender' *Sun*

'After reading this memoir in essays by the warm, wise, wry and wonderful CJ Hauser, author of the viral *Paris Review* essay "The Crane Wife", you'll have to go fix your face. Were you crying laughing or just crying? Both? Splash some cold water on your cheeks. That's it. Now, go forth in peace with a new understanding of what it means to live and love' *Garden & Gun*, Best Southern Books of 2022

'A deeply personal and vivacious memoir . . . eye-wateringly funny . . . [and] intensely introspective as they focus on what they are looking for and what they feel is missing' *Irish Examiner*

'Compassionate and funny and brave. The book is a masterclass in life writing, and a lesson in how to live a life outside the narratives that would contain us. CJ is a master story weaver. I was left wanting more, in the best way possible' Charlie Gilmour, author of *Featherhood*

'In this perceptive and probing work, Hauser brilliantly parses the myths that shaped their understanding of love . . . Sparkling . . . A thrillingly original deconstruction of desire and its many configurations' *Publishers Weekly*, starred review

'Sometimes a viral essay is just a viral essay. Other times, as with Hauser's story of breaking off their engagement (written for the *Paris Review*), a piece that spoke to millions will lead to something bigger – in this case, an absorbing memoir in essays' *New York Times Book Review*, Editors' Pick

'Intimate, wry, compassionate, filled with imaginative connections drawn between art and life. Reading it feels like talking to an unusually articulate and well-read friend . . . Hauser has a gift for spinning stories from their life and unpretentiously interpreting them through the prism of art. They have written a book that proves their viral success was no flash in the pan, a book you want to press into friends' hands. Invigorating, vulnerable, generous, it is a liberation'
Irish Mail on Sunday

'Wise, funny and oh-so true about dating' *i*

'Stunning and interrogative . . . Brilliant . . . Calling Hauser "honest" and "vulnerable" feels inadequate. They embrace and even celebrate their flaws, and they revel in being a provocateur . . . Much has been written on the themes Hauser excavates here, yet their perspective is singular, startlingly so. Many narratives still position finding the perfect match as a measure of whether we've led successful lives. *The Crane Wife* dispenses with that. For that reason, Hauser's world view feels fresh and even radical'
Oprah Daily

'Intimate, all-too-relatable magic. Hauser writes like they're whispering hard-earned secrets to a friend, picking apart how they have been held hostage to their own fantasies about love and happiness in warm and vulnerable scenes . . . What a gift it is to have the curtains lift and let us all in' Electric Lit

'If you ever ask yourself why you fell for, left, stayed too long, chose badly, questioned your instinct, then this blazingly clever memoir will be a revelation . . . this is a near-genius look at the search for love' *Sainsbury's Magazine*

'As Hauser grapples with the changing shape of their life story, it's fitting that the shape of each essay and, indeed, the shape of the collection itself, are self-consciously experimental in form . . . Reading *The Crane Wife* is a bit like following Hauser into the Mirror Maze, their voice as narrator guiding the way through and out. Whether writing about familial or cultural stories, each text becomes a mirror in which Hauser sees their own self reflected back. And in their willingness to turn inward, to truly face their own self, Hauser's essays open outward, becoming themselves mirrors into which readers might gaze' *Ploughshares*

'Smart, poignant stories . . . all threaded with snort-out-loud wisdom' *Grazia*

THE
CRANE WIFE

| A MEMOIR IN ESSAYS |

CJ HAUSER

PENGUIN BOOKS

PENGUIN BOOKS

UK | USA | Canada | Ireland | Australia
India | New Zealand | South Africa

Penguin Books is part of the Penguin Random House group of companies
whose addresses can be found at global.penguinrandomhouse.com.

First published in the United States of America by Doubleday 2022
First published in Great Britain by Viking 2022
Published in Penguin Books 2023

001

Grateful acknowledgement is made to New Directions Publishing Corp. for permission to
reprint an excerpt from "Tell Them No" from *Be With* by Forrest Gander, copyright © 1995,
2010, 2012, 2013, 2015, 2017, 2018 by Forrest Gander. Excerpt from "The Ivy Crown" from *The
Collected Poems: Volume II, 1939 – 1962* by William Carlos Williams, copyright © 1953 by
William Carlos Williams. Reprinted by permission of New Directions Publishing Corp.

Several pieces originally appeared in the following publications:
Electric Literature: "The Man Behind the Curtain" (December 12, 2019)
The Guardian: "This Is Small Talk Purgatory: What Tinder Taught
Me about Love" (December 7, 2019)
Lit Hub: "My Niece Is Probably the Reincarnation of Shirley Jackson: CJ Hauser
on Motherhood and *The Haunting of Hill House*" (July 2019)
The Paris Review: "The Crane Wife" (July 2019);
"The Second Mrs. de Winter" (October 13, 2020)
Slice Magazine: "The Mechanicals" (Winter 2014)
Tin House: "Blood: Twenty-six Love Stories from Life" (Winter 2016)

Printed and bound in Great Britain by Clays Ltd, Elcograf S.p.A.

The authorized representative in the EEA is Penguin Random House Ireland,
Morrison Chambers, 32 Nassau Street, Dublin D02 YH68

A CIP catalogue record for this book is available from the British Library

ISBN: 978-0-241-50378-2

www.greenpenguin.co.uk

in gratitude for

the family we are given
the families we are choosing
& ideas of home with room enough for both

Stumbling again
dumbly
home into the
line of my
own questioning.

—FORREST GANDER, "TELL THEM NO"

CONTENTS

III

IV

» *For readers who would like content warnings,*
an annotated Table of Contents appears on page 307

– I –

. . . *sometimes not even our mouths belong to us. Listen, in*
the early 1920s, women were paid to paint radium
onto watch dials so that men wouldn't have to ask

the time in dark alleys. They were told it was safe,
told to lick their brushes into sharp points. These
women painted their nails, their faces, and judged

whose skin shined brightest. They coated their
teeth so their boyfriends could see their bites
with the lights turned down. The miracle here

is not that these women swallowed light. It's that,
when their skin dissolved and their jaws fell off,
the Radium Corporation claimed they all died

from syphilis. It's that you're telling me about
the dull slivers of dead saints, while these
women are glowing beneath our feet.

—PAIGE LEWIS, "THE MOMENT I SAW A PELICAN DEVOUR"

Blood

I | PUT YOUR BOOTS ON, 1918

Cap Joyce was a cowboy who ran an Arizona dude ranch called the Spur Cross because acting like a cowboy, for tourists, was more lucrative than the actual herding of cattle. He had a trick horse named Patches that could bow, roll over, and nod the answers to math questions. Sometimes Cap stood on Patches's back and played guitar. Then the Great War came. He sold Patches and left his wife in charge of the ranch and went off to fight in France, where he was mustard-gassed, but survived, and was heavily be-medaled for the trouble. He was my great-grandfather.

Cap had been home a week when the ranch hands took him aside and said that his wife had been carrying on with the foreman. They wouldn't have mentioned it, the ranch hands said, except they didn't seem to be stopping.

Cap said, "Where is he?"

Cap went to the bunks. The foreman was dressing.

"You fuck my wife?" Cap said.

The man froze. "Yes," he said.

Cap said, "Put your boots on."

The foreman put on his boots.

Cap shot him dead. He did not bleed much, they say.

II | UNION MAID, 1984

My first kiss was a communist. His name was Jack. He was part of a kids' playgroup in New York City. All the mothers were part of the International Ladies' Garment Workers' Union except for mine. Her involvement remains a mystery.

In the playgroup, the babies crawled over the carpet and the mothers shared pots of coffee and by and large the babies were naked and if they were not naked they were wearing overalls. Good communist babies wear overalls.

Here are some of the things that I wore: a tiny pair of lederhosen (Germany), a real silk kimono with a red bird stitched on the breast (Japan), a rabbit-fur coat with wood fasteners (Russia). My grandparents had been traveling and always sent me, the first grandchild, souvenirs.

There is a picture of this first kiss. Jack, in overalls, is on hands and knees, long black hair in ringlets. I am practically bald, bending toward him, hands planted on the rug. I am wearing a pink velveteen jacket (Paris).

A week later the union ladies said: "You can't keep coming if you dress her like that." The week after, my mother brought me to the group in the rabbit-fur coat, not thinking the union ladies were serious. They were.

III | THE LAND OFFICE, 1921

When Cap got out of prison he went to the land office with a mind to start a new ranch in Wyoming. There was a woman at the front desk, a secretary. Her name was Robbie Baker.

"Can I help you?" she said.

"I'm going to marry you," Cap said. "And I need some land."

That was my great-grandmother.

IV | BEESTING, 1989

Brian Katrumbus could run faster than any boy in kindergarten and had hair like corn silk. It was Valentine's Day. A week earlier, when I'd been stung by a bee while daydreaming out the window and then cried quietly, not knowing what to do, it was *Brian Katrumbus* who told the teacher that something was wrong with me. He poked the teacher and said, "Something is wrong with her."

I'd picked out a very special valentine for Brian Katrumbus. I wore a Band-Aid over my small wound the day I watched him open his envelopes, waiting to see how he would receive my card. But Brian Katrumbus had a system. He ripped open each envelope, and then shook it, so whatever candy was inside tumbled out onto his carpet square.

Then he tossed the valentine away. Like shucking peas.

V | TRADES, 1932

Cap and Robbie married. They spent the Depression living out of a car with their two sons. One of these sons was my grandfather Eddie. Cap drove across the country, trading with

Native peoples. He offered ad space for their "trading posts" in his "wild west" magazine in exchange for the tourist-intended crafts—headdresses, bows, and beads. Cap later sold these crafts, or traded them for food. Fake "Indian" crafts. Fake "cowboy" magazines.

"What did Robbie think about all this?" I ask. "Where is the woman in this story?"

"Robbie stuck with him the whole time," my family says.

A job came through for Cap, in New York.

Cap hated the city, the job. He drank.

(This is a family tradition that filters through the generations. We hate things, so we drink. We love things, so we drink. We have bad luck, so we drink. We fear good luck, so we drink. It has to do with a kind of sadness that is blood-born. My mother keeps a scrap of paper taped to her diary, a quote from Yeats that reads: "Being Irish, he had an abiding sense of tragedy, which sustained him through temporary periods of joy," and the first time I read that line it hummed over my mind like a diviner's stick.)

Cap almost landed a role in a cowboy movie, but was beat out for the part by Tom Mix.

Cap was disappointed. He drank.

"But about Robbie," I say. "Did she want Cap to be an actor?"

"Still, Robbie stuck," my family says.

I want to learn from what went wrong in the past but sometimes it seems everything worth knowing has been redacted. As if ignorance is the only thing that allows each successive generation to tumble into love, however briefly, and spawn the next.

VI | ALL CACTI ARE SUCCULENTS BUT NOT ALL
SUCCULENTS ARE CACTI, 1994

My parents go on vacation to Arizona. They bring back souvenir cacti for my sister, Leslie, and me. Little furry stumps, potted in gravel.

Within a month, both our cacti are dead.

My sister's cactus is desiccated and shrunken. Dead of thirst.

Mine is slumped over, rotten through. I have overwatered and flooded the roots.

Our parents exchange a look. As if they know already that love will not be easy for us. That we are differently but equally screwed.

VII | AS SURE AS THESE STONES, 1948

My grandparents met in the theater.

Cap failed to become an actor, but years later his teenage son, my grandfather Eddie, would play the role of "crippled boy healed by a miracle" in a play at the Blackfriars Guild. Maureen Jarry was the props mistress. She was older than he was. We still don't know by how much. She refuses to say. Eddie lied about his age, of course. He told her he was twenty. Maureen told him to buzz off. At the time she was dating the lead actor—older, and quite successful.

My grandfather has always been a persistent son of a bitch.

He worked on my grandmother for weeks.

Nothing.

Then this happened:

One of the props for the play was a handful of gravel Maureen gathered from the empty lot behind the theater each night. In the final scene of the play the lead actor's character held out the gravel and said, "As sure as these stones do fall to the ground, I heal thee," and he would turn over his hand and the stones would fall and by this miracle my grandfather's character could walk again. But one winter night, my grandmother gathered what she thought was gravel from the back lot but was actually, as my grandfather enthusiastically describes it, "frozen dog turds."

And so, hours later, when the older actor spoke his line and turned his hand over, no stones fell, and he found himself instead with a handful of recently thawed dog shit.

"I am healed!" my grandfather called out, all the same. He danced around the stage without his crutches. "Oh, I am healed!"

VIII | CORN SYRUP, 1997

My middle school put on *Macbeth*. Danny played the second murderer.

The second murderer was my first proper kiss.

I was the director's assistant and liked skulking backstage in all black and carrying a clipboard. It was opening night. Danny ran offstage after killing Banquo. He found me in the dark, and we whispered. It had gone well. He was triumphant. He was covered in red corn-syrup blood.

"I want to hug you, but—" he said.

"Hug me," I said.

Then I was covered in fake blood. This is what love is like.

My best friend started dating his best friend and we would all talk on the phone at night. It was an elaborate process, getting all four of us on the line, and once we did, we were often confused about who was who.

"You're so funny," I would say, to who I thought was Danny.

"That wasn't me," he would say.

After these conversations, my best friend and I would call each other directly. Which one said he liked Nirvana? Which one wanted to be a cook? Whose mother could drive us to the movies? We were never sure.

IX | BLOOD, 1967

My mother has told me a hundred times about the boy who sold his blood to buy her flowers. "He had a motorcycle," she says. "He had no money, but he wanted to take me on a date so he went out and sold pints of his blood so he could do it."

Pints.

"He was woozy at dinner," she says. "He couldn't eat at all. He seemed like he was going to faint. But he'd bought me flowers. Lilies. Isn't that romantic?"

This story bothers me. It intrudes upon my father, and that's part of it, but it's also the way my mother wields those flowers as some false barometer of love.

As if her generation were worthy of blood and mine only backstage corn syrup.

My mother has asked me on every Valentine's Day since I was fourteen, "Did he buy you flowers?"

"I told him not to," I say.

"Why would you do that?" she says. "What kind of standards are you setting?"

"I don't want that kind of relationship," I say. "I don't want flowers."

I want to say: Stop pretending that the point is the lilies and not the blood.

X | SCRABBLE CHAMPION, 2000

The first time I slept with the boy, I thought I would bleed because that's what virgins do, but there was nothing on the sheets. No red banner for him to hang out the window or whatever grand gesture was meant to make you feel how important a moment it was. I had grown up riding horses. The moment had passed years before without my knowing it.

We'd thought his mother would be out all afternoon but she came home early and knocked on his door in the middle of it.

"What are you doing in there?" she said through the door, not because she was concerned but because she was the sort of woman who liked company.

"Playing Scrabble," the boy said.

"Who's winning?" she said.

"Both of us," he said.

XI | NOTHING WILL COME OF IT, 1969

My mother, Brenda, Boo for short, was going on a blind date, in a group, with a man named Doug Bush. But Doug Bush got sick, and my mother's friend wouldn't come unless Boo had a date, too. So the man who is now my uncle Paul enlisted his little brother, Tom, my dad, to stand in.

"It wasn't a date," my mother says, which is news to me.

It's news to my dad, too.

"What do you mean it wasn't a date?" he says. "It was our first date—of course it was a date."

My father remembers that at dinner they ran into some friends, and he was talking to one of the guys about the little green Triumph my father had recently bought from him on the cheap. About how it kept breaking down and he was trying to fix it.

He remembers my mother saying something like: "How typically male to be talking about your cars."

He remembers saying back: "How typically female to complain about car talk."

"There was banter," my father says.

My mother remembers almost nothing except that when she was dropped home that night by my uncle Paul . . .

"By me!" my father says.

"Was it you?" Boo says. Either way, when she was dropped home, my grandmother Maureen asked her how it went, and she said: "Nothing will ever come of it. He's down at school in DC."

"The fact that you said that shows that it was a date," my father says.

"I remember what I wore."

"Of course you do," I say. "Of course *that's* what you remember."

"Do you remember?" she asks my father.

My father is a practical man. My father keeps T-shirts from the seventies in his active rotation.

"It was a blue dress," he says. "With a collar, and a belt like this." He mimes a kind of cinching.

"Yes," says Boo. "My mother made that dress."

Why has she redacted what she felt that night but kept the dress? Why is the very thing that is missing here the bit I most need to know?

A year after this maybe-first-date my father would graduate and my mother would be at college and my father would burn out his Triumph going to see her so many times. It would literally explode on the side of the highway.

XII | THE MANLIEST SPORT, 2001

I am at a friends-and-family picnic when I meet Doug Bush, the man who was meant to be on that blind date with my mother. I am sixteen and have been trying to flirt with the only boy at this picnic who I can say with absolute certainty is not related to me: the hired fiddler, playing in the barn. When this proves unsuccessful, I wind up drinking beers and playing horseshoes with Doug Bush.

"Horseshoes," Doug Bush tells me, "is the manliest sport because you never have to put your beer down to play it."

Doug Bush sounds like a robot when he tells me this because he had throat cancer from smoking and his vocal cords have been replaced with a box he has to press with one finger to speak.

Doug Bush pushes his button and tells me, "I could have been your father."

XIII | GEODE MAN, 1970

When my father drove three hours north to my mother's all-girls' college in upstate New York, he did not complain about the distance or the cold. They went to a bar called the Tin & Lint, where my father drank Schlitz and my mother drank gin rickeys. They went to the racetrack and bet on horses, my father paying and my mother favoring the dapple grays, no matter what their odds. But if their romance, and my existence, hinges upon a single moment, the geode is it.

"Where are we going?" my mother asked.

"The parking lot," my father said. "I have a present for you."

Up in the dorms, my mother's friends spied from the windows.

He hefted something from the trunk of his car. A rock the size of a small melon.

"Thanks for the rock," my mother said.

"It's a geode," my father said. "It has crystals inside." He took a hammer from the trunk and handed it to my mother.

"What color are the crystals?" my mother asked.

"I don't know," my father said. "They could be blue, or purple, or brown, or gray. We have to crack it open to find out."

"You crack it," my mother said. "And I sure hope those crystals aren't mud brown."

(The thing you have to understand about my mother is this: she meant it.)

My father swung. The rock split. My mother inspected.

Amethyst crystals.

She kissed my father and they went to the bar.

Hours later, as he walked her back to the dormitory, they heard giggling from the third floor. Girls hung from the windows.

"Geode Man!" they called. "Come back and give *us* a rock, Geode Man."

The geode sits in my parents' living room.

It frightens me. The rock. The story. Because I wonder: If those crystals had been any other color, would I have made it into this world at all?

XIV | KNIVES, 2002

A tarot reader comes to the house and lays cards for my sister and me. She tells my sister that she will marry a man who works with knives.

My sister thinks: a doctor.

I think: a butcher.

We resolve to be on the lookout for handsome chefs.

"What about me?" I ask. "Who am I going to wind up with?"

"I see a plane," the reader says. "I see you going far away from here."

"What am I supposed to do with that?" I say.

XV | WHAT WE'RE IN FOR, 1950 & 1973

My grandfather got married when he was seventeen—so young he needed his mother to sign the marriage certificate for him. My mother married my father a month after her college graduation. I'm sure it's hard to marry young and synchronize your growing up with another person's. But I imagine it is easier, too.

It is amazing that those of us who do not find love young muster the strength to try again—years of history clattering behind us like so many tin cans dragged behind a wedding sedan.

XVI | NEWPORTS, 2003

I worked as a waitress at a tiny restaurant where I made almost no money. The kitchen staff called me "The Russian" because my handwriting was so bad they assumed it was Cyrillic. The chef was thirty-eight and I was nineteen but I didn't care because he was wonderful and I had fantasies of his following me into the walk-in freezer and untangling me from my apron and fucking me against the bags of frozen shrimp and tortellini. This never happened. But I did try.

By "try," I mean I became convinced that if only I could go out on smoke break with the other waiters and the chef, I would get to know him, and despite the fact I never spoke, he would *intuit* that I was pining for him to do this.

So one day I showed up with a pack.

"You smoke?" the chef said.

"Since forever," I said.

I lit my first cigarette. They were Newport menthols.

Ten years after my first cigarette, I stopped the way I started: for a boy.

I texted an old smoking friend:

I QUIT. FOR A BOY. PREDICTABLY.

She texted back:

THE ONLY THING YOU SHOULD EVER QUIT FOR A BOY IS SEX WITH OTHER PEOPLE.

XVII | GUYS AND DOLLS, 2004

I go to college and join a theater troupe, which troubles my mother. It is Christmas break, and we are sitting on the couch in our living room.

"Never date a man who knows more show tunes than you," my mother says.

My father, in the next room, hears this. He enters the living room, stage right, doing the Charleston.

"I got the horse right here!" he sings. "The name is Paul Revere!"

He Charlestons out of the room, stage left.

"I'm serious," my mother says.

My father reenters, somehow, stage right again, singing:

"Getting to know you! Getting to know all about you!"

XVIII | THE FIXER, 1999

My uncle Randall, my mother's brother, is a journalist. In the late nineties he was traveling through the Balkans to cover the problematically unserious prosecution of Serbian war criminals. He wanted to go undercover to interview a man who was known to have committed numerous rapes and murders, and who was living, quite openly, in a small Bosnian village with a personal militia for protection. Every local fixer told him this was a batshit-crazy, terrible, likely lethal idea and turned him down. Then, one day, someone said:

"Have you talked to Goca Igrić? I think she's who you're looking for."

Goca is also a journalist. She is Serb and chain-smokes Marlboro Reds and drinks several pots of Turkish coffee a day and was, at the time, under threat of death from all manner of political and criminal organizations after spending the war years defiantly speaking out against Slobodan Milošević.

I once asked my uncle when he fell in love with Goca.

Though they didn't start dating till ages later, he said perhaps it was that first time they met, in a café, when he told her what he wanted to do and asked her to be his fixer. He said Goca paused after he'd described his batshit-crazy, terrible, likely lethal idea. She exhaled all the smoke from her lungs and said, "I don't think I can *not* do this."

"Maybe that was when I knew," my uncle said.

It was the first thing my family ever taught me about love that felt as honest as blood. I can't *not* do this.

XIX | LITERACY, 2004

Stanley was a wonderful actor and liked to read aloud and once, when things were already almost over, he read to me from *The Iliad*.

He'd been reading for fifteen minutes when I suddenly understood that sometimes people are not so much in love as they are in need of an audience. I was a backstage person who sewed and welded and toggled light boards and perhaps this is why I was slow to understand this—but once I did, I began disappearing myself. A good backstage person. A good woman.

It was not Stanley's fault I thought this was what I was meant to do. It was years of family stories that hid the ways women knew in their blood what was wrong or right. Hid truth behind the scrim of romance or, worse, fate.

I disappeared myself the way you slowly ease the light-board controls. Down and down, so the spots dim, and fade to black, and then go out completely.

XX | COLOR-BLIND, 2003

My sister, Leslie, commits the greatest act of love I've ever seen.

She had been seeing Doug for some time when she found out he was color-blind.

My sister lost her shit because all her perfectly coordinated outfits were ruined. My sister takes her outfits very seriously.

"The way you see me," Leslie told Doug, "I clash. I look terrible."

"You're beautiful," Doug told her.

But for my sister's reds to become greens was unacceptable. She hated green.

The next time I saw her, Leslie was wearing a green sweater. She was wearing it with a navy skirt.

"Nice sweater," I said.

"It's atrocious," Leslie said.

"Then why are you wearing it?"

"Because to Doug this looks like navy and red," she said. "And nautical colors are really in right now."

XXI | THE BLACK CAT, 2006

A gang of girls was going to the Black Cat for Brit Pop Night so we could dance to The Smiths and the Sex Pistols and smoke and wear too much eyeliner and not give a shit about the boys or the fact that in another few months most of us would be graduated and adrift. I was going because I wanted to dance but maybe also because of a tall girl named Maggie, who wore big glasses and button-down shirts with the sleeves rolled up in a let's-get-down-to-business manner that filled me with longing. In our theater meetings, Maggie took copious notes like I took copious notes, and she always seemed to be looking up from those notes to stare at me at the precise moment that I was looking up to stare at her.

But then we didn't make it to the Black Cat, because there was a snowstorm.

(Eventually, we would kiss. Eventually, we would go to bed together. Eventually, I would fail to say bisexual, would fail to say queer, would fail to speak the truth and come out the way

I should have, would fail *her.* Eventually, I'll tell you this whole story.)

We were so disappointed by the snow. The canceled plans. And so we all went to the same tired party we'd been trying to avoid and went through the motions of having a good time.

I went out on the balcony to smoke and watch the snow come down. There was a small crush of people out there. I spotted Maggie. She was not wearing glasses. She was wearing a black tank top. She waved at me from across the balcony. I waved back. Then we stared at each other like we did in meetings and she lifted up her shirt a little. On her stomach, she'd written, in red lipstick

I'D RATHER
BE
AT
THE BLACK CAT

XXII | ASHOKAN FAREWELL, 2007

A friend of mine was working on one of those farms where he dressed in old-timey clothes and wire-rimmed glasses and pretended to be a tinsmith, a banjo player, a man from 1901, for tourists, who loved that sort of thing. But he was actually wearing the clothes, and smithing the tin, and playing the banjo, so where the performance ended was hard to tell.

I went to visit him. "I'm going to introduce you to Frank," my friend said.

Frank was a short-order cook who chain-smoked and had hair that fell in actual fucking ringlets and lived at the farm.

But the thing was, there was *also* a donkey named Frank on the farm, so when my friend brought me to meet "Frank" I wasn't prepared because I'd been anticipating meeting a donkey, and then here was this man with actual fucking ringlets.

One thing led to another.

Frank led me downstairs and as he took off my shirt I said, "Wait!"

I'd spotted a giant sepia photograph of two people holding a baby, framed over the fireplace, and I asked who those people were, because they were beautiful.

He said that they were his parents, and that the baby was him, but that when his parents got divorced his parents hated each other so much that neither of them could stand to look at the picture anymore, and were going throw it away, so he took it.

I put my shirt back on, because maybe everything just winds up terrible in the end and there's no point at all and we couldn't possibly fuck with all that tragedy watching over us, could we?

Frank took my shirt back off, but not unkindly.

XXIII | HOPE, 2008

My relationship with Bob lasted a full year longer than it should have because Barack Obama was running for president and had so raised our expectations of what redemptive things were possible that we thought perhaps he could save us from the petty, insidious ways we'd been hurting each other. We, too, could change.

Thanks, Obama.

When I left Bob, he wrote a short story about it and gave it to our writing workshop. In the story, he was a rock star and I was a baker. In the story, he'd invented that I'd been infected with chlamydia by my first boyfriend and had to have my ovaries removed and was now barren. In the story, I was called Zoë and screamed at the rock star in the middle of the street. Screamed things I'd actually screamed in the middle of the street the week before.

"This dialogue is so *alive*," the teacher said. "A real breakthrough in your work."

"But do you have your ovaries?" my friends asked.

XXIV | BENDER, 2009

Al invited me out to Long Island in the middle of winter because I had never had a 7-Eleven Slurpee before. This was absurd, but I said yes, because of how he asked, formally:

"Would you care to join me on Long Island this coming Saturday at two for a Slurpee and perhaps a walk on the beach?"

I took the train two hours past places with names like Wantagh and Islip. In the station bathroom I applied lipstick and the woman next to me, whose boobs were all but out of her shirt, made eye contact in the mirror and said, "Honey, you don't need that." Al picked me up and we got Slurpees and we drank them on the beach in our winter coats.

Our parents were different but had shaped us the same way. I think we were afraid of becoming them. I think we were afraid that what we found in each other was more than we deserved.

On the beach that first day, Al had a flask of whiskey. He asked me if I'd like some. I said yes.

What he actually said was: "Have you ever been on a bender?"

What I actually said was: "I have always wanted to go on a bender."

We bent for four good years.

XXV | "THE IVY CROWN," 1979

"What was that poem you read at your wedding?" I ask my mother. "That sappy Rilke poem?"

"It was not a sappy Rilke poem," my mother says. "It was William Carlos Williams and your grandfather cried when he read it."

"What was it called?"

"I can't remember the title but it was something about 'Love is cruelty,' blah blah blah."

"Love is cruelty?" I say.

My mother says, "It's a good poem."

Sure
love is cruel
and selfish
and totally obtuse—
...
But ...
  ...
we have,
no matter how,
by our wills survived.
  ...
We will it so
and so it is
past all accident.

XXVI | REMEMBER THE WILSONVILLE BEE
MASSACRE, 2013

I hopped a plane to Oregon after seeing Arlo, an old boyfriend, and deciding we were still in love, and meant to be married. We thought perhaps I should forget my plans of getting a PhD in Florida and move to Oregon instead.

We drove three hours to the coast to sit on the dunes and stare at the Pacific, a romantic evening, but then there were these helicopters shining their searchlights down on the waves. We covered our ears as we watched the lights truck over the water's surface, searching for a body.

I flew home, confused. I tackled my friend Cora to the bed and cried on her and said: "I love him but I'm not in love with him! But maybe we should just get married anyway! Maybe I should move to Oregon! Maybe this is just what true love feels like!"

Cora is a good friend, and so she did not point out that I had just used the words "true love."

"It's okay," she said. "You're going to shut up and then you're going to move to Florida, where you know no one, just like you planned. And sometimes you'll call me and tell me about it. And this will be good."

"But—" I said.

"Shush," she said. "Shut up now, and everything will be fine."

On my last day in Oregon, on our way to the airport, we'd driven past a crowd of people dressed like honeybees, yelling. The people in the bee suits were protesting a pesticide sold at the local hardware store that was damaging to bees. We were both so tired by then. We were failing but we were hopeful and we didn't know what would happen once I got on that plane so we were primed for hysterics when we saw one bee-man who was holding a sign that read:

REMEMBER THE WILSONVILLE BEE MASSACRE!

It is easy for some massacres to seem small in hindsight. For all the blood spilled to seem less in memory. But there are others that go around with signs and shout at you every day of your life, pointing, *Look at all this blood. Just look at it.* There are some massacres you make yourself.

We looked at each other and we asked: "Will you remember?"

We said: "How could we ever forget the Wilsonville Bee Massacre?"

XXVII | CYCLICAL, 2013

I am in a largely deserted mall in Tallahassee, Florida, where, until a few weeks ago, I'd known no one. I am about to see a movie with a group of new friends, including Nick, a man I think I like, and to whom I am trying not to pay an obvious amount of attention.

I walk past the dead mall's many blanked-out storefronts, and then I see them, a ways off, these new, kind people. They are waiting for me, but before I can reach them, my sister calls me on the phone, crying.

"What's wrong?" I say.

It's her boyfriend, she says. She loves him but she's not *in* love with him.

Leslie says: "But maybe this is just it. Maybe this is all love ever feels like and I'll never feel anything more than this."

I don't cry when she says this, even though my sister is like a limb of my own body and when she is unhappy, I feel it keenly. I do not cry, even though I feel the family blood-sadness rising within me, whispering about the futility of everything. Because it seems unfair that I should have made these very same mistakes but not spared her them. That everything that has happened before, to our family and our friends and even to ourselves, is so heavy to carry, and yet is in no way a protection against our future stupidity and pain. Is in no way a promise that we will not make these mistakes again.

I don't laugh when my sister says this, even though I am overcome by the absurdity of my own words echoed back at me in the hallways of a dead mall in Tallahassee, Florida. The absurdity of how my world seemed to be ending just months ago, and yet, here I am, in this new, ordinary place, and quite happy.

What I do is say to her: "Explain to me what you mean when you say love-but-not-in-love."

Across the way my new friends are still waiting for me. I watch as the man I think I like bends to tie his shoes. His graceful stoop gives me a pang and I pretend I do not feel the blood pulse quick in my wrists.

What I do is say to my sister: "Tell me all about it."

What I do is I pretend that none of this has ever happened before.

I have to act as if all of this is happening for the very first time.

Act One: The Mechanicals

You remember they were building a wall by his house. You were always speeding, almost missing the turn, when you'd spot the men with their stones, and back up, and take the right. It seemed like the two of you had always been in love, but the whole time you were together they were building that wall, so how long could it have been, really?

The boy wore Hawaiian shirts in winter. He had a mouth that never stopped moving. He had a dumb dog with short legs who was always getting lost, and one time, before you'd met, your parents found her by the side of the road, and drove her back to him. He could sing like Freddie Mercury. He could sing like Paul McCartney. He could sing like Tom Waits. You were seventeen and you didn't stand a chance.

He had boy habits like collecting *Star Wars* figurines and farting under blankets and speaking in silly voices when he needed to say serious things. He had grown-up habits like a bad back that required orthopedic sneakers and a painkiller addiction. Like listening to Wagner while slowly driving his mother's sedan down the back roads when he had insomnia.

He took you to the lake. You sat in a lifeguard chair together and he told you he loved you and it was all very romantic until you realized there was another couple ten yards off, fucking in the sand. Honestly, it was still pretty romantic. Honestly, you still think lifeguard chairs are some kind of sacred.

You had an agreement to pull over any time you saw a toy store. You threw dodgeballs at each other and adopted stuffed-animal children and tried to fit your lanky teen bodies into the plastic race-car beds until someone yelled at you to leave. That was the deal. You never left without first getting at least one person to yell at you.

He got you into bad situations. Forgetting about you at his friends' parties so you had to find your own ride home. Getting you into fights with your parents. Always, always telling the waiter it was your birthday when it wasn't, just for the piece of free cake, even though he sometimes left without paying anyway. When you cried he'd ask if some ice cream wouldn't make everything better. Like girls' problems were that easy to fix. You'd hit him and curse but then he'd drive you to the twenty-four-hour Carvel on the side of the highway, and once he had you sitting on a picnic bench, watching the cars do eighty, eating vanilla soft-serve with rainbow sprinkles, smelling the exhaust, he would say, "Admit it, you feel better, don't you?" You'd hit him again.

His mother taught Shakespearean acting to middle-schoolers. Her troupe rehearsed at the local farm, which had too few cows to be a good dairy but enough acres of garden that when she put on *A Midsummer Night's Dream* it looked just like it was supposed to. You liked the parts where the young lovers got confused in the woods and fought and kissed but you didn't understand the other half of the play where the builders and tinkers, the mechanicals, tried to stage their own show within the show. The mechanicals were neither young nor beautiful and the show they tried to make was very bad. It was called

Pyramus and Thisbe. In it, a man played a woman and a woman played a wall and they kept on talking about a lion's terrible roar. You found the whole thing extraneous. He thought it was the best part, and you wondered what you were missing.

You cracked up your car and had to go to the hospital. He came to see you even though your parents didn't like him. He brought you a dirty traffic cone stolen off the road with wildflowers stuck in the top. This meant, *I love you.* This meant, *Be careful.*

His house had a sauna and a pool and a collection of African masks. The two of you sat in the sauna, then ran outside across the grass, to jump in the water naked. You paddled around, him chasing you under the Tibetan prayer flags that flew from the tree line, and when he caught you, he pressed himself against you until you couldn't stand it anymore and then he took you inside and laid you on the floor and fucked you while you stared up into the carved-wooden faces of those masks. He was your first, and the sex always felt safe and it always felt good, and the fact of this, the safety and goodness of it, has proved lethal down the line.

And yet, if you had to compare your dynamic to something, you think he probably thought of himself as Jean Reno in Luc Besson's *The Professional* and you as his Mathilda, his sad baby Natalie Portman. Except you were actually fucking. Except you were only a year apart in age. You know you're not supposed to like that movie anymore now that you're old and overeducated but you still love looking at her—love looking at him looking at her—in all the problematic ways you're not supposed to look at a bruised peach and find it beautiful. Not supposed to want to *eat* or *be* that peach. This particular ouroboros of saving and being saved has also proved lethal down the line.

. . .

You could make it to his house inside of ten minutes if you blew through one stop sign. If you didn't miss the turn. If you didn't have to wait for all the men building the wall to clear their tools and their stones from the street.

When the boy went away to college he told you he was scared, but you were the one left behind with your parents, who were so mad you'd had sex. Left behind with all the fights defending this relationship you didn't even *have* anymore because he was gone. You were so angry and you didn't have anyone who understood and so you made him into everything. Your defining story. It had to be a story that mattered, otherwise what was it all for?

Most people thought of what you had as teenage infatuation, but it wasn't. Even now you sometimes think of the high-octane intimacy that passed between you and wonder if someone older could have survived it. You're not saying that this was unique, just that it was real.

The boy sounded far away on the phone when he called you from college, even though he was only in California. Sometimes he was weird and would apologize and say it was just the pills the pills the pills. He'd say he was going to quit them, and you'd help him talk himself into doing it, and he would. He'd flush them down the toilet and you would hear him dropping them in, *plink,* and flush. You'd wonder whether he'd really done it because he was at acting school after all. A few days later, though, you would know it was for real, that he'd gone cold turkey again, because he would say flippant, cruel things and be listening to Frank Zappa.

You broke up with him the summer before you went to college because you were tired of trying not to reciprocate the advances of the boys back home, who just wanted to sit with you on a rock with a bottle of bourbon and make up names for the stars while they tried to cop a feel. Later, at college, the boys had all gone to Catholic preparatory schools and they did things like ask permission to touch you. You weren't able to appreciate that at the time. They planned dates they called dates and bought you flowers in cellophane and you couldn't appreciate this, either, so you lied and said you were a virgin waiting for marriage.

The boy wrote you letters. You wrote him back.

You almost got together again after college, when he came to visit you in Brooklyn and you spent a week together, cutting up like old times. Sprinting through the Arms and Armor section at the Met and getting yelled at by security. Dancing in your bedroom at night because you'd both had sugary cocktails and you could hear the guy upstairs practicing his bass.

You were in your twenties now, so grown, and there was no one to stop you from being together. This was it, you were sure. But then he broke it off. You were wearing a blue neckerchief that must have seemed like a very cool thing to be wearing in Williamsburg, Brooklyn, in 2006 but when he told you he'd slept with a yoga instructor he'd met while visiting a friend two nights before, the neckerchief compounded how stupid and lacking in dignity you felt and you vowed to never again wear any article of clothing that you could not survive the mortification of being dumped in. This has proved to be a good rule.

After he returned home, he posted long Facebook meditations about the Brooklyn morning light coming through your windows, how it illuminated your beta fish, who lived on the mantel, all this to describe the melancholy of having fucked you and left you naked in bed for what would be the last time. Later, he began posting photos of the yoga instructor.

The shame of having been wrong about him, doubled down on being wrong, on and off, for six years, was almost worse than the heartbreak. Almost.

You didn't return his letters. You cut things off and didn't cave until he became a twelve-stepper, another five years later, writing you one of those long apology notes that are part of the making-amends step. You have received, in this human life, too many of these letters. The letter enumerated a million things he'd done that you hadn't even remembered. There was no mention at all of how callous he'd been after you chose him over your friends and parents when he went away to college, or the phone calls after the pills, or the yoga instructor after that.

A year later you were both invited to the same wedding in a vineyard. You were smoking cigarettes and drinking bourbon and he had quit everything, which, no matter what had passed between you, you acknowledged as a very good and impressive thing. The two of you walked down rows of grapevines and he asked you to let him make amends. You said amends were made. Check it off the list. Consider it done. You crushed a cigarette under your boot and ground it into the soil. You kissed the boy on the cheek when he drove you back to your shitty motel and you thought that was a pretty good way to say goodbye to someone forever.

The next morning the woman at the front desk said a man had come looking for you in the middle of the night, around four a.m., and she'd told him there was no one by your name staying there. You gave her back your key on its plastic ring and thanked her. You realized that this generous woman working the night shift at the goddamn Sea Breeze motel had more sense than you, and she'd met him for only two minutes.

You visit your hometown. You are driving aimlessly when you see the wall. You stop and slowly back up to the right-hand turn. It is built. There it is, all real and caked together with stones, and you feel a pang. You can get rid of everything else, the phone numbers and the photos, and still you will have these stories banging around inside you.

This is the first time you understand that, when people talk about *moving on,* they don't mean that you won't remember or bleed anymore. Just that you'll go on to do other things. Meet other people. And yet, in the middle of a normal day, something as simple as a stone wall can still suddenly and invisibly destroy you. And because it's too much to explain, most days, when this happens, you'll just keep driving along. You won't mention the wall or what it summons to anyone. And it's this silence, more than anything else, that defines *moving on.*

The wall they've built is highly mediocre.

You think of the one funny part in the mechanicals' *Pyramus and Thisbe.* Pyramus has killed himself, and Thisbe has killed herself, and still the play does not end there. Not only because it is insufferable but also because, next, the person playing the wall falls down as if dead. A dead wall and *even now* the play is not over. Because still left is the moonshine, represented by a paper disc, and the lion with a mop for his mane. The play is over. For years and years, it has been over. And still, here you are, stuck with these sad props.

Hepburn Qua Hepburn

I t was always apparent to me that Tracy Lord wasn't meant to marry George Kittredge. George is a caricature of by-your-own-bootstraps wealth—not so much a real man a person might love as the embodiment of A Correct Choice a woman might make in the realm of Good Marriages. To marry a George was to acquiesce to what the world thought of as success at the expense of what I thought of, rather grandly, as true love.

In my defense, I was thirteen.

The summer I romantically imprinted on the 1940 film adaptation of *The Philadelphia Story,* it was 1998, and I spent most of my time in the holy neon aisles of the local video store fighting with my friends over what to watch. It was because I was sick of being subjected to whatever cassette the boys in my life held up and rhapsodized about that I turned to the American Film Institute's list of "The 100 Greatest American Movies of All Time." I assumed academy experts would deliver me from the tastes of dumb-shit boys. The irony of this is not lost on me.

These days *The Philadelphia Story* clocks in at number forty-four on the AFI list, though back then it was certainly closer to the top (where *Citizen Kane* has been squatting for nearly twenty-five years). But the rankings are immaterial—because no film I watched during that time has altered the way I see the world so much as *The PS* has.

The PS is at once a love story and a comedy of errors. The dialogue moves at breakneck pace. It's a screwball three-act in which old-money society gal Tracy (Katharine Hepburn) is getting married to new-money eligible bachelor George (John Howard). Their wedding is complicated by the fact that it will be covered by short-story-writer-turned-reluctant-tabloid-reporter Macaulay "Mike" Connor (Jimmy Stewart), whose pronounced distaste for the rich is reasonable even as it smacks of the kind of Bolshevik cosplay so common among men of a certain education. Mike manages to find Tracy attractive, nonetheless, and vies for her affections. "The young, rich, rapacious American female," he says, moments before he goes all goo-goo-eyed. "No other country where she exists."

Tracy has been blackmailed into having her wedding covered because the tabloid is threatening to expose an affair Tracy's father had with a dancer (a *dancer*) and the pickle is even picklier because Tracy's first husband, fellow old-money Philadelphian C. K. Dexter Haven (Cary Grant), has brought the tabloid folks to the Lords' house under the guise of their being friends of Tracy's absent brother. He confesses the ruse to the Lords immediately but takes great pleasure in the scrutiny the tabloid brings to the occasion because he still loves Tracy and doesn't want her to marry this new guy. So Dex participates in the pre-wedding festivities, which would seem strange if everyone in the family didn't adore him so much.

The question the viewer follows throughout the movie is

this: Of the three available men in the movie—George, Connor, and Dex—which one is the right one for Tracy Lord?

In 1998, this issue of Which One was very much on my mind, as a kissing-aspirant human. I immediately accepted *The PS* as a kind of instructive text to show me the ways of women and love, and I adored every part of it.

Except the ending.

Because it was so totally clear to me, back then, that Connor, the Jimmy Stewart character, was the person Tracy should wind up with. And yet, in the end, Tracy winds up back with Dex (Grant).

"What the hell!" I shouted in the empty TV room above my parents' garage. I chucked the cassette case across the room. Then I rewound the ending and watched it again, trying to keep up with the dialogue as Hepburn made her choice. Trying to decide if I agreed with it. Looking for clues.

The PS is still my favorite movie and I am still rewinding and rewatching. Every time I'm sure I've seen all its truths, and every time it shifts on me again. The movie stays the same, and I change. I am never sure who I am going to root for, or what I'm going to take away.

Part of the unsavory thrill of *The PS* is that Hepburn's Tracy is so assured, so powerful, and yet her uncertainty in the face of a major life decision, her marriage, is debilitating to her. To watch a confident woman falter is a kind of spectator sport the film relishes. Hepburn is both the movie's star and its spectacle. She gets to be the heroine for the price of being the butt of most of its jokes.

I didn't notice this when I was thirteen, of course. I just saw her strength and her wit and her beauty. Internalized that a woman must slim her ego if she wants to fit into a wedding dress.

What was most compelling to me was the way the movie allowed the three men to pitch Tracy versions of her future by pitching her versions of herself. My friend Olivia once perfectly described *The PS* as: "Men explain Katharine Hepburn to Katharine Hepburn," and, indeed, this is the whole bag. She is described as a goddess, a queen, and a golden girl over the course of the movie, and we come to understand that if Tracy chooses one man over another, she will not only have a different life, she will *be* a different version of herself. She will *become* a different person. And so, in this way, Tracy can choose who she wants to be . . . insomuch as she can choose her husband. The range of options for her identity is limited to those presented by the men. And as a result, the options are less than ideal.

To conflate the choice of a romantic partner with the choice of one's own identity might strike you as retrograde, but as a fourteen-year-old girl trying on various identities of my own, it made total sense. Who was I, anyway? I was looking for someone to tell me. I was used to a limited range of accessible identities being presented to me—this was how the other teen-girl things I liked worked: mood ring shades and astrology signs and nail-polish colors and birthstone earrings and personality quizzes. I accepted these cheap placeholders for any kind of realer, deeper understanding of who I was or might be. You never got to choose freely. All you could do was pick from the options presented to you. Why should love be any different?

———

CONNOR: Hey, Tracy, you can't marry that guy.
LORD: George? I'm going to. Why not? . . .
CONNOR: You just don't seem to match up.

The PS is absolutely and completely about class. Connor himself is perpetually broke in an elective, artistic kind of way and comes from a middle-class family in Indiana. C. K. Dexter Haven, as the name perhaps implies, is from the old-money "upper crust," like the Lords, who are also comically rich. George Kittredge grew up poor and is now self-made nouveau-riche.

But when Connor talks about *matching up,* he is not referring to the fact that George grew up poor, but rather the fact that he is not Tracy's intellectual or spiritual equal. George, Connor implies, is a good, solid man who understands hard work, but Tracy *understands the deeper truths of life.* Understands suffering. Like, say, just for example, Connor does.

In a scene with so much tension and chemistry it still floors me, Connor finds Tracy in the public library, reading his short stories, which, she is surprised to find, are wonderful:

LORD: I can't make you out at all now.
CONNOR: Really? I thought I was easy.
LORD: So did I, but you're not. You . . . you
    talk so big and tough, and then you write like
    this. Which is which?
CONNOR: Both, I guess.
LORD: No. No, I believe you put the toughness on
    to save your skin.
CONNOR: You think so?

LORD: I know a little about that.
CONNOR: Do you?
LORD: Quite a lot.

We suffer the same! We are special in the same, dark way! It's fucking catnip to me.

I have been notoriously dickish in my life about men with habits or interests I do not enjoy. And it's because I've shared Jimmy Stewart's impassioned artist's sense of the necessity of *matching up* with the person you love. Of feeling the same kinds of feeling. Of moving through the world in the same kind of way.

How could I possibly date a man who loved football? Who liked Blink-182? A man who played video games? Who thought Adam Sandler was funny? Who wore khakis? Who did not enjoy spicy food?

For years I conflated tastes with identity, with depth.

I pretended this was a compatibility issue, but the reality is that I was threatened by men's tastes *because I assumed they would have to become mine*.

By this same warped logic, I dated people whose interests I did not share but aspired to. I loved people who were more outdoorsy than me. People who knew more about art. People who were better at building and creating things with their hands than I was. As if through the transitive properties of dating, I, too, would become and learn these things.

My friend Sean went to seminary to become a Jesuit before falling in love and deciding he would rather be in love than be a Jesuit. But some of that Jesuitical energy still surrounds him, and perhaps this is why I sometimes find myself telling him secrets. *Confessing*, even.

I once dated a man who had very different tastes from me and I started singing that old "Is This a Threat to My Identity" song to Sean, and Sean told me I was being ridiculous.

"This is the problem with the way people date now," he said. "People are always trying to date people who have the same tastes as them."

"So you can share things," I said.

So you don't need to give up your things for theirs, I did not say.

"Fans of Swedish death metal date other fans of Swedish death metal," Sean said. "And that's cool. But then you don't know if you share anything real, any values, with the person you're marrying."

"'Values,'" I said, "sounds very religious."

"It doesn't have to be," Sean said. "Sure, like, that was one of the reasons Catholics used to marry other Catholics: because you assumed you and another Catholic shared values. But it doesn't have to be part of a religion. You can just be with someone who happens to value the same things as you. Otherwise all you have to go on is Swedish death metal."

The assumption underlying Sean's good advice was that another person's identity would not have to become mine if we fell in love. That their identity would not subsume me.

But I find other people contagious. I have difficulty not mirroring cadence when talking to British friends. Three years in the South left me addicted to "y'alls" and liable to lapse into semi-drawl. I am porous to the world, a kind of joyful sponge for the affectations and interests of the people I love. It has been the work of my life to build slightly firmer boundaries around myself so that I can figure out where I end and the people I love begin.

In hetero relationships my choices and desires always seem

to yield more readily than men's. I am not confident I won't bend myself into whatever shape it is the next man requires of me. Can't be sure that the way he sees me won't become the way I see myself.

———

For all the strength Hepburn brings to the role, Tracy Lord is a character who absolutely believes in the versions of herself the men present to her.

C. K. Dexter Haven is the first man to explain Hepburn to Hepburn. They are poolside at the Lord estate, Dex in a suit, Tracy vulnerable in a swimsuit and robe.

LORD: You seem quite contemptuous of me, all of
   a sudden.
DEXTER: No, Red, not of you, never of you. . . .
   I'm contemptuous of something inside of you
   you either can't help or make no attempt to.
   Your so-called strength. Your prejudice against
   weakness. Your blank intolerance.
LORD: Is that all?
DEXTER: That's the gist of it. Because you'll
   never be a first-class human being or a first-
   class woman until you've come to have some
   regard for human frailty. It's a pity your own
   foot can't slip a little sometimes, but your
   sense of inner divinity wouldn't allow that.
   This goddess must and shall remain intact. . . .

Tracy responds to Dex defiantly, but during this speech her eyes well, her nostrils flare, her mouth sets and resets. The difference between what Hepburn is saying and what she's telling the viewer with her body, with her face, is enormous, and it is her genius. On Dex's part, he's trying to hurt Tracy, sure, but he also really wants her to hear what he's saying. He delivers the lines with a kind of calm urgency. *Look at yourself,* he seems to say.

When Tracy's fiancé, George, shows up a moment later, Dex makes himself scarce. Tracy is still shaken from the conversation. She doesn't want to be the woman Dex tells her she is. And so, for one glorious moment she tries to dream up the kind of self *she'd* like to be. Tracy Lord is rich, and blind to her own privilege, but she is also smart, and in pain, and her dreaming does not seem, to the viewer, ridiculous. She tries to answer the question Who Am I and What Do I Want *for herself,* for just a second:

LORD: Oh, George, to get away and somehow to be
     useful in the world!

This does not last long.

KITTREDGE: Useful—you, Tracy? I'm going to build
     you an ivory tower with my own two hands!

Hepburn looks stricken as George goes on to all but echo Dex's speech of a moment ago:

KITTREDGE: That's the wonderful thing about you,
     Tracy.
LORD: What? How?
KITTREDGE: Well, you're like some marvelous,

distant, well, queen, I guess. You're so cool
and fine and always so much your own. There's a
kind of beautiful purity about you, Tracy, like
a statue. . . . Oh, it's grand, Tracy. It's
what everyone feels about you. It's what I first
worshipped you for from afar. . . . Only from a
little nearer now, eh, darling?
LORD: I don't want to be worshipped. I want to be
loved.
KITTREDGE: Well, you're that, too, Tracy. . . .
LORD: I mean really loved.
KITTREDGE: But that goes without saying, Tracy.
LORD: No, no, now it's you who doesn't see what I
mean . . .

Her fiancé's loving speech maps onto her ex-husband's critique. Tracy recoils from what George says everyone believes: that for her to ever be useful in the world is a joke. That like some "cool and fine" statue, she should just stand still and mean something.

And tomorrow, of course, Tracy's meant to marry George and commit to this version of herself, till death do they part.

———

It would be easy to label *The PS* a boy-crazy romp, but the script, laid bare, reads more like a Hitchcockian thriller.

———

When I watched *The PS* as a teen, and then in my twenties, I didn't see the cruelty. I was too busy trying to figure out which man Tracy should pick.

Was it George, who wanted to worship at her feet as if she were a statue on a pedestal, or Dex, who spited her for being a goddess with unreasonable standards?

Of course it wasn't.

The right answer, I knew back then, was Macaulay Connor, who, like Tracy, is hard on the outside, but sensitive inside. A kind of soul twin, despite their class differences. And if I was so fervently wrong about Connor being the right choice back then, perhaps it was because a funny, fast-talking, gangly man is my kryptonite, and Jimmy Stewart is the king of these.

Or perhaps it was because Connor and Tracy share the film's most iconic scene, and how could the biggest scene belong to them if he wasn't the right answer?

———

After being read for filth by her ex-husband and her fiancé, Tracy—who, by the way, has been wearing a very goddesslike tunic/bathing robe this whole time—stumbles around the corner of the house like a wounded animal, while the rehearsal dinner celebration is taking off without her. Tables are set with drinks. She considers them. She downs, in succession, three dainty coupes of Champagne. And so, the night is afoot. The goddess, that queenly statue, our own moon, will be taken down. She'll do it herself. And she'll do it to prove she's not who the men think she is. In its own way, it's a bid for freedom. But as with most bids for freedom that begin with cocktails, it goes poorly.

When Tracy and Connor cross paths again much later that night, they are both quite drunk. Thus begins the famous scene where, full of Champagne, Stewart and Hepburn woo each other.

CONNOR: Tracy . . . you're wonderful. . . .
   There's a magnificence in you. . . .
TRACY: Mike . . .
CONNOR: A magnificence that comes out of your
   eyes and your voice and in the way you stand
   there and the way you walk. . . . You've got
   fires banked down in you. Hearth fires and
   holocausts. . . .
TRACY: I don't seem to you made of bronze?
CONNOR: No, you're made out of flesh and blood.
   That's the blank, unholy surprise of it. You're
   the golden girl, Tracy. You're full of life and
   warmth and delight. . . . What goes on? You've
   got tears in your eyes.
TRACY: [Quickly] Shut up, shut up, oh, Mike, keep
   talking, keep talking, talk, will you? . . .
CONNOR: What good is talk? Tracy, Tracy.

[They embrace]

TRACY: Golly, golly Moses. Nobody's ever kissed
   me like that.

I want to kiss Jimmy Stewart for saying these things about
Tracy—never mind what I'd do if he said them to me. But, more
important, he has made her human again. A golden girl, sure.
But a human full of warmth and so capable of feeling. In a
movie where Tracy has no power to transform herself, Connor
allows her to see herself in a way that does not horrify her, just
for a moment. And then he kisses the girl he's described.
   (An aside: Connor and Tracy kiss and then take a naked

swim but they do not fuck, and the reason Connor does not sleep with Tracy is that she is drunk. He carries her to her bed, makes sure she is safe, and *then leaves her alone*. The next day, when everyone is shocked to hear things didn't go any further between them, Connor says it was because Tracy was "a little, little . . ." "Pixilated?" Dex supplies. "Yes," Connor says, "and there are rules about that!" Indeed, there are. And thank you, Jimmy Stewart, for this 1940s PSA.)

Connor says all the right words in his scene with Tracy. And he says them beautifully. More important, he creates A Moment for them, which makes them feel alive and special and full of possibility. Never mind that Connor is dating Liz Imbrie, the photographer from the tabloid. Never mind that she's two verandas over (how many verandas can one estate possibly have?) busily typing up a story for the paper to save the day at the very moment this scene is going on. Never mind all that.

I've spent most of my life dating Macaulay Connors.

Because what I believed when I was thirteen, and for many years afterward, was that *this* was what love was about. This kind of one-soul-seeing-another-soul synchronicity. This kind of Big Moment of Feeling and Drama. And so I have courted these kinds of loves.

They've been marvelous, like that scene is marvelous, while they lasted.

Unfortunately, what happens with a Macaulay Connor is that you don't ever get to be a golden girl for very long. You get to be a golden girl for only as long as you are In a Big Moment of Feeling and Drama. And eventually the moment passes. And then you transform into Liz Imbrie, tabloid photographer by day, painter by night, Macaulay Connor's longtime situation-ship. A daily, lived-in sort of girl, with daily, lived-in sorts of concerns.

At one point, Dex asks Liz why she and Connor aren't married.

```
LIZ: He's still got a lot to learn. And I don't
    want to get in his way for a while. . . .
DEX: Suppose another girl came along in the
    meantime?
LIZ: I'd scratch her eyes out. That is, unless
    she was marrying someone else the next day.
```

I was in my mid-twenties when I started seeing, in Liz Imbrie's face, both pain and the stifling of the pain, as Connor, not unlike Tracy, continually trots after the next thing that will make him feel like the kind of person he wants to be. Connor rails against the injustice of an artist being forced to work to earn a living wage, while Imbrie quietly does her photography job instead of doing her painting, the art *she* wants to do, because she accepts the necessity of eating and paying rent.

It took me almost a decade of being Liz Imbrie to notice her standing there.

And once I had, it took the shine off Connor. Which was why, watching *The PS* at the end of my twenties, I began to succumb to the movie's logic. That it is Cary Grant, C. K. Dexter Haven, who is the right choice for Tracy after all.

———

The PS convinces us Cary Grant is the right choice for Hepburn at the end of the movie because he understands her the most deeply. Through her drunken antics Tracy has come to know and accept human weakness, and so, the next morning, toppled from her pedestal, she is now someone Dex is prepared to love for her flaws and humanity instead of for her perfection, and Tracy is grateful for it.

TRACY: I'm such an unholy mess of a girl . . .
But never in my life, not if I live to be a
hundred, will I ever forget how you tried to
stand me on my feet again.
DEXTER: You? You're in great shape.

That's what I wanted, I decided. A Dex. Someone who sees you for the horror show you are, and *opts in*. Someone who relentlessly sees what's wrong with you, and pushes you to be better. *That,* I decided, was the most honest way of being in love.

I took this worldview out for a whirl. I got back together with an ex, Arlo. Because I loved him, sure. But also because he was the only person in my life who had ever actively told me that I was a bad person. He was my Dex.

To be clear, he wasn't telling me I was a bad person for no reason. This was not a manipulation, just an accounting of the past. I had done bad things to Arlo in high school. And I did bad things as part of us getting back together, too. This is not a casual self-flagellation. The sins are real.

He reminded me of them, often. *And it made me feel seen.* Feel known. It made me feel like any other person I might date, who would see me as a good person, your George Kittredges, your Macaulay Connors, were merely fools for whom the scales had not yet fallen. They, too, would eventually see the bad person I really was, and when they did, they would leave.

Or worse, they would never see the real me at all. And I'd be alone with myself, forever.

But Arlo already knew the worst of me, and still wanted to stay. The fact that he thought so little of me was a comfort. So completely did I believe this that I was on the verge of bailing on graduate school and moving across the country to be with him.

I would like to tell you I stopped the relationship because I realized this wasn't what love was supposed to look like. But even as I decided to stick with graduate school, and not move across the country to be with Arlo, and in so doing caused one more grievous hurt to this person I'd hurt before, I told myself this was another failure on my part. That I was just too weak to be with a person who saw me truly. And here I was, hurting him again. One more bad thing.

It took a very long time for me to understand that while, yes, I had behaved badly in this relationship multiple times, and yes, I was full of sins and flaws, being loved by a person who saw the worst in me wasn't the same as being honest and sorry about my failures. That it was possible to own and admit your mistakes without building a relationship around them.

To say that Dex and Tracy belong together because they love each other's flaws is a charitable reading. A more cynical way of seeing things is that Dex has orchestrated the debacle of the night before to teach Tracy a lesson, and now that she's in the muck with the rest of them, she feels she deserves no better. Dex takes sport in knocking the goddess/statue/golden girl from her pedestal, and once he has dislodged her from this perch, like some sort of carnival target, he takes her home as his prize.

All of which is to say the possibility of Dex as the right answer has faded for me, too.

If I sound overly suspicious here, perhaps it's because the reason C. K. Dexter Haven and Tracy Lord got divorced in the first place was that he hit her. It is, in fact, the very first thing that happens in the movie, though it's easy enough to forget about it.

The movie opens with a silent newsreel–like clip from the backstory of Tracy's marriage to Dex. In the scene, they seem to be shouting, arguing. Tracy throws his golf clubs out the front door, cracks a putter over her knee. Dex then climbs the front steps back to her, considers himself, and then palms her face. He pushes her down to the ground in one, clean shove.

In a condensed radio production of *The PS,* based on the movie, the announcer accounts for this silent scene by saying, "Tracy Lord's first marriage to C. K. Dexter Haven was dissolved by a vigorous right to the jaw."

Twice during the movie, Tracy's kid sister, Dinah (played by scene-stealing Virginia Weidler), spies on Tracy and Dex and wonders if he's "going to sock her again."

The implication of all this is that, yes, theirs was a fiery and passionate and bickering sort of marriage. But it also implies that Tracy left Dex because he hit her. Got a divorce because she did not want him to hit her again.

Beyond the instances I mention, the violence is never addressed in the movie. It goes unspoken. No part of the movie's arc, which ultimately brings Tracy and Dex back together, includes a reckoning with this violence.

Again, everyone in Tracy's family just loves Dex.

What to do with the information that Cary Grant himself

was accused of being abusive to multiple partners in his own life? In what ways is the movie asking us to both see and know that Cary Grant is violent, and then *forgive him* for this, in the name of accepting our lovers as messy and flawed? After all, the movie so clearly believes he is the good guy in this story. He's the right answer for Tracy. He's goddamn Cary Grant.

There's a difference between a person loving you for the person you really are and a person who sees the worst in you and relentlessly calls it out. I'm on the fence about Tracy's relationship with Dex. Of course I don't think a person should stay with a violent partner. Of course not. But in *PS*-land it is 1940, and so the movie has no problem using this violence *as a metaphor instead of a fact*. And metaphorically speaking, the movie is asking what it means to forgive a person you love for a very bad thing they did to you. Can you do it? Can you ever be with that person again? Is there a way that those experiences can be a boon to a relationship instead of ruining it?

If you strip all the particulars away, it's a good question.

In a scene that's easy to miss, Dex finds Tracy curled up in the backseat of a car outside his place. She is drunk and has fallen asleep. Dex climbs in, and their two faces shot against the car seat make them look like lovers facing each other in bed. Dex speaks to Tracy lovingly. She flutters her eyes open and closed as he invites her inside.

DEXTER: You look beautiful, Red. Come on in.
LORD: Why?
DEXTER: Hmm. No particular reason. A drink,
   maybe?

LORD: I don't drink.
DEXTER: That's right, I forgot.

[A pause; Tracy opens her eyes, sure of herself]

LORD: I haven't.

There is a long pause between when Dex says he's forgotten and Tracy says she hasn't. Whereas a moment ago she was a sleepy girl full of Champagne, when she says, "I haven't," she is wide awake.

I am in my late thirties now, still making *The PS* into my own personal Rorschach blot, and these days, it's this moment that slays me.

Because when Tracy shakes her head, when she considers going inside with Dex, when she says she hasn't forgotten, she is talking about *everything that has passed between them*. She is saying that she would like to come in, but she remembers, she remembers, she remembers the past, the hurt of it, and the caution it taught her, and so she can't. Even if some part of her would like to.

What she hasn't forgotten is enough to stop her.

This scene is about so much more than what Dex did to Tracy. It's about everything from the past she can't stop from guiding her choices, her actions, her possibilities.

Earlier in the movie, Tracy's mother, Margaret, starts to say: "The course of true love . . ." but before she can finish with the *never did run smooth* part, a drunk Macaulay Connor supplies, "Gathers no moss!"

It's a throwaway line. A gag in which a drunk man mixes up his proverbs.

But what would it mean for the course of true love to gather no moss?

Would it not look a little like forgetting?

Isn't it another way of saying that the thing one most needs in true love is a blank slate? To carry nothing from the past terrain you've covered with you into the future? To be, in essence, a stone with no history?

There is another mention of "true love" in *The PS*.

The *True Love* is the name of a boat Dex and Tracy once, long ago, sailed up the coast of Maine for their honeymoon. Dex brings Tracy a scale model as a wedding gift, and George is the one who unwraps the present, and gives the little boat to Tracy as she's swimming about her pool, in a one-piece and bathing cap.

She holds it up:

TRACY: Why, it's a model of the *True Love*.
KITTREDGE: The what?
LORD: A boat he designed and built, practically.
  We sailed it down the coast of Maine and back
  the summer we were married. My, she was *yar*.
KITTREDGE: *Yar*—what's that mean?
LORD: It means . . . Oh, what does it mean? Easy
  to handle, quick to the helm. Fast, bright.
  Everything a boat should be. Until she develops
  dry rot.

———

On the morning of Tracy's wedding day, *The PS* presents to us, the audience, a kind of macabre multiple-choice question in which we must answer, once and for all, Who is Tracy Lord?

Or maybe even, how should one ideally be, as a Love Object?

Tracy herself must make a choice, inasmuch as she must decide whether she's getting married, and to whom. So which version of Tracy Lord should Tracy Lord choose to be?

A) A GODDESS
B) A STATUE AND/OR QUEEN
C) A GOLDEN GIRL OF FLESH AND BLOOD
D) AN UNHOLY MESS OF A GIRL
   (the flip side of this coin reads: A WOMAN WHO
   BELIEVES THE MAN WHO HURT HER IS THE
   MAN WHO UNDERSTANDS HER BEST)

The scene that unfolds at the end of the movie goes something like this:

George proves himself unworthy by writing Tracy an uptight middle-school letter about deserving answers about what's gone on with Connor the night before. Then, everyone collectively gaslights George into thinking he's a bad person for suspecting Tracy had an affair with Connor, even though Tracy herself was convinced she'd probably slept with him. But never mind that. Tracy rejects him for making this assumption, and in this way we dispense with George, whose truest crime was being very boring as a result of being once poor and thusly so busy making his own money through actual work that he had no time to develop a unique style of veranda banter to call his own and make him worthy of our love.

Despite George's departure, no one has remembered to actually stop the wedding, and so guests are now seated, and a priest is standing with his bible at the ready, and the wedding march is playing and Tracy is supposed to be walking down the aisle *right now . . .*

In a Grand Romantic Gesture, more about saving the wedding than anything else, Connor then proposes to Tracy. Says he'll marry her right there on the spot. Tracy says no, because she has the good sense not to read into their one night of kissing possibilities greater than the fantasy can bear. She also mentions that she *DOESN'T THINK THAT LIZ WOULD LIKE IT.* That is, Connor's girlfriend, who is, again, and always, standing right there.

With Connor rejected, this leaves us with option D)ex.

Dex has implied to Tracy that other people are always getting her out of jams, which, while it seems like a fair critique of a rich girl in general, is not something we've actually seen happen in this particular movie, but at this point *Tracy has accepted Dex as the authority on who she is,* and so she decides he's right and that she herself should do the awkward business of telling the guests that the wedding is off.

She opens the door to the hall, and shouts for attention, but then gets tongue-tied, and pleads with Dex for help. And so Dex starts feeding her lines. He has Tracy tell them that there's going to be a wedding after all, that she's going to remarry him, Dex.

She says: "Oh, Dex. I'll be *yar* now. I'll promise to be *yar.*"

And Dex says: "Be whatever you like. You're my redhead."

And it's all extremely romantic. And they get married. And it's in the tabloids. She has made her choice. The end.

It would be easy to say that this story, in which a woman confuses her choice of a partner with her choice of an identity, is ridiculous, of another era. How awful, we might say, that in 1940, we still thought of women's identities in this way.

Boys, boys, boys! Which will Tracy choose? How silly for a woman to put so much stock in men, to speak of them so much! Why not focus on Tracy? Why not give us Hepburn Qua Hepburn? Let her choose her own identity!

Unless, of course, your last partner did a number on you, and afterward you didn't feel quite like yourself anymore. Weren't sure, anymore, who you were.

Unless, of course, you remember. Remember every not-great experience you've ever had with a partner. How they made you feel wary and angry and fearful and then, how they also told you to stop acting like you were made of bronze or something. To be a little warmer, and kinder, and more forgiving of human frailty.

It's awfully hard to be *yar* when you've already been up and down the coast a few times.

Barbara Walters once got a bad rap for asking Hepburn if she were a tree, what kind she would be. (An oak.) I think what made people laugh at the question was not just how softball it was, but the fantasy of it. As if, when it came to identity, a person just got to choose.

The PS is still full of romance and mystery for me. It is still my favorite movie. And these days, when I turn it on, it's not the men, and it's not even Tracy, whom I'm watching. It's Hepburn. I'm watching and I'm asking Hepburn how she manages to move Tracy through the scenes with so much power and grace.

Barbara Walters's tree question was ridiculous, but she redeemed herself in an another interview, ten years later, with this exchange, as good an answer as I'll ever get:

WALTERS: You cry very often in films. Do you ever cry in real life?

HEPBURN: Cry?

WALTERS: Cry.

HEPBURN: No. I don't cry. . . .

WALTERS: In films you do.

HEPBURN: Yes, so they'll know I'm sad.

WALTERS: Are you ever in doubt?

HEPBURN: Practically always. . . .

WALTERS: Yet you're so definite!

HEPBURN: Yes, I am, but you might as well be.

The Man Behind the Curtain

*"All the magic isn't in fairyland," he said gravely.
"There's lots of magic in all Nature, and you may
see it as well in the United States, where you and
I once lived."*

—L. FRANK BAUM, *TIK-TOK OF OZ*

My friend and I went to the Yellow Brick Road Casino, looking for a good time. We were not optimistic about this, but we thought it might be a laugh. Neither of us was a gambler. We set ourselves a twenty-dollar budget because we did not trust ourselves with more.

I had been driving by this casino in Chittenango, New York, for almost two years. It is painted emerald green and has a wide yellow awning. Above the awning, the Yellow Brick Road's sign of neon bricks blink in a spiral. I was hoping that, inside, the YBR would have a little bit of Oz-y magic to it. You'll think this was naïve of me, but I was hopeful because I used to *know* the Wizard of Oz. We were in communication for many years. I had my eye on the casino because, when the wizard died, he left me short on a kind of magic I've been looking for ever since.

. . .

In any given room, my grandfather would find the smartest, strangest child and put himself in league with them against the adults. He loved: hand buzzers, trick horses, fake vomit, squirting daisies, cowboy truisms, knock-knock jokes, and scatological humor. On grandparents' visiting day in the third grade, he promised every child at my lunch table a strawberry-shortcake ice cream bar, against the wishes of their parents. Instead of simply handing out the ice cream, he gave us each a dollar, so we could feel the power of exchanging the currency ourselves.

I thought of him as a wizard. This is not a metaphor. The thing my grandad Ed Joyce loved most was *The Wonderful Wizard of Oz,* and when I was a child he perpetrated an obvious but persuasive prank upon my little sister and me in which he convinced us, methodically, and across multiple media, that the Land of Oz was real.

Is it fair to call it a prank if he never hoped for a gotcha moment? If he hoped we'd believe in him forever?

Inside, there was nothing Oz-like about the YBR at all. It looked like clip art of a casino. Worse, it had been so long since I last gambled that everything about how a casino worked had changed. At the problematic Disneyland that is Mohegan Sun I'd once been given a velvety pouch of chips, heavy with possibility. On a riverboat in Natchez, Mississippi, that looked like the set of *Maverick,* I'd received a foam cup of golden tokens with a lovely jingle to it. There'd been a kind of magic in the transubstantiation of money into these new currencies that had the power to multiply themselves into something more.

This was not the case at YBR. At the info desk, we were

given loyalty cards with our legal names on them. We took these to the slots, which were mostly digital: Lobstermania, Snow Leopard, Sexy Viking Lady—none of them Oz-themed. I put my card into a slot and tried to load money onto it, only to discover the card did nothing other than earn rewards points at a local gas station.

I approached a pair of nicely dressed workers who were milling about the floor, to ask them how I was supposed to give the casino my money. The workers were called, I shit you not, *munchkins*.

The munchkins told me that YBR was now a state-of-the-art casino, just like Atlantic City, just like Vegas.

"What does that mean?" I said.

"It means," the munchkins said, "you can put your cash directly into the machine."

My friend and I returned to the digital slots, which, it turned out, were boring. You pressed a button to pledge your dollar amount, and the digital wheels spun. The button was unsatisfying. It offered no illusion of guiding my own fortunes.

The analog slots were better. Their tumblers rolled and glowed: bar, cherries, dollar sign. Was it the thunking of the machine that appealed, or was it that I had seen people win money this way in a movie? Or was it maybe that this machine had not a button, but a handle? It took some heft to pull it—you had to *try*. There was even some technique to it, I told myself. I developed a slow-then-quick maneuver that got me closer to the triple cherries than I'd come before.

I liked how the old-gen machines made it seem like maybe I was a tiny bit in charge of my own fortunes. I could decide how to pull the bar, and how hard, and each time I fed the machine a dollar, I became a little more convinced I'd gotten my technique down.

Soon, I was going to pull the handle and the triple cherries would come, because I'd earned it. I'd put in my time with this machine, and America had raised me to believe that time invested would always pay off. I lost again. I had found myself in the space where the reality of the American Dream collides with the truth that the House Always Wins.

My grandad's Oz origin story was the Depression. He was the son of a war hero/ex-con called Cap, who, when his Arizona dude ranch went bust, took his family on the road. My grandfather spent much of his early life on the move, sometimes even living out of the family car, as Cap joined the Civilian Conservation Corps and ran his "wild west" magazine. My grandfather often found himself parked in the library of whatever town they landed in, where he found his only friends: Dorothy and the Scarecrow and Tik-Tok and Polychrome and the whole cast of characters in L. Frank Baum's *Oz* series. He told himself that someday, if he ever had any money, he would buy all the *Oz* books. The thirteen originals written by Baum, and twenty-six written by other authors.

As it turned out, as an adult, he did have money. Quite a bit of it.

The story of how this happened is the sort of "up by his bootstraps" American Dream tale people can't resist, and it was as ubiquitous in my childhood as the story of Oz. Ed Joyce went from being a child of the Depression living out of a car to working in radio. He hosted a jazz program as Jazzman Joyce!

After that there was a live children's television show sponsored by a cake company, *Breadtime Stories,* which featured a real monkey named Cookie. There was a radio interview show, *The Talk of New York,* where he brought on guests like Malcolm X and Timothy Leary. When he moved into hard reporting, he was responsible for breaking the story of Ted Kennedy at Chappaquiddick. In the 1980s, he became the president of CBS News, where he gained a reputation for being so simultaneously brutal and charming that he was known as "the velvet shiv."

Across these years and successes, he went about acquiring a complete set of first-edition *Oz* books. He read them to his own children, and while we were growing up, he read them to my sister and me. We all lived in the same small Connecticut town.

There was nothing I loved more than these stories. He had a radioman's flair and performed the chapters as a madcap, polyphonic one-man show. I can tell you *exactly* what the Nome King, and Princess Ozma, and Tik-Tok are supposed to sound like.

The *Oz* readings were only briefly discontinued when my grandparents retired back west to a horse ranch in Santa Ynez, California. I was seven and my sister was four.

The radioman's solution to the distance, of course, was recording.

Every day, after school, my sister and I checked the mailbox for a padded mailer with a cassette tape inside. An *Oz* chapter. My grandad included photocopies of the illustrations that went with the reading. He set the scene at the beginning of the tapes—telling us where he was sitting and whether any of his dogs were around. At the end he always let us know what he was doing next, normally feeding his horses, and then he told us to be good to our parents and stay "frisky and jolly."

This was when my grandfather began convincing us that Oz was real.

There is one bit of tape to this effect still extant. Mid-chapter, mid-recording, he receives a phone call, the line bleating stagily in the background. He apologizes for interrupting our reading. "I think I have to take this . . ." he says, and pretends to turn off the tape. Then he says: "Oh, hello, Wizard!" in a tone of absolute delight. He proceeds to make a date to hang out in a poppy field, assuring his caller, *the fucking Wizard,* that he has indeed been practicing the magic he'd taught him so he could perform tricks for us kids that coming Christmas. Has he told the kids that Oz is real? Oh, no, no, he hasn't yet. But he will, when the time is right. "Goodbye, Wizard!"

When my sister and I first heard this bit of tape we turned to each other and said *nothing.* To even repeat what we had heard would break the spell.

It was possible to believe. Because my grandad *did* do magic tricks. He pulled scarves from his nose and guessed the color of dice in secret boxes and erased images from coloring books with flourishing gestures.

Why wouldn't we think he was in league with the wizard?

With each trip to California, the illusion grew. He took us to Figueroa Mountain and led us waist-deep into a legitimate poppy field. We collected pine cones bigger than footballs, which he soaked in Borax so that when we threw them into the campfire they turned the flames green. He pretended he could talk to animals (in Oz, animals talk) and taught his own horse to nod and stamp responses to his questions—an old dude-ranch trick learned from his father. He hid gemstones around the garden, insinuating that the Nome King had left them there and would be very angry if we took his treasure. We always took the treasure, and often found notes in the same spot a day later threatening, thrillingly, to "stomp your curly toes off."

My grandad was the sort of man who was always pulling your leg while simultaneously doing *real* things too amazing to be believed, so where the truth might lie was hard to parse. Back then, I think I knew I was supposed to believe, but only halfway, the way a good scene partner might. Instead, I believed it desperately, recklessly, as if asking too many questions might scare the fantasy away.

I had my reasons for wanting to believe that the world my grandfather was spinning for us was possible. I was a very ordinary girl who feared I might never become anything different, and in the *Oz* books even very ordinary girls from Kansas could be whisked away from chores and schoolwork to have adventures with robots and queens. It didn't matter that Dorothy wasn't remarkable—she could still do incredible things. Back then, I made no distinction between believing in Oz and believing in an American Dreamish world where the poor son of an ex-con cowboy could rise through the ranks of American life. America would see something in you that no one else did and give you a chance at whatever marvelous future you aspired to! Oz was for everyone!

Late capitalism is not a good moment for believing in either of these kinds of magic.

As an adult, the real world often disappoints me. I am a person who prefers to live in my head, in books and fantasies, where everything shines slightly brighter than reality. I've often wished to go back to the times when some of the Nome King's rocks might appear on my front stoop, when some animal would speak to me its secret.

The first cracks in the illusion came in the sixth grade, when we were asked to read a biography by a significant person. It is perhaps telling that, in my Oz-mania, I did not choose to read a biography of Baum and instead chose Judy Garland, who, of course, played Dorothy in the 1939 movie production of *The Wizard of Oz*. We were meant to come to school on Biography Day dressed as the subject of our chosen book and to report to the class about our lives . . . *in the first person, in character.* We would then go on to mingle with our famous compatriots at a "Character Brunch."

My mother helped me locate *Little Girl Lost: The Life and Hard Times of Judy Garland* by Al DiOrio, Jr., at the local library.

I was horrified and obsessed by Garland's tragic biography and was determined to bring her truth to the people. And yet, in a totally warped choice, *I still chose to appear at school dressed as Dorothy that day,* not as Garland. I was all pigtails, glitter-glue heels, and blue ankle socks when I stood in front of my fellow sixth graders and introduced myself as "Judy, Judy, Judy." I told the class that the rigors of my film shoots required me to take "uppers," which were *drugs,* which also helped me lose weight, which was "good for Hollywood," and about the difficulty I then had sleeping, which required "downers" (also *drugs*!), and how this cycle of uppers and downers eventually killed me.

I then whispered that there were rumors that my death wasn't really an accident but a suicide.

When the bell rang, my teacher suggested I playact as Dorothy instead of Garland at the impending Character Brunch.

"Can I *at least* tell people about Carnegie Hall?" I asked.

"Sure," she said.

I understand now that I was meant to read and report on something uplifting, to behave like the other children, who'd come dressed as Jackie Robinson and Marie Curie and whose families had presumably found them biographies that did not dwell on the other Black ballplayers who were robbed of the chance to make good on their talent, or on the effects of radiation exposure. We were all meant to be Dorothy and not Judy that day—to recite the shiny, Oz-y dream version of our biography's subject. Given my predilection for fantasy, it might surprise you to learn that I was also the kind of kid who hated a lie. But I knew there was a difference between a fantasy and a lie even then. And that day in sixth grade, I smelled a rat.

"Hi, Grandad. I was Dorothy at school this week," I told him on our regular phone call.

"How did it go?" he asked

"Not too great," I said. "Not too great at all."

When I told him what had happened, he positively cackled.

I am a teacher, and I once spent an entire semester, with my undergrad literature students in Florida, accidentally calling the American Dream the "American Myth." It was November before a Cuban-American student I'd known for a couple semesters felt comfortable enough to correct me, mid-lecture. I thanked her.

"What an embarrassing and strange thing to get wrong," I told the class.

"I mean you were wrong but you're not *wrong*," she said, plonking her copy of *Winter's Bone* on the desk. We all laughed. It was funny but it wasn't funny.

I suppose something about the word *dream* doesn't sit right with me.

In Baum's books, Dorothy's adventure with the Wizard is only the first of many times she goes to Oz—in later stories she even brings her family with her, an uplifting example of chain migration—and Oz's reality is asserted by these return visits. The movie sends a different message, not for lack of sequels, but because, in the end, Dorothy wakes up. It was all a dream, her family tells her. "But it wasn't a dream," Dorothy says, "it was a place." All the Gales' farmhands are gathered around her bedside when Garland says she saw them in Oz, as the Scarecrow, the Tin Man, and the Cowardly Lion. And yet *here* they are. Bolger and Haley and Lahr, now in the reality of black and white. They are dressed sensibly, the dirt of their work on their gorgeous faces.

Were men such as them ever in such a place?

Oh, no honey, their looks say, *not us—we never got to go anywhere like that*.

They are still down on the farm.

I've always hated the way the movie gives us the promise of Oz only to snatch it away in the end, and the three friends break my heart most of all.

I've taught undergrads at five very different schools over the past decade. I am essentially an optimist and I earnestly believe in my students' futures. Some of the students I've taught came up rough like my grandfather, some rougher, some of them were middle-class kids who never doubted they'd get a degree, some of them were scrappy farm kids, some of them survived lifetimes of hardship and were finally going back to school in their sixties, some of them were veterans, some of them had escaped gangs, some of them came from intense privilege, and many of them were first-generation Americans. I think that *all* of these different kinds of students wound up in my classroom in no small part because they had bought into an American Dream that promised a college degree would open doors.

And maybe this is why my belief in the dream crashed and burned.

Because it is easy enough to believe a dream for yourself, and quite another to speak it out loud to a room of students who trust you to tell them the truth.

These days, I cannot bring myself to sell my students any kind of American rhetorical goods that claim to be equally available to all of them. I cannot bring myself to tell them about the Technicolor future, and say, *I see* you *there, and I see* you *there.* Because, even if I do think I see it, there's a chance that someday we're all going to wake up and I will have betrayed them by dreaming too vividly at the front of the classroom.

I think my mouth said "myth" when it couldn't say "dream" because to describe our collective American story to students as an available goal and not a particular generation's narrative-shape-of-choice makes me feel like I am back in the sixth grade, Dorothy on the outside but Judy on the inside. Like I am smelling a rat, and the rat is me.

When we were at the casino, we were in the current-day town of Chittenango, most of which is on Oneida, or Onyota'a:ká, lands. Chittenango is also the birthplace of L. Frank Baum. Presumably, it is for this reason that the Oneida Nation decided to name its casino Yellow Brick Road, and its adjoining liquor store the Tin Woodman's Flask.

Had I read a biography of Baum, instead of a biography of Garland, back in sixth grade, I would have learned what I found out the morning before our casino journey, when I looked up his Chittenango connection.

At the top of my search results I found this, from a recent NPR story: "L. Frank Baum, before he wrote *The Wonderful Wizard of Oz,* ran a newspaper in South Dakota. This was in the early 1890s during the Indian Wars. When Baum heard of the killing of Sitting Bull and the massacre at Wounded Knee, he wrote editorials calling for killing each and every last Native American. From his Sitting Bull editorial: *'The Whites, by law of conquest, by justice of civilization, are masters of the American continent, and the best safety of the frontier settlements will be secured by the total annihilation of the few remaining Indians. Why not annihilation? Their glory has fled, their spirit broken, their manhood effaced; better that they die than live the miserable wretches that they are.'*"

Why would the Oneida Nation create a casino inspired by the work of the man who'd published this monstrous op-ed? I'm dumb enough to hope someone decided turning Baum's world profitable for native people would be a satisfying irony. Dumb enough to hope maybe no one knew. I have the good sense not to call the Oneida Nation or the casino and ask. To spare whoever I'd get on the other end of the line my awful question and to instead ask myself what to make of all this.

I ask myself: Why, if I've called myself an Oz-freak all these years, a superfan, have I never googled Baum?

Perhaps I knew better than to try to look for the man behind the curtain.

I'm sure my grandfather wouldn't have been surprised by the facts of Baum's life and prejudices. There are inconvenient truths behind the curtain of most American Dream stories. Capitalism seldom offers a free balloon ride. Stories of someone rising up are usually at the expense of someone else we don't talk about. That's the wizardry of most lovely stories—the sleight of hand, the misdirection, the "look over *here,* not over *there.*"

I think these were ideas my grandfather understood. Because, as it happens, I do own a biography of Baum. *The Real Wizard of Oz* by Rebecca Loncraine had sat unread on my shelf since my grandfather gave it to me, years ago. When I flipped it open, my grandfather's inscription read: "I know you thought I made up all those stories. But this is really the guy. Love, Grandad."

I don't know what to do with Oz anymore. I want to tell you that it was real when I was small, when my grandfather was alive, but that would mean that it was only real so long as it was easy to believe in.

For as long as my grandad and the rest of the greatest generation were still alive, recounting their greatest magic tricks, it was easy enough for me to believe in the American Dream. But without my grandad around pulling silks from his ears, hiding quartz in the garden, coaxing horses to nod and stomp with sugar cubes, the illusion falls flat. The chances of an American Dream–style success in this world begin to feel dinky, random. And yet, even though there's nothing beyond the façade of the Yellow Brick Road Casino that promises any kind of Oz, here I am, in Chittenango, on Oneida land, in Baum's birth-place, feeding my money directly into those state-of-the-art machines.

My friend and I called it quits and put on our winter coats. It was November and there was snow on the ground. On the way out, I asked him to take a picture of me. In the parking lot there was a larger-than-life emerald-green mural of Doro-thy's friends: Scarecrow, Tin Man, Cowardly Lion. They were rendered almost like the old illustrations I knew. My friend backed up and backed up, almost all the way into the road, to take the picture. But they were simply too large. It was impos-sible to fit both them and me in the shot.

The Crane Wife

Ten days after I called off my engagement I was supposed to go on a scientific expedition to study the
whooping crane on the Gulf Coast of Texas. Surely, I
will cancel this trip, I thought, as I shopped for nylon hiking
pants that zipped off at the knee. Surely, a person who calls off
a wedding is meant to be sitting sadly at home, reflecting on
the enormity of what has transpired and not doing whatever
it is I am about to be doing that requires a pair of plastic clogs
with drainage holes. Surely, I thought, as I tried on a very large
and floppy hat featuring a pull cord that fastened beneath my
chin, it would be wrong to even be wearing a hat that looks like
this when something in my life has gone so terribly wrong.

Ten days earlier I had cried and I had yelled and I had packed
up my dog and driven away from the upstate New York house
with two willow trees I had bought with my fiancé, Nick.

Ten days later, and I didn't want to do anything I was supposed to do.

I went to Texas to study the whooping crane because I was
researching a novel. In my novel there were biologists doing
field research about birds and I had no idea what field research

actually looked like, and so the scientists in my novel did things like shuffle around great stacks of papers and frown. The good people of the Earthwatch organization assured me I was welcome on the trip and would get to participate in "real science" during my time on the Gulf. But as I waited to be picked up by my team in Corpus Christi, I was nervous—I imagined everyone else would be a scientist or a birder and have daunting binoculars.

The biologist running the trip rolled up in a large white van with a boat hitch and the words BIOLOGICAL SCIENCES stenciled across the side. Jeff was fortyish and wore sunglasses and a backwards baseball cap. He had a beard and a neon-green cast on his left arm. He'd broken his arm playing hockey with his sons a week before. The first thing Jeff said was: "We'll head back to camp, but I hope you don't mind if we run by the liquor store first." I felt more optimistic about my suitability for science.

Not long before I'd called off my engagement it was Christmas.

The woman who was supposed to be my mother-in-law was a wildly talented quilter and made stockings with Beatrix Potter characters on them for every family member. The previous Christmas she had asked me what character I wanted to be (my fiancé was Benjamin Bunny). I agonized over the decision. It felt important, like whichever character I chose would represent my role in this new family. I chose Squirrel Nutkin, a squirrel with a blazing red tail—an epic, adventuresome figure who ultimately loses his tail as the price for his daring and pride.

I arrived in Ohio that Christmas and looked to the banister

to see where my squirrel had found his place. Instead, I found a mouse. A mouse in a pink dress and apron. A mouse holding a broom and dustpan, serious about sweeping. A mouse named Hunca Munca. The woman who was supposed to become my mother-in-law said, "I was going to do the squirrel but then I thought, That just isn't CJ. *This* is CJ."

What she was offering was so nice. She was so nice. I thanked her and felt ungrateful for having wanted a stocking but not *this* stocking. Who was I to be choosy? To say that this nice thing she was offering wasn't a thing I wanted?

When I looked at that mouse with her broom, I wondered which one of us was wrong about who I was.

The whooping crane is one of the oldest-living bird species on earth. Our expedition was housed at an old fish camp on the Gulf Coast next to the Aransas National Wildlife Refuge, where five hundred of the only eight hundred whooping cranes left in the world spend their winters. Our trip was a data-collecting expedition to study behavior and gather information about the resources available to the cranes at Aransas.

The ladies' bunkhouse was small and smelled woody, and the rows of single beds were made up with quilts. Lindsay, the only other scientist, was a grad student in her early twenties from Wisconsin who loved birds so much that when she told you about them she made the shapes of their necks and beaks with her hands—a pantomime of bird life. Jan, another participant, was a retired geophysicist who had worked for oil companies and now taught high school chemistry. Jan was extremely fit and extremely tan and extremely competent. Jan was not a lifelong birder. She was a woman who had spent two years nursing her mother and then her best friend through cancer. They had both recently died and she had lost herself in caring for them, she said. She wanted a week to be herself. Not a teacher or a mother or a wife. This trip was the thing she was giving herself after their passing.

At five o'clock there was a knock on the bunk door and a very old man walked in, followed by Jeff.

"Is it time for cocktail hour?" Warren asked.

Warren was an eighty-four-year-old bachelor from Minnesota. He could not do most of the physical activities required by the trip, but had been on ninety-five Earthwatch expeditions, including this one once before. Warren liked birds okay. What Warren really loved was cocktail hour.

When he came for cocktail hour that first night, his thin silver hair was damp from the shower and he smelled of shampoo. He was wearing a fresh collared shirt and carrying a bottle of impossibly good Scotch.

Jeff took in Warren and Jan and me. "This is a weird group," Jeff said.

"I like it," Lindsay said.

In the year leading up to calling off my wedding, I often cried or yelled or reasoned or pleaded with my fiancé to tell me that he loved me. To be nice to me. To notice things about how I was living.

One particular time it was because I had put on a favorite red dress for a wedding. I exploded from the bathroom to show him. He stared at his phone. I wanted him to tell me I looked nice, so I shimmied and squeezed his shoulders and said: "You look nice! Tell me I look nice!" He said: "I told you that you looked nice when you wore that dress last summer. It's reasonable to assume I still think you look nice in it now."

Another time he gave me a birthday card with a sticky note inside that said BIRTHDAY. After giving it to me, he explained that because he hadn't written in it, the card was still in good condition. He took off the sticky and put the unblemished card into our filing cabinet.

I need you to know: I hated that I needed more than this from him. There is nothing more humiliating to me than my own desires. Nothing that makes me hate myself more than being burdensome and less than self-sufficient. I did not want to feel like the kind of nagging woman who might exist in a sit-com.

These were small things, and I told myself it was stupid to feel disappointed by them. I had arrived in my thirties believing that to need things from others made you weak. I think this is true for lots of people but I think it is especially true for women. When men desire things, they are "passionate." When they feel they have not received something they need, they are "deprived," or even "emasculated," and given permission for all sorts of behavior. But when a woman needs, she is *needy*. She is meant to contain within her own self everything necessary to be happy.

That I wanted someone to articulate that they loved me, that they *saw* me, was a personal failing and I tried to overcome it.

When I found out that he'd slept with our mutual friend a few weeks after we'd first started seeing each other, he told me we hadn't officially been dating yet, so I shouldn't mind. I decided he was right. When I found out that he'd kissed another girl on New Year's Eve months after that, he said that we hadn't officially discussed monogamy yet, and so I shouldn't mind. I decided he was right.

I asked to discuss monogamy and in an effort to be the sort of cool girl who does not have so many inconvenient needs, I said that I didn't need it. He said he thought we should be monogamous.

Here is what I learned once I began studying whooping cranes: only a small part of studying them has anything to do with the birds. Instead we counted berries. Counted crabs. Measured water salinity. Stood in the mud. Measured the speed of the wind.

It turns out, if you want to save a species, you don't spend your time staring at the bird you want to save. You look at the things it relies on to live instead. You ask if there is enough to eat and drink. You ask if there is a safe place to sleep. Is there enough here to survive?

Wading through the muck of the Aransas reserve, I understood that every chance for food matters. Every pool of drinkable water matters. Every wolfberry dangling from a twig, in Texas, in January, matters. The difference between sustaining life and not having enough was that small.

If there were a kind of rehab for people ashamed to have needs, maybe this was it. You will go to the Gulf. You will count every wolfberry. You will measure the depth of each puddle.

More than once I'd said to my fiancé, "How am I supposed to know you love me if you're never affectionate or say nice things to me or *say* that you love me?"

He reminded me that he'd said "I love you" once or twice before. Why couldn't I just *know* that he did in perpetuity?

I told him this was like us going on a hiking trip and his telling me he had water in his backpack but not ever giving it to me and then wondering why I was still thirsty.

He told me water wasn't like love, and he was right.

There are worse things than not receiving love. There are sadder stories than this. There are species going extinct, and a planet warming. I told myself: Who are you to complain, you with these frivolous extracurricular needs?

On the Gulf, I lost myself in the work. I watched the cranes through binoculars and recorded their behavior patterns and I loved their long necks and splashes of red. The cranes looked elegant and ferocious as they contorted their bodies to preen themselves. From the outside, they did not look like a species fighting to survive.

In the mornings we made one another sandwiches and in the evenings we laughed and lent one another fresh socks. We gave one another space in the bathroom. Forgave one another for telling the same stories over and over again. We helped Warren when he had trouble walking. What I am saying is that we took care of one another. What I am saying is we took pleasure in doing so. It's hard to confess, but in the time after I called off my wedding, the week I spent dirty and tired on the Gulf, I was happy.

On our way out of the reserve, we often saw wild pigs, black and pink bristly mothers and their young, scurrying through the scrub and rolling in the dust among the cacti. In the van each night, we made bets on how many wild pigs we might see on our drive home.

. . .

One night, halfway through the trip, I bet reasonably. We usually saw four, I hoped for five, but I bet three because I figured it was the most that could be expected.

Warren bet wildly, optimistically, too high.

"Twenty pigs," Warren said. He rested his interlaced fingers on his soft chest.

We laughed and slapped the vinyl van seats at this boldness.

But the thing is, we did. We saw *twenty pigs* on the drive home that night. And in the thick of our celebrations, I realized how sad it was that I'd bet so low. That I wouldn't even let myself *imagine* receiving as much as I'd hoped for.

What I learned to do, in my relationship with my fiancé, was to survive on less. At what should have been the breaking point, but wasn't, I learned that he had cheated on me. The woman he'd been sleeping with was a friend of his I'd initially wanted to be friends with, too, but who did not seem to like me, and whom he'd gaslighted me into being jealous of, and then gaslighted me into feeling crazy for being jealous of.

The full course of the gaslighting took a year, so by the time I truly found out what had happened, the infidelity was already a year in the past.

It was new news to me but old news to my fiancé.

"Logically," he said, "it doesn't matter anymore."

It had happened a year ago. Why was I getting worked up over ancient history?

I did the mental gymnastics required.

I convinced myself that I was a logical woman who could consider this information about having been cheated on, about his not wearing a condom, and I could separate it from the current reality of our life together.

Why did I need to know that we'd been monogamous? Why did I need to have and discuss inconvenient feelings about this ancient history?

I would not be a woman who needed these things, I decided. I would need less. And less.

I got very good at this.

"The Crane Wife" is a story from Japanese folklore. I found a copy in the reserve's gift shop among the baseball caps and bumper stickers that said GIVE A WHOOP. And there are so many versions of this story, but in the one I found, there is a crane who tricks a man into thinking she is a woman so she can marry him. She loves him, but knows that he will not love her if she is a crane so she spends every night plucking out all of her feathers with her beak. She hopes that he will not see what she really is: a bird who must be cared for, a bird capable of flight, a creature, with creature needs. Every morning, the crane wife is exhausted, but she is a woman again. To keep becoming a woman is so much self-erasing work. She never sleeps. She plucks out all her feathers, one by one.

One night on the Gulf, we bought a sack of oysters off a passing fishing boat. We'd spent so long on the water that day I felt like I was still bobbing up and down in the current as I sat in my camp chair. We ate the oysters and drank. Jan took the shucking knife away from me because it kept slipping into my palm. Feral cats trolled the shucked shells and pleaded with us for scraps.

Jeff was playing with the sighting scope we used to watch the birds and I said, "What are you looking for in the middle of the night?" He gestured me over, and when I looked through the sight, the moon swam up close.

I think I was afraid that if I called off my wedding I was going to ruin myself. That doing it would disfigure the story of my life in some irredeemable way. I had experienced worse things than this, but none threatened my American understanding of a life as much as a called-off wedding did. What I understood on the other side of my decision, on the Gulf, was that there was no such thing as ruining yourself. There are ways to be wounded and ways to survive those wounds but no one can survive denying their own needs. To be a crane wife is unsustainable.

I had never seen the moon so up close before. What struck me most was how battered she looked. How textured and pocked by impacts. There was a whole story written on her face—her face, which from a distance looked perfect.

It's easy to say that I left my fiancé because he cheated on me. It's harder to explain the truth. The truth is that I didn't leave him when I found out. Not even for one night.

I found out about the cheating *before* we got engaged and I still said yes when he proposed in the park on a day we were meant to be celebrating a job I'd just gotten that morning. Said yes even though I'd told him I was politically opposed to the diamonds he'd convinced me were necessary. Said yes even though he turned our proposal into a joke by making a *Bachelor* reference and giving me a rose. I am ashamed by all of this.

He hadn't said one specific thing about me or us during the proposal, and on the long trail walk out of the park I felt robbed of the kind of special declaration I'd hoped a proposal would entail, and, in spite of hating myself for wanting this, hating myself more for fishing for it, I asked him: "Why do you love me? Why do you think we should get married? Really?"

He said he wanted to be with me because I wasn't annoying or needy. Because I liked beer. Because I was low-maintenance.

I didn't say anything. A little farther down the road he added that he thought I'd make a good mother.

This wasn't what I hoped he would say. But it was what was being offered. And who was I to want more?

I didn't leave when he said that the woman he had cheated on me with had told him over the phone that she thought it was unfair that I didn't want them to be friends anymore.

I didn't leave when he wanted to invite her to our wedding. Or when, after I said she could not come to our wedding, he got frustrated and asked what he was supposed to do when his mother and his friends asked why she wasn't there.

Reader, I almost married him.

Even now I hear the words as shameful: Thirsty. Needy. The worst things a woman can be. Some days I still tell myself to take what is offered, because if it isn't enough, it is you who wants too much. I am ashamed to be writing about this instead of writing about the whooping cranes, or literal famines, or any of the truer needs of the world.

But what I want to tell you is that I left my fiancé when it was almost too late. And I tell people the story of being cheated on because that story is simple. People know how it goes. It's harder to tell the story of how I convinced myself I didn't need what was necessary to survive. How I convinced myself it was my lack of needs that made me worthy of love.

After cocktail hour one night, in the cabin kitchen, I told Lindsay about how I'd blown up my life. I told her because I'd just received a voice mail saying I could get a partial refund for my high-necked wedding gown. The refund would be partial because they had already made the base of the dress but had not done any of the beadwork yet. They said the pieces of the dress could still be unstitched and used for something else. I had caught them just in time.

I told Lindsay because she was beautiful and kind and patient and loved good things like birds and I wondered what she would say back to me. What would every good person I knew say to me when I told them that the wedding to which they'd RSVP'd was off and that the life I'd been building for three years was going to be unstitched and repurposed?

Lindsay said it was brave not to do a thing just because everyone expected you to do it.

Jeff was sitting outside, in front of the cabin with Warren, as Lindsay and I talked, tilting the sighting scope so it pointed toward the moon. The screen door was open and I knew he'd heard me, but he never said anything about my confession.

What he did do was let me drive the boat.

The next day it was just him and me and Lindsay on the water. We were cruising fast and loud. "You drive," Jeff shouted over the motor. Lindsay grinned and nodded. I had never driven a boat before. "What do I do?" I shouted. Jeff shrugged.

I took the wheel. We cruised past small islands, families of pink roseate spoonbills, garbage tankers swarmed by seagulls, blowing fields of grass and wolfberries, and I realized it was not that remarkable for a person to understand what another person needed.

— II —

So, in the face of overwhelming odds, I'm left with only one option:
I'm going to have to science the shit out of this.

—ANDY WEIR, *THE MARTIAN*

Kind of Deep Blue

I did not intend to be single in the rural village where I live. I'd moved there with my fiancé after taking a good job at the local university. We'd bought a house with room enough for children. Then the wedding was off and I found myself single in a town where the nonstudent population is 1,236. I briefly considered flirting with the cute local mailman, the cute local bartender—then realized the foolishness of limiting my ability to do things like get mail or get drunk in a town with only 1,235 other adults. For the first time in my life, I decided to find a date online. I was thirty-four.

The thing about chatting with people on Tinder is that it is boring. I am an obnoxious kind of conversation snob and have a pathologically low threshold for small talk. I love people who fall into the category of Smart, Sad People Flaunting Their Intelligence with Panache. I love Shakespeare's fools and Elizabeth Bennet and Cyrano de Bergerac. I love the *Gilmore Girls* and *The West Wing* and *Rick and Morty*. I long for a conversation partner who travels through an abundance of interesting material at breakneck speed, shouting over their shoulder at me, "Keep up!" Someone who assumes I am up for the challenge, someone who assumes the best of me.

It will not surprise you to learn that this is a totally batshit way to approach Tinder and that, for my snobbery, I paid a price.

The first person who seemed to share my conversational ethos over chat was an academic, a musician. He had a dark sense of humor, he was witty, and he laid all his baggage out there on the line right away. Even through our little chat window it was obvious he was fully and messily human. I could not wait to meet him.

But reality was different. What had seemed passionate and daring online turned out to be alarmingly intense. There were multiple bouts of tears, there were proposed road trips to meet his mother and dog, there was an unexpected accordion serenade, and there was the assertion that I would make a beautiful pregnant woman. Please know that I think a man who can cry is an evolved man. I hope to someday have a kid, which might entail being, for a time, a pregnant woman. I even like the accordion. None of this was bad on its own, but altogether it was *so much*. After I said I didn't want to date anymore, he sent me adorable letterpress cards in the mail that said he was upset, no, angry, that I wouldn't give us a shot.

My next date had just moved to New York by way of Europe and was a collector of stories and observations. Our chats took the form of long blocks of text—anecdotes swapped and interrogated. Offerings dropped at each other's feet. And I loved this.

But these stories became grotesque in real life. My date spent most of our dinner trotting out anecdotes about how Americans were "very fat," which made it difficult to enjoy my chiles rellenos. When we went back to his apartment for a drink, it was beautifully decorated—full of plants and woven hangings and a bicycle propped against a shelf full of novels. He was smart and handsome and sort of an asshole, but perhaps in a way that would mellow over time in a Darcy-ish manner, I thought. We drank some wine and when eventually I said I should probably go home, he got up and kissed me, which I enjoyed, and so I told myself that this was what online dating was like. That I should carpe diem and have an experience.

During sex, he choked me. Not for long, and not very hard, but his hands manifested very suddenly around my throat in a way I know was meant to be sexy but which I found, from this relative stranger, totally frightening. I had not indicated this was something I liked, and neither had he. I know people are into that. *I* could even be into that. But not as a surprise.

Afterward, as he talked to me, I counted the appropriate number of minutes I needed to wait before making an exit that wouldn't seem like I was running away. I was still counting when he said that he was really interested in mass shooters and the kinds of messages they left behind. Still naked, he brought his phone to bed and showed me a video from 4chan. I sat there, his sheets twisted around my waist, as he held his phone out so I could see this compilation of mass shooters' video manifestos, set to comically upbeat music. "It's hilarious," he asserted. And I said I had to go. The next day, and a few times after, he messaged asking why I had run away and gone dark.

What seemed interesting online was pointing me toward wild extremes in real life. I knew I had to stop obsessing over people's banter. But once I gave up the banterers, my Tinder chats read like a liturgy: where are you from, how do you like our weather, how old is your dog, what are your hobbies, what is your job, oh, no, an English teacher, better watch my grammar winkyfacetongueoutfacenerdyglassesface.

For a civilian, I know kind of a lot about robots. Specifically, I know about chatbots and other AI meant to perform through language. In fact, at the time I began online dating, I was teaching a class of undergrads about representations of robots in science writing and science fiction. In class, we discussed how an artificial intelligence that manages, through a text-based conversation, to pass as human can be said to have passed a Turing test.

A Tinder chat was its own kind of test, wasn't it? One in which we were trying to prove to each other that we were *real,* were *human,* were *fuckable,* or possibly even *lovable.* This was also a kind of Turing test, I decided. Or maybe online dating just seemed more bearable when I thought of it this way. It was easier to pretend I was a woman conducting a scientific investigation of language than it was to admit that I was lonely. Than admitting that an algorithm someone had made to sell ads to singles was now in charge of my happiness. Easier than admitting that this was a risk I was willing to take.

I was teaching one of my favorite books at the time: *The Most Human Human* by Brian Christian. Christian goes to participate in the world's most famous Turing test, the Loebner Prize, in Brighton. He serves as a human blind, chatting through an interface with people who then have to decide whether he is a human or a chatbot. The true point of the Loebner Prize is to see whether any of the chatbots can convince the judges of their humanity—but as Christian's title suggests, there is also a jokey prize offered to the human confederate whom the fewest participants mistake for a robot. Receiving the Most Human Human award was Christian's goal. In the book, he asks: What could a human do with language that a robot could not? What are the ways of expressing ourselves that are the most surprisingly human? How do we recognize our fellow humans on the other side of the line?

And so, as I attempted to find the lovely and interesting people I was sure were lurking behind the platitudes of the average Tinder chat, I asked myself Christian's question: What could I do that a robot couldn't? How could I be a person who both understood that she was online, on Tinder, and still communicate like a humane human being?

I was thinking metaphorically, but there *are* real chatbots on Tinder. I never encountered one (to my knowledge. Actually . . . was Dale with the six-pack and swoopy hair and the photo on a yacht who wanted to know if I was DTF RN, only ever a beautiful amalgamation of 1s and 0s?). But this is such a common problem on Tinder that a culty test has emerged—a kind of CAPTCHA for humans to deploy if a match seems suspiciously glamorous or otherwise unreal. In the Potato Test, you ask the person you're speaking with to say "Potato" if they're human. And if they don't, well, you know. One of my favorite screenshots of this going down (the Tinder subreddit is a glorious place) reads as follows:

TINDER: YOU MATCHED WITH ELIZABETH

ACTUAL HUMAN MAN: OH LORD. GOTTA DO THE POTATO TEST.

SAY POTATO IF YOU'RE REAL.

"ELIZABETH": HEYY! YOU ARE MY FIRST MATCH. I DARE YOU
TO TRY TO MAKE A BETTER FIRST MESSAGE AHAHA

ACTUAL HUMAN MAN: SAY POTATO ELIZABETH

"ELIZABETH": AND BTW, IF YOU DON'T MIND ME ASKING THIS,
WHY ARE YOU ON TINDER? PERSONALLY I THINK I'M NOT
MUCH INTO SERIOUS STUFF AHAHA

ACTUAL HUMAN MAN: SAY POTATO

Meanwhile, the conversations I was having with true potato-tested men and women weren't much different from Actual Human Man's conversation with Elizabeth. These conversations never resolved into anything more than small talk—which is to say that they never resolved into anything that gave me a sense of who the hell I was talking to.

I started taking hopeful chances again, and many of my conversations yielded real-life dates. I could write you a taxonomy of all the different kinds of bad those dates were. Sometimes it was my fault (blazing into oversharing and rightfully alienating people), sometimes it was their fault (bringing his own chicken sandwich and commenting on my tits within the first fifteen minutes), and sometimes it was nobody's fault and we had a fine time but just sat there like two nonreactive elements in a beaker. One way or another, though, what it always came down to was the conversation.

The chapter I have always loved most in Christian's book is the one about Garry Kasparov "losing" at chess to Deep Blue, IBM's chess-playing computer, in which he explains the concept of playing in "book." In short, the book is the known series of chess moves that should be played in sequence to optimize success. In most high-level chess matches, the first part of any game is played in "book" and a knowledgeable observer will know which moves will follow which until a certain amount of complexity and chaos necessitates improvisation—at which point the players begin to play in earnest. Some might say *play as themselves.* Kasparov holds that he did not lose to Deep Blue because the game was still in book when he made his fatal transposition error and so, while he flubbed the script, he never truly even *played* against the algorithmic mind of his opponent during that particular match.

Christian makes a brilliant comparison between most polite conversation—small talk—and the "book," arguing that true human interaction doesn't start happening until one or both of the participants diverge from their scripts of culturally defined pleasantries. The book is necessary in some ways, as it is in chess (Bobby Fischer would disagree), in order to launch us into these deeper, realer conversations. But it is all too easy to have an entire conversation without ever *leaving* the book these days—to talk without ever accessing the other person's specific humanity.

This was my trouble with Tinder. No matter how hard I tried to push into real human terrain, over chat, and some-times on real-life dates, I always found myself dragged back into a scripted dance of niceties. I might as well have been on dates with Deep Blue, ordering another round of cocktails and hoping its real programming would eventually come online.

After these dates, I felt pretty low. Like I would never find what I was looking for.

What was I looking for?

Sometimes I thought about Elizabeth Who Wouldn't Say Potato and her suitor. I thought about how he asked her not if she was human, but if she was *real*. There's a passage from *The Velveteen Rabbit* which my sister asked me to read at her wedding. I thought I was up for the task—it's a children's book, for fuck's sake—but when the time came, I cried all the way through:

> "Real isn't how you are made," said the Skin Horse. "It's a thing that happens to you. When a child loves you for a long, long time, not just to play with, but REALLY loves you, then you become Real."
>
> "Does it hurt?" asked the Rabbit.
>
> "Sometimes," said the Skin Horse, for he was always truthful. "When you are Real you don't mind being hurt. . . . You become. It takes a long time. That's why it doesn't happen often to people who break easily, or have sharp edges, or who have to be carefully kept. Generally, by the time you are Real, most of your hair has been loved off, and your eyes drop out and you get loose in the joints and very shabby. But these things don't matter at all, because once you are Real you can't be ugly, except to people who don't understand."

This was what I wanted: for someone to prove to me not only that they weren't a robot, but that they were *real,* and would make me real, too. But it's not like I could put that in a Tinder bio. *CJH, 34, not carefully kept, will keep it real 'til our eyes drop out <3*

It had been, by this point, a year of on-and-off Tinder dating. At one point I even googled Brian Christian to see if he was single. And alas, he was not.

"That's it," I told my friends, for whom I always performed

the stories of my bad dates. "I'm ghosting everyone in my in-box and deleting my account."

But there was one man I kept talking with, despite my resolution.

ME: I'M LAUGHING AT THE PART OF YOUR BIO WHERE YOU SAY YOU'RE "HOPELESSLY EXTROVERTED." ARE YOU THE SORT OF PERSON WHO MAKES FRIENDS ON AIRPLANES?

JOEY: NO, BUT I'M A CHRONIC OVER-SHARER!

ME: I'VE ACTUALLY GROWN INTO OVER-SHARING. IT'S THE ONLY WAY TO AVOID INFINITE SMALL-TALK PURGATORY.

JOEY: TINDER IS BY DEFINITION SMALL-TALK PURGATORY.

ME: HOW DO WE ESCAPE?

JOEY: GET AWAY FROM CELL SIGNALS AND HEAD FOR THE HILLS.

We were out of book. It was as if he had gestured to the conversational matrix we were talking inside of, the one I'd been trying to escape, and said, Hey, I see it, too.

We developed our own language. There were inside jokes, callbacks, patterns of engagement. After that first day, a robot couldn't have replaced either of us, because our speech was *for* each other. It revealed who we were together: goofy, honest, heartbroken, funny about our sadness, a little awkward. The language we spoke in was what Christian would call "site specific," meaning it was a language meant to exist in a certain place, at a certain time, with a certain person.

Eventually, I agreed to go on a real-life date with Joey—bargaining us down from dinner to drinks because I'd come to anticipate needing an exit strategy. I made no effort to look nice. I drank two beers with friends beforehand to numb myself to the disappointment I anticipated. But as soon as I showed up at the brewery we'd picked, I immediately regretted these decisions. The man sitting across the bar was even cuter than I'd anticipated, and more than that, as I approached him, thinking about our conversations over the past weeks, I was able to admit to myself how much I liked him already. How much I hoped he might like me. How much I hoped I hadn't already blown this. But as soon as we started talking, my ratty shirt and snow boots, my buzz and other defenses, didn't matter. Our date was all of the things our chats were—awkward, funny, honest, and backandforthy, which is to say *human*.

"I actually hate this brewery," I told him. "Their beer is so bad."

"Me, too!" Joey said.

"Then why did we pick it!"

"It just seems like the sort of place you're supposed to meet."

On our first anniversary, Joey gave me a present. It was a novelty blanket, and woven into it was a screenshot of our first Tinder conversation. He laughed very hard, and I laughed very hard, as he offered it to me, because it was ridiculous. It was meant to be. But it was undercover-earnest, too. It was sweet and it was dumb and I could not have loved that blanket more.

Joey and I split up before we could reach a second anniversary, but as I went about the breakup torture that is boxing up all your ex's things, the photos and gifts too painful to stare down, I couldn't give up the blanket. It was a reminder that being human is risky, and painful, and worth doing. That I'd rather lose everything as Kasparov than succeed as Deep Blue.

The conversation on the blanket is actually quite long, and one of our friends teased us: "You talked for *this* long before you locked it up? You both need better game."

It is true that neither of us had any game. It is also true that this wasn't the point. The point was that we both understood how easy it is to let your life pass along, totally in book, unless you take a risk, disrupt the expected patterns, and try to make something human happen.

Act Two: *The Fantasticks*

Your parents are New Yorkers and raise you a theater kid. They take you to see *The King and I* and *Les Misérables* and *The Phantom of the Opera* and *Cats* and *Rent* but nothing, nothing makes you feel the way *The Fantasticks* does. You see the show three times, and each time, it floors you. It's the longest-running musical in the world. For forty-two years, a person could walk off of the street and into the perfect, timeless moment of the little Sullivan Street Playhouse, with the curtain on a clothesline and the paper moon and the enormous costume trunk and the piano and the harp.

The third and last time you see *The Fantasticks*, you go with the boy. The one who'd always liked the mechanicals in *A Midsummer Night's Dream*. The one who was first in every way that could matter. First love, first sex, first wounds. First time you thought the way you were in love was special, different, something no one else could ever possibly understand.

Do you remember one of the first things The Girl in *The Fantasticks* says? It's this:

I'm sixteen years old, and every day something happens to
   me. . . .

Oh, ohhhh, ohhhhh! I hug myself till my arms turn blue,
    and then I close my eyes, and I cry and cry until the tears
    come down and I can taste them. I love to taste my tears.
    I am special. I am special! Please, God, please, don't let
    me be normal.

Can you remember how you were back then?

You are a senior in high school. It is Connecticut, and it is fall,
and you are walking the hallways between classes. Your high
school is always under construction and so the ceiling panels
are opened to exposed wire and the lighting is sort of dim and
flickery but the floor is clean and well waxed because the janitor, Sandro, takes waxing very seriously. He sings operatically
as he tends the floors at night. You know this because you are
always lingering at the school at night for some activity or play
or club, *in theory*. In practice you are usually sitting on a desk
with chairs turned upside down on top of it, listening to Sandro sing.

He calls you his Bella. The floor-waxing apparatus gets
strapped to his back and he uses a wand with a fuzzy blade to
apply it. The machine makes an enormous sound and Sandro
sings loudly, against the noise. He sings in Italian. You think of
what he sings as opera but it could have been anything in Italian and you would have said that.

For reasons that are hard to explain, you write your college
admissions essay about Sandro. It doesn't matter what prompt
the college gives you, to each school you send this weird little

vignette about how nice it is when Sandro sings in Italian at night and how he calls you Bella and how very beautiful the floors of the school are when properly waxed. It seems obvious to you now that this was not a great move. That this was, maybe, at least part of the reason why your dreams of going to college at Pomona to study with David Foster Wallace were crushed.* Why almost none of the schools you applied to let you in. Because, honestly, they probably thought you were sleeping with Sandro. Or, still not great, thought your only extracurricular activity was shooting the shit with the janitor. Or, also bad, that your essay was a kind of virtue-signaling about how, sure, you were applying to their fancy school but you weren't *like that really; some of my best friends are janitors.* Or, more likely, most egregiously, the Sandro vignette told them you had too big an ego to follow a prompt or instructions. Was proof that you couldn't swallow your desire to write whatever the hell you wanted for even one minute because you were privileged enough to think of an assignment as *restricting your creativity.* To think the rules somehow *didn't apply to you.*

But of course, it turned out, they did. They always do.

The point is you remember how beautifully waxed the floors were that day, because as a classmate goes running down the otherwise empty hallway toward you, his reflection stretches out in front of him, across the shiny floors. He is quite tall to begin with, and now this long, stretched-out version of him is in the floor, reaching toward you, as he flaps his arms and sort of skips down the hallway shouting in a comically performative voice, *"A plane hit the towers, a plane hit the towers!"* He isn't tell-

---

* Yes, you hear yourself, but the loss of this alternate future, even now, gives you the howling fantods.

ing you specifically. He isn't noticing or speaking to you. But this is how you hear about the attack. He doesn't even understand what he is saying yet, you're pretty sure. He just knows he is in possession of some kind of dramatic news and is trumpeting it. And that's what you'll always think about when you think about 9/11: the way this classmate seemed to stretch out forever as he was reflected in Sandro's perfectly waxed floors.

This isn't a 9/11 story. But it matters that it was just after 9/11, because after the attacks a lot of Broadway was struggling, since tourists were too scared to go into the city. Your former–New Yorker parents definitely thought George Bush could shove his capitalist jingoism right up his butt when he said that the best thing Americans could do in response to the tragedy was *shop,* but also, the highest form of patriotism they could think of was donating blood and then buying a lot of theater tickets to save Broadway and making reservations at Sardi's. Was going into the city and acting like New Yorkers *immediately.* Let's call it Patriotic Thespianism.

You see a lot of shows that season.

In December, the boy comes home from college for Christmas. Is he still your boyfriend? You've decided to keep dating long-distance, and you talk on the phone all the time, but when you think about it now, it's clear he was fucking other people and you were not. But you believe he is your boyfriend hard enough to reject the advances of the boys at school, who are probably infinitely better choices, but do any of them want to take the train into the recently attacked city to see a musical with you over winter break? No, they do not. And so they don't stand a chance.

You want to see *The Fantasticks* with the boy because he is also a theater kid. Had been, in fact, the king of the theater kids. The first time you'd ever properly seen him was before you even started dating, when he played Harold Hill in the middle-school production of *The Music Man*, and right away you loved him so fucking much.

The boy has never seen *The Fantasticks* and you think of it as terribly romantic, and so you get tickets. The lights go down in the little theater, a moment that never doesn't thrill you, and the overture plays. It gives you goose bumps.

You know all the lyrics to the show by heart, so it shouldn't come as a surprise, but when the narrator eventually starts singing the musical's most famous song, you hadn't seen it coming:

Try to remember the kind of September
When life was slow and oh, so mellow
Try to remember the kind of September
When grass was green and grain was yellow
Try to remember the kind of September
When you were a tender and callow fellow
Try to remember and if you remember
Then follow . . .

You cry, and the boy cries, and the whole audience and most of the cast and even the harpist cries. The song hasn't changed, but everything around it has.

The Fantasticks is a musical in two parts. The first act consists of an entire happy love story, at the end of which the cast assembles into an intricate blocking arrangement resembling a family portrait, and from these poses, they conclude a great, swelling number called "Happy Ending." When the lights come up on Act Two, the cast appears frozen in these same postures. As if you had left them there all intermission. Several ominous minor keys are played as they fidget and grimace and attempt to hold together their tableau. Then, The Girl picks an imaginary plum from a tree in her father's garden.

She bites it and says, "This plum is too ripe."

The Girl and The Boy split up and go out to see the world. "I'd like to be not evil, but a little worldly wise," the girl sings. They suffer, they learn, they return home. And they are different now, but they fall in love again.

After the show, you and the boy leave the playhouse, and walk around the village holding hands and looking at all the Christmas lights and you feel very worldly and grown-up. Then the boy realizes he's lost his wallet. You turn back toward the playhouse to look for it. It's hard to describe why this lost wallet feels like such an emergency but that's how fragile your happiness seemed back then. A lost wallet was the sort of thing that could sour the mood and ruin the whole day. You try to trace your steps back to the places you've been.

You walk all the way back to the theater and still have not found the wallet, but they are nice enough to let you go inside and look. All the houselights are up, which makes the stage look a little sad and stripped of its magic and there is an old man sweeping the floors. The boy starts looking for his wallet, but you decide to ask the old man, perhaps because, as we've established, you believe in the powers of janitors.

You tell him why you are there and he asks where you were sitting. You rattle off your seat numbers and he moves to the row without having to look at any of the labels; he knows the theater's coordinates by heart. He lifts the boy's wallet from the floor and you both thank him, for finding the wallet, for saving your day, saving the mood, saving the moment—just all of it. You leave the theater arm in arm, almost skipping.

Imagine how sweet the plum still was.

The planes hit the towers in September, and by January *The Fantasticks* is gone. Your mother is watching the news in the kitchen and she yells out to you, "The Sullivan Street Playhouse is closing!" You rush in and there, on TV, is the man who'd been sweeping the floor and gave you back the wallet. It's Lore Noto. The producer who'd put up the show in the first place. Who ran the Sullivan Street Playhouse all those years. Lore Noto gave you back the day by finding the wallet.

You call the boy at college and tell him about the playhouse closing. About Noto. And he also freaks out over the sadness and magic of it all. This is such a satisfying reaction that you are sure, all over again, that the two of you will last forever. Because *he gets it*. He understands about things like *The Fantasticks,* and Sandro's singing, and your classmate's reflection, and every painful-beautiful bit of the world you are convinced no one else understands because whenever you try to explain how keenly you feel it all, people look at you funny (*I am special! I am special!*).

It is infinitely preferable to believe that you and the boy are special than to accept that going around feeling lonely and misunderstood and out of sync with other people is just what it feels like to be a person. To be alive. That this is what life is like for *everyone*.

To this day, listening to *The Fantasticks* overture on a pair of headphones is enough to seize your arms with gooseflesh. But most of the time, when you tell people about *The Fantasticks* they've never heard of it. Even people who like theater.

And this mystifies you because it seemed like they were always there, conjuring magic every night on Sullivan Street. But things can disappear just like that. Even the longest-running musical in the world.

The boy is your longest-running relationship. The person who appeared and reappeared and mattered for the longest stretch of your life.

Did you take the boy to that show to prove to him that you and he, like the second-act Fantasticks, could be separated and then find each other again? Did you imagine that the rules of the world, all its Septembers and buildings fallen down, didn't apply to you? You did. It never occurred to you that when you tried to return to the theater where you and the boy put on your best shows, it would be gone. That the two of you could change so much that you wouldn't be able to trace your steps back to the kids you once were.

The Lady with the Lamp

I am standing at a NASCAR track, full of robots and roboticists, in the suburbs of Miami, Florida, and I am watching an Atlas bot, a humanoid first-responder robot, attempt to open a heavy metal door.

Atlas bot fails to open the door.

It is 2013. I am getting sunburned. It is almost Christmas. "When are you coming home?" my mother asks on the phone. "Not yet," I tell her. "But I'll try to be there for Christmas Eve dinner." She sighs.

I felt I needed to come here. To see this. *This* is the DARPA Robotics Challenge (DRC) trials. Sixteen teams competing to design robots capable of tasks typically carried out by first responders.

I am not a roboticist or an engineer or a programmer or any kind of scientist. I am not even a science writer. I'm a rinky-dink novelist who has paid too much for a rental truck, an enormous black F-150 with the windows stuck down, to drive out to this weird suburb and stay at a motel room, in which, the night before, when I had turned on the heater, it very efficiently burned something inside of itself and set off the smoke detector. I have recently started dating a man, Nick, whom someday I will fail to marry, and I send him text messages about the robots because he really loves an anime called *Evangelion,* in which tiny people in giant, sentient robot mecha suits battle one another, and I think these texts will charm him, but he does not seem terribly charmed. I am wearing a Day-Glo orange vest that says PRESS across the back of it as well as a hard hat, which I was told I was required to wear at all times while in the press zones, which were closer to the robots than the regular stadium seats, and where there might be *flying debris or squirting hydraulic fluid, haha, probably not! But do wear your hard hat.* What I am trying to say is that I feel incredibly foolish in just about all the ways a person can feel foolish.

Atlas bot fails to open the door again.

I have pitched an essay about what it might mean for the American government to fund the development of robotic first responders. The magazine has arranged my press pass. But standing here, in my Day-Glo vest, trying to figure out what to write in my notebook, I am at a loss. What I want to write in my notebook is something someone, most people, might find interesting about all of this. When *I* look at the robots, *I* feel an enormous welling up of some unspecified feeling, *I* find myself moved, almost to tears. But of course I can't write about that for the magazine. This strain of unresolved personal strangeness I know better than to speak aloud, much less to write about.

What would another person think about all this? I keep asking myself, as I watch Atlas bot, notebook ready.

What would someone, most people, find interesting?

What would charm them?

Atlas bot fails to open the door again.

I will try and fail to write this essay for the next eight years.

———

I first became obsessed with robots in 2010. My mania started with research for a story I was writing about a woman who serves as a drone operator, which led me to an incredible book by P. W. Singer called *Wired for War,* a history of robotics in the military. It was Singer who taught me that the majority of all robotics funding in the United States comes from the Defense Department, specifically, DARPA.

ARPA, the Advanced Research Projects Agency, was founded in 1958, not long after the Russians launched Sputnik 1, to be the U.S. program in charge of technology and science research. When the Nixon administration absorbed ARPA into the Defense Department, it became DARPA: The *Defense* Advanced Research Projects Agency.

There are scientific reasons why DARPA has decided to hold these particular trials in 2013. The event is meant to incentivize developing a robot *that can perform the tasks of a human first responder attempting to save human lives in a disaster scenario.* We are, after all, in the wake of the Fukushima meltdown.

So, yes, it is a robotics competition, but it is also a publicity stunt. Robots recast as saviors—part firefighter and part EMT, rushing into burning buildings to save the day. Robots can be the good guys. The Defense Department can be the good guys.

In the press release for the DRC trials, Dr. Gil Pratt, the program manager, said:

> the technology we're trying to develop [will] allow human beings and robots working together to have an effect on evolving disasters in environments that are too dangerous for human beings to go into by themselves.

The trials included eight tasks:

- Drive a utility vehicle at the site
- Travel dismounted across rubble
- Remove debris blocking an entryway
- Open a door and enter a building
- Climb an industrial ladder and traverse an industrial catwalk
- Use a power tool to break through a barrier
- Locate and close a valve near a leaking pipe
- Attach a connector, such as a wire harness or fire hose

The DRC was a casting call for a robotic savior, and I wanted to be there to learn from them. Because saving people was something I thought I knew a little bit about. Back then, I thought that was what it meant to be in love.

———

There is a kind of man I tend to date.

This man is considered undatable by the more reasonable public.

He is considered difficult. He is the sort of man who, when you say his name, those who have met him say, "Oh, him." He is known by everyone in broad strokes and intimately by no one. He seldom has many close friends. He is eccentric or ornery or sad. He is a loner but he also has a big mouth. He does not like many people. He does not let people get close. If you date this kind of man, and meet a friend or relative of his, without fail they will say, "We're just so glad X finally found someone!" and there will be an edge of disbelief or perhaps *relief* in their voice.

If this man is in a band, and he often is, he is most likely the lead guitarist. If he is not in a band, he is still, spiritually, the lead guitarist.

The average person, when encountering such a man, will think, *Oh, boy,* and keep a distance. They will not have figured this man out, per se, but the fact of the man seeming mysterious, seeming to have something *up* with him, is not a thing that is intriguing to them. They do not feel the need to find out what is *up.* They have a suspicion that, whatever is *up,* it will not bring them joy or peace to know about it. And for this reason, they go no further.

To reappropriate language from Dr. Pratt of the DRC, these men are "disasters in environments that are too dangerous for human beings to go into by themselves."

And yet I always go. Why?

Meeting this kind of man activates an impulse. It is not lust. It certainly isn't love. It's the sense that someone has fallen by the wayside and I am the only Samaritan around who might stop. That perhaps by virtue of noticing or being intrigued by him, I am uniquely suited to helping—practically obligated, in fact. I can save this man, I tell myself.

My method for doing this is by dating him.

None of this is reasonable or wise or kind. These men have not asked for help. They have issued no SOS. I am a bit like the Defense Department, deploying troops to some new country I insist needs my help to become democratic and peaceful and free. I occupy the land. I misunderstand the local culture. I create new policies and systems no one asked for. I bungle things. I buy a leather jacket and put up a MISSION ACCOMPLISHED banner and will later regret both. I stay too long. Only years later do I slink away in a defeat I refuse to call defeat.

When we break up, these men and I, and I ask friends whether they had thought we were well suited for each other, they always say: *No one knew why you were with that guy! We assumed there must have been something wonderful about him we didn't know about because you were with him.*

But the *something* was that I was narcissistic enough to think he needed me.

For years, I have convinced myself that love is meant to be an act of extreme and transformative caretaking. And so I've been more savior than partner. More robot than girl. More nurse than lover.

———

For a long time, I referred to my addiction to "saving" difficult men as "Florence Nightingale Syndrome."

Florence Nightingale was called "The Lady with the Lamp" for her tireless insistence on doing nursing rounds during the night, checking in on her patients, most famously wounded soldiers in Crimea. Nightingale is credited with creating many of the methods that spawned uniform modern nursing practices and is also famous for being a kind of statistician—she collected data about her patients and used it to inform future care. She carried a literal lamp, but the sobriquet also implies she was a woman who showed us the way somewhere.

I hope all of this is what she is most famous for, anyway. Because until I looked her up, all *I* knew was that she was a nurse, and that she fell in love with her patients.

"Florence Nightingale Syndrome" (sometimes called the Florence Nightingale Effect) is a trope of pop-psych storytelling in which a caregiver falls in love with their patient, even if there is very little real exchange between them. Caretaking is conflated with love and so the syndrome takes hold.

But it turns out that this is, truly, a bum rap for Florence. Because Nightingale *never fell in love with any of her patients.*

In fact, Nightingale felt that love or romance might get in the way of her nursing career and so specifically avoided romantic entanglements. A man she purportedly loved once proposed to her, and she turned him down so that she could focus on her work.

So where does the term come from?

As best I can tell, the first usage seems to occur in a profile of the actor Albert Finney (yes, that is Daddy fucking Warbucks from *Annie*) in *People* magazine, in 1982:

> In addition to wanderlust, the actor for a while bet heavily on horses (today he owns eight Thoroughbreds). He was equally passionate about drinking, too. "But my digestive tract couldn't cope," he says. "After a few whiskeys I used to throw up—but I'd come back to the party and drink more Pernod anyway. Then my appendix burst. I got peritonitis and realized I couldn't take it. It was what I call 'the John Barrymore syndrome,'" Finney adds sardonically, pouring himself another glass of Chassagne-Montrachet. "You know—you're more interesting and romantic if you seem bent on self-destruction. There may even be some ladies drawn to you who suffer from 'the Florence Nightingale syndrome.' And then, you see, if you don't live up to their expectations, you have the get-out clause."

Get-out clause.

Reading a dinger like that is enough to make a woman conspiracy-minded.

When I think about how my understanding of Florence

Nightingale was corrupted because one rogue comment from a man can eclipse the whole truth of a woman's life . . . it makes me shaky with rage.

And the thing about the Florence Nightingale Syndrome is that it doesn't imply that women should *stop* taking care of people. Rather, it looks at this devoted, persistent care and says: All that is fine so long as you don't *feel a way about it*. By the effect's logic, the way female care goes from saintly to disordered is when a woman develops an emotional relationship with the object of her care or perhaps even with the idea of the care itself. The disorder is not being able to devote yourself to this kind of caretaking without having feelings about it and thereby becoming distractingly human.

This was precisely the kind of logic I was operating under in 2013 when I went to the trials.

And *this* was why I was texting Nick about robots.

This was what I thought the robots of the DRC had to offer me.

They were saviors, offering aid and care, and they could not become disordered, the way I thought I was, with an inconvenient abundance of feelings about it, because they were robots, and they had no feelings. At the DRC, I hoped to witness the glorious thing I might someday become: a perfect, dispassionate savior.

But of course that's not at all what I found in Miami.

————

On the first day of the trials, I must pass through the expo tents in the parking lot to get to the racetrack. Robotics, AI, and VR companies show off projects and products. There is a tent where a remote-controlled robotic snake coils around my ankles and wiggles to music. There are recruitment tents for universities like RPI and MIT. Recruitment tents for first-responder organizations.

I pause at a tent in front of which the robot called Atlas is slumped. The tent has a banner that invites me to experience a virtual-reality simulation of what it feels like "to be Atlas." Atlas is the bot DARPA/Boston Dynamics has issued to competitors developing only their own programming. Another set of teams have elected to design their own physical robotics in addition to the programming work, a significantly more complex challenge. Behind Atlas, a man dangles a pair of VR goggles from his hand. "Want to try?" I make my apologies. I don't want to be late for the trials.

At the racetrack, the event stations for the tasks are set up in the infield. Each one looks like the stage for a strange apocalyptic play. Radioactive symbols and broken metal scaffolding and crumbled bricks. Walls marked with what looks like the aftermath of an explosion. Above the events is a giant Jumbotron carrying the daylong feed of events and the leaderboards.

The outside of the track is ringed by open garages, but instead of being populated by NASCAR drivers and crews, the garages are set up as the home bases of the sixteen teams. Each garage is the place from which a given team's robots will be controlled, and the communication systems used to control them will be "degraded" to simulate a disaster. I see the names I have studied online. RoboSimian from the NASA Jet Propulsion Lab, IHMC, Tartan Rescue, MIT, SCHAFT, HUBO, CHIRON, Mojavaton. Some team garages have ratty couches outside, where team members are unabashedly napping. I notice the IHMC team, mostly twentysomething men, chain-smoking in their garage, Christmas lights and little red felt stockings strung across the bay door.

It is hot, and the garages are open on both sides so a breeze can pass through. I tug at my plasticky vest. My hair is sweaty under my hard hat.

Suddenly there is music, and I look up at the PA, and I swear to you the song playing, which will be on heavy rotation for the next forty-eight hours, is "Harder, Better, Faster, Stronger" by Daft Punk. The trials are about to begin.

———

A case study: the end of a relationship that lasted almost two years, with Joey, the man I had met on Tinder, who had given me the blanket with our conversation on it. This was almost six years after I had attended the DARPA trials.

Joey saw himself as a tragically doomed sort of person. He wasn't. He was lovely and capable. And because I saw how lovely and capable Joey was, I ignored the fact that he spoke about himself in this doomed sort of way. I ignored the fact that he preferred to think of himself as a person to whom bad things beyond his control happened.

I thought: I love this person, and all the things he says are making him unhappy are so easily fixed! We will fix them together! And then we will be happy!

He wanted to make more time for his band. I deferred to the practice schedule and went to every show. He was unable to focus, to relax, and so we went to a meditation class to learn how together. He felt it was bad luck he'd never traveled abroad, gotten a stamp in his passport. I said, "Where do you want to go?" He said, "Thailand," so I bought us two tickets to Thailand.

I was helping, I was fixing, and I was solving, so that eventually he could be happy.

Once he was happy, I was sure, he would love me.

Joey was miserable at work, wanted a different job, so I asked if he wanted a job at *my* work. He said yes.

I said, "Are you sure? I do not care if you work making Creamsicles at the Stewart's Shop if that's what makes you happy. I just want you to be happy and also I need you to be pretty sure about this before I call in favors."

Joey said, "Yes, I'm sure."

So I got him an interview. He did the interview and said it seemed like a good job.

While we awaited news on the job, it was time for our trip to Thailand.

During our trip, we went on a boat and kayak excursion Joey had found for us on Phang Nga Bay. It was a place out of a dream, a long-tail boat, islands rising up from a brilliant teal sea, clouds that rolled alongside our boat like sentient storm gods. We paddled into a stand of mangroves and saw hundreds of bats, as big as our forearms, with adorable faces, bickering in the trees. On the shores of small islands, we saw monkeys cocking their heads at us while grooming their young, kingfishers of all colors in the branches overhead. One night we camped on a literal deserted island. Our two badass and hilarious tour guides, a naturalist and a boatman, set up camp and said goodnight and we were on our own. We ate noodles and shrimp on top of a cooler and as we did, smaller bats emerged, a stream of them from the woods, rushing over our heads as we ate, which was, for me, heaven.

"I love this," I said.

"Yeah," he said. We'd finished eating.

Then Joey got up and started walking. He left silently. I lost track of him around the island's bend in the evening dimness. When he didn't come back after a few minutes, I got up to try to find him. I trekked around the island a bit more. There were gelatinous neon anemones throbbing in the tide lines and fat little urchins stranded in the tide pools like purple grenades. Crabs scuttled around suspiciously. I couldn't find Joey. When I eventually gave up and circled back, I found he had returned to our campsite. I found him in our tent. In his sleeping bag.

"You're going to bed without me?" I said, through the mesh of the tent door.

"I'm tired," he said, from the other side.

He was obviously in a bad mood. And I tried to think why.

I had been playing whack-a-mole with his problems. I had brought us all the way here, to the other side of the world, to solve them. There was nothing left for me to fix, to heal, and yet, even here, in this literal paradise, he was unhappy.

He had not said goodnight to me, on a desert island.

He had managed to leave me alone, *on a desert island.*

And even then, miserable, crouched outside the tent, I was still trying to find a way to fix it.

Two weeks after we got back from Thailand, Joey was offered the job at my work. The job I had asked a senior colleague to look for, for him. The job other people had spent time organizing and interviewing for, for him. When they offered it to him he said he needed to think about it.

A few days later, they asked if he had an answer for them. And then he started panicking. I asked what he was thinking, and when he said he didn't want the job after all, I lost it.

I said, "But why did you let me ask for it, then?"

Joey said he was worried about where his band would practice if he moved for the job. He was wondering if maybe he wanted to get into marketing instead. He was wondering all sorts of things, and I was so fucking upset. I was upset that he was acting this way but I was also upset that I had played a large part in creating this job-offer situation. How wrong I'd been to think it would ever go well.

I said, "It's fine if you don't want this job but I need you to be in charge of things a little more after this, okay? It's my fault for trying to fix things for you and I'm sorry, but you need to be a little more in charge of figuring out what's going to make you happy. I need to know you're going to do that."

Joey said he didn't think he could do that.

He said he couldn't ever promise to take care of me the way I took care of him. This was an observation he volunteered, freely.

Almost two years into our relationship and this happened over the phone in the middle of the workday.

He sent me an email finalizing our breakup the next day. And I never saw him again.

This is a sad story only inasmuch as stories about people like me, who delude themselves, are sad. So maybe it's not so sad at all.

I tried to help Joey because I thought that without the distraction of all his miseries—which seemed to me so easily solvable—he would finally love me *properly*. He would take care of me the way I'd been taking care of him. I would fix and fix and fix until he was able to notice that I was standing there, hoping to be loved. But of course it doesn't work that way.

What is the wisdom here? That I was a shit nurse?

That it is hard to heal someone who does not want to get well?

That nursing is seldom repaid with love?

Or perhaps, more honestly: that you cannot actually ethically love someone you see as your patient.

———

Throughout the first day of the DRC trials, spectators watch from the bleachers as the robots cycle through the task stations. There are always eight events happening at once, and at first I worry that I will miss something. I scuttle around with my notebook trying to find the station where the most action is.

I needn't have worried. They are slow, these robots. So slow that the broadcast on the Jumbotron speeds the footage up in time-lapse, a method typically reserved for the blooming of flowers and melting of glaciers.

I cannot explain why the door task becomes my favorite, but I spend hours, literal hours, watching this particular trial, described in my press materials as: "Open a Series of Doors: Moving the doors in an arc challenges the robots' perception and dexterity. The robots must figure out how to align and move themselves as they open each door."

The robots must pass over a field of debris to arrive at a series of doors. The first of three doors has a metal bar handle that must be pressed down and then pushed to open the door. The robots must then pass through the door and close it behind them. And that is just the first of three doors, each with a different opening mechanism. Some pull, some push. Some weighted, others not. This is all happening in a diorama-like disaster scene. The walls behind the robots are a deep teal color menacingly spackled with what looks like residue from an explosion. A yellow radioactive symbol sign hangs on the wall.

The robots try to scale the debris or clear it, and they tip over and fall. The robots make it to the door and reach for the handle but miss, or fail to grasp it, the handle slipping from their pincers. Their inability to grab on has a quality familiar to me from nightmares, in which simple tasks like these feel impossible: *just grab the handle, there's a way out of here, just open the door.*

Everything changes once SCHAFT's S-One robot enters the door challenge. SCHAFT is a gangly, blue-bodied robot with an enormous square blockhead and black claw hands. We watch and SCHAFT moves through the rubble like it's nothing. He is moving at the speed a very slow and cautious human might move. Which is to say, compared to the other robots, he is moving at light speed. It is thrilling to watch him go. Technically SCHAFT is the Japanese company that has made the S-One robot, but everyone just calls the robot SCHAFT, because the jokes are too good to pass up. We sing, the journalists, and engineers, and I:

> *Who is the man that would risk his neck for his brother, man?*
> *(Shaft)*
> *Can ya dig it?*
> *Who's the cat that won't cop out when there's danger all about?*
> *(Shaft)*
> *Right on*

SCHAFT approaches the first door. He grips the handle. We gasp. He loses it. We gasp. On the third try he opens the door. The journalists and roboticists scream with disbelief. He moves to the second door and passes through it as well.

He did it. He did it. Everyone is saying this. He did it!

He approaches the third door. He grabs, grabs, and then latches on to the third and final handle, the hardest one, because it is weighted, and requires pulling inward instead of pushing, which can unbalance the robot. The drama in this, such a small task, becomes enormous because of how impossible a barrier this door has become.

And then SCHAFT opens the door. SCHAFT stands there holding the handle, door open.

Everyone is losing their minds. It becomes emotional, watching him open this door, his pathway to safety.

And then, the wind blows.

SCHAFT loses his grip, and the door slips from his grasp, and slams shut again. There is an audible *Awwwww* or *Ohhhh* from the crowd. He will still get high marks, but he was so close to completing this task.

I slip away so no one will see me crying in my hard hat.

The DRC robots are not the perfect heroes I'd hoped for, but I love them anyway. I love them *specifically*. I love them *right now*, without assuming they will someday be better at doing the things they're meant to do. I love them for reminding me that when you are working toward a large good thing, it's the small stuff that often feels impossible.

Just turn the handle.

Just open the door and walk through it.

Just change the motions. Just rewrite the programming.

How hard could it be?

It turns out, really fucking hard.

I hide in one of the shady entry tunnels beneath the speedway bleachers to cry about SCHAFT. A man with a rosacea-red nose, wearing a green wool blazer despite the heat, approaches and begins telling me how the Defense Department is murdering people with drones.

"I know," I say.

He keeps telling me anyway. He is not put off by my crying. Eventually he asks me to sign his petition. I do.

My beloved friend Marta is a person so kind, so willing to see the best in others, that she often attracts unlikely friends and winds up having elaborate social interactions a woman of less generous spirit might not indulge. For this reason, Marta's sister calls her "Friends Without Borders," after the medical organization Doctors Without Borders, which brings medical care to people who need it in dangerous and remote places. I like to think that if Florence Nightingale had been born in this generation she might have been part of Doctors Without Borders.

Marta and her sister are from Spain, and so the phrase, as it's come to be used among us is actually, *Amigos Sin Fronteras.* For example, Marta will announce she's going to a deathly-sounding dinner party of total strangers or will offer to drive someone she met yesterday to get their snow tires put on and we will shout, "Why! Why did you agree to this!" When she tries to explain, we throw our hands up.

"Amigos Sin Fronteras!" we chant. "Amigos Sin Fronteras!"

A little while back, this same lady-friend-group was catching up, and I was describing my recent dating life.

This was *years* after the DRC in 2013.

Years after I had called off my wedding to Nick in 2016.

Ages since Joey had left me alone on that desert island in 2019.

I thought I'd come to understand a few things about how I behaved in love.

But here I was, talking to my girlfriends, *in 2020,* explaining how I was trying to overlook small incompatibilities in new, prospective partners' dating profiles in order to see their deeper potential. "I'm trying to understand the difference between being petty and spying a true red flag," I said. I listed a few of the dubious incompatibilities from online profiles I'd decided not to consider insurmountable: profile says his favorite food is chicken nuggets; profile says his main interest is video games; profile includes quotes from three different Will Ferrell movies; profile says he is unemployed but working on a screenplay; in profile pics he appears to live in a camper van; in profile pics he appears to exist nowhere but his own bathroom mirror; in profile pics he appears to be a Civil War ghost.

I was deeply and clearly not interested in any of these qualities, or men. I knew this.

And yet . . .

Would a good person be deterred by these things? I asked myself. Was it ethical to disqualify a person as a partner for any of these reasons? How would someone, most people, react to these profiles?

I told myself that someone, most people, would be fine with them. Excited, even. They would go on dates with these men. They would enjoy these dates. And so I forced myself to hover outside my own mind, and override my own, true, human reactions with what I thought a good and ethical and generally less-strange person would do.

As I was explaining all this to my girlfriends, I started laughing so hard I was crying.

"Am I . . ." I said, laughing so hard I couldn't even get out what I wanted to say, "am I . . . Novios Sin Fronteras?"

Novios Sin Fronteras.

Boyfriends Without Borders.

Four years after the whooping cranes, and I was having an "epiphany" again. I was understanding something new. Even as I am rolling my eyes at myself, I can remember the excitement of the "epiphany":

What if boundaries and borders are actually the only way people can love each other equally and freely? What if, without those boundaries, love becomes an act of humanitarian aid?

The thing I have most wished for in this world is a love that has no borders. Which is to say *un*conditional love. And I thought that if I generously gave unconditional love to a difficult person, I might receive it back. And so I loved the people I thought I could do the best job of loving. As if it were a vocation, a calling, a duty.

I never asked myself how I wanted to be loved or by whom. I never asked myself whether the people I was well suited to care for were well suited to care for me. And most of the time they were not. This was not their fault. I never asked.

Doctors and nurses offer unconditional care—they treat whomever it is their job to heal. In order to be ethical they must be impartial. A robot is, theoretically, impartial, unless it is programmed with skewed data. But to be in love is to be partial. It is to be specific.

All romantic love is conditional in that the condition is a person's essential nature. Their them-ness. If your love for a person isn't predicated on the condition that they are them right now as they are, and is instead predicated on their need for that love, or on your thinking that you could do a good job of making that person happier or "better," then you are a nurse, you are a robot hero, and maybe you can save the day. But you are not a lover. You are not in love.

Why did I think it was ethically necessary to imagine my way out of my own opinions and judgments? To fall in love the way someone, most people, might, the way some imaginary, "good" person might?

Perhaps, to enjoy being the hero who swoops in and saves the day is to have a deep desire for self-annihilation. Saving someone feels easy, compared to asking yourself who the hell you are and what you want and how you want to be loved and by whom. Compared to asking, How might I care for myself?

In my life, the answers to these questions have never been clear. Back in 2013, the questions had never even been asked.

For a while, having these sorts of "epiphanies" convinced me I was going to be okay. Because *I knew things now*. And yes, knowing how warped I had been in the past was important—but identifying a problem, and then knowing the solution, and then putting that solution into practice, it turns out, are not all one wholesale kit and fucking caboodle.

They are three differently weighted doors, and you have to pass through all of them, or else, of course, you get stuck.

———

Toward the end of that first day of the trials, I return to the Atlas bot VR tent. The one with the banner that asks: WHAT DOES IT FEEL LIKE TO BE ATLAS?

"Let's get you in there!" a man says. He helps me put on a VR headset and adjusts the straps so it's snug around my face. The headset has two giant googly eyes affixed to the front.

The simulation begins. Wearing the goggles feels like being inside a video game. And inside the game, I am in Atlas's body. In front of me, I see a grayish blocky room. I turn my head, and there is a hallway leading off somewhere farther away than any part of the tent is in real life. I turn back to the room, and it rushes around me, the world of the simulation filling my peripheral vision as well as my straight-on sightlines. Nothing about the room I'm in is realistic but the experience of being in it feels incredibly real. My body feels that I am, at once, there, in that room, but also, I feel the weight of the goggles on my face, the heat of the tent. I tip my head down, and there are my hands. I lift them in real life and in the simulation I lift my hands, too. My hands are Atlas's hands.

What does it feel like to be Atlas?

I attempt to walk by pressing a button I'm holding and I bump into a wall. I free myself and turn around. I see a table, or a pedestal with objects on it. I press my button. Try to approach it, but I get dizzy, and before I know it, I am trapped in a flashing corner of another wall.

For a person who came into this event thinking she might have some kinship with these robots, I am very bad at being Atlas.

I turn around again and find a walkway that will lead me to the table with the objects. I walk again. My stomach lurches. Only now do I realize that this was not a good idea.

In my real life, I am extremely unable to process directions and objects in space. I have no sense of direction in a way that is alarming to people who know me well. I cannot rotate an object in my mind. Once, as a teenager, I attempted to play GoldenEye 007 on Nintendo at a friend's house, and found the first-person perspective so disorienting and dizzying that it made me feel sick. I had to abandon my controller and run to the bathroom to puke.

In the Atlas simulation, I see a gray wall in a greenish landscape and there again is the table with the objects. I successfully walk up to it. I feel lightheaded, but I've made it. I hold out my robot hand and I can see it there in front of me. I open it. I close it. I wonder whether I might pick up the wrench or the block or the . . . who are these things for? Who needs what? I look around the world of the simulation once more, and I realize part of what makes it so uncanny: I am the only one here. This is a world of one room, one me, and these objects. I am as completely alone with myself as I've ever been before. I reach for the table with Atlas's hands. My hands. I'm supposed to pick up an object, but how do I know which one?

I open my hand.

I close it.

My head swims.

I pass out and collapse. In real life.

When I come to, the demo man is taking the very expensive googly-eyed VR set off my face. Then he lifts me up and gives me a chair to sit in while I collect myself.

"I'm so sorry," I say.

"Just take a minute," he says.

"I'm so embarrassed," I say. I sit there, forehead to knees, trying to do deep, stomach-settling breaths. I am still dizzy. I feel motion-sick. I should have known my brain and guts couldn't handle a first-person simulation.

Because that's what broke me.

When I put on those VR goggles and tried to be Atlas bot, I was forced into the one role I had relentlessly trained myself to avoid.

A subjective first-person gaze on the world.

The role of myself.

Seeing the gray room in the simulation, I wanted to do what I always did in life: to imagine what this room meant for the person I was taking care of. For someone. Anybody. I would see it how I thought they would see it. I would imagine what they would need from it, and then proceed through the space accordingly. But in the Atlas simulation I was alone. I was only my gaze. My own robot hand. And whatever object I picked up from the table, it was *for me*. Which object, then, did . . . I . . . want to . . . pick up? I had no idea. My own subjectivity was terrifying.

I hustle away from the tent. From its WHAT DOES IT FEEL LIKE TO BE ATLAS? banner.

What did it feel like to be me? I had no idea.

———

The trials are over, and I am sunburned, and I go to the restaurant/karaoke bar across the road from my motel. I sit at the bar and order a beer and a basket of fried clams. I have my notebook out but I don't even know what I should write in it. Whatever it was I thought I was going to learn about how to save a person without feeling a way about it has not come to fruition. Whatever it is that *someone, most people,* would have found interesting about this escapes me.

A man in his sixties is singing an old cowboy song in front of the karaoke screen. He isn't singing the words on the screen behind him—it's some other song entirely—but he sounds great. There's a warm vibe to the bar, twinkling lights strung around, shelves full of tchotchkes. Tomorrow is Christmas Eve everywhere, but especially at my mother's house, where I will be asked how this article that has delayed my participation in the Christmas festivities is coming. I stare at my notebook. The man finishes his song and we applaud him. *Karaoke* means "empty orchestra" —did you know that? I learned that from one of my robot books but now I can't remember which.

I am in the middle of my ridiculous pity party when a group of men wearing DARPA badges walk in. A bearlike guy in wire-rimmed glasses, huge hands, comes up behind me and orders eight drinks for his group. The others settle themselves at a picnic table outside and start yelling at him to hurry up, changing their drink orders, good-naturedly hassling him. The waitress starts pulling their drinks from the tap and lining them up, one by one, next to my elbow.

"I'm sorry," the guy says to me. "I don't mean to crowd you."

"It's okay," I say. "You're celebrating. Are you part of the trials?"

He looks at me excitedly. "Are you Janice?" he asks.

This is the fourth time I have been asked this in the past three days. Apparently there is a lone female engineer participating in the trials. I never got to meet her. But every time someone seems surprised by my femaleness, they ask if I am Janice, hoping to be meeting this mythical being.

I wish I were Janice. I really do.

I want to be anyone else. As if this might save me from having to figure out what I actually want. As if, by being no one, I could be good to everyone. As if love could possibly work like that. I consider pretending to be Janice. I really do. But I also feel a flicker of understanding that I can't avoid becoming a first-person person forever. So I tell the truth.

"I'm not," I laugh. "I'm a writer." I pause, and then confess, "A fiction writer, not a journalist, even. What team are you on?"

Admitting to who I actually am for the first time in days, I can feel my spine unhitching, my guts settling pleasantly into my pelvis, can feel the gentle swim of being tipsy in my head and the heat of being sunburned across my forearms, and this is what it feels like to be me. Saying who I am, out loud, I am back in my body again. I am myself. I am a first-person person. Oh, hello, there you are, here I am.

"The design team," he says. "We designed the trials. The task stations."

"No fucking way," I say. "Congratulations. It was really cool how they looked like movie sets." And then I rapturously describe how I'd seen SCHAFT open the door and then lose it to the wind.

One of the other guys from the table comes over to grab the forgotten drinks, shaking his head at the wait. "You should ask her if she wants to hang out with us," he says, ferrying away all the pints but one. Nodding at it as he goes.

The man I've been talking with looks at me and sticks out his hand. "RJ," he says.

I shake his hand. "CJ," I say. He laughs.

"Do you want to hang out with us?" He gestures to the beer on the bar.

I look at the beer there on the counter. Do I?

I do.

I pick it up.

As RJ and I approach the table, someone points at me and says, "Janice!"

"Unfortunately not," I say.

We shoot the shit until almost four in the morning, this whole group of roboticists and EMTs and DOD lifers, talking about the trials and robots and Miami, and past war stories from other jobs. There are tequila shots. They show off for me. I am thrilled. I bum a cigarette from one of the guys, who speaks only a little English and has a plush Totoro character key chain on his backpack.

I light the cigarette and say, "I love Totoro," pointing at his key chain. He smiles, but does not understand, so I do the dance Totoro teaches the little girls to do in the movie, the one that makes their garden grow overnight. A dance that is also an enchantment, that makes the world turn faster, turn in time-lapse, acorn to seedling to tree in minutes. Progress and growth and knowing, happening so quickly. Happening as impossibly fast as we scientists and human girls might wish it would. One door, and then a second door, and then the third, all in a rush. He laughs, understanding, and squeezes the little Totoro. "Yes," he says.

Mulder, It's Me

I'm never again dating anyone who dislikes any of these three things . . .

I had written the three things, which had come to me, like a unified field theory of shitty men, on a cocktail napkin. The napkin said:

1. BIG DOGS
2. THE SEA!
3. MUPPETS

I flapped the cocktail napkin at my friend, who was laughing so hard she was blotting her eyes. I was drunk but I wasn't unserious.

"To dislike any of these things is sociopathic," I said, studying my napkin. "Something is *broken*," I said, "in a person who doesn't like these things."

"I'm not wild about the Muppets," my friend said.

"But do you hate them?" I said. "Do you wish them ill?"

"I do not wish the Muppets ill."

"From now on this is the rule."

A Muppet-oriented relationship theory is potentially more sociopathic than not liking Kermit the Frog. But I was looking for answers. Trying to understand what had gone wrong in the past.

Back then, I was in the autopsy business. Dissecting my failed relationships in search of answers. From every relationship postmortem came new rules about what I should and should not do in the next one. My autopsy rules multiplied over time, until there were so many I could hardly keep track of them. But I kept doing it, because maybe, if I investigated my own failures closely enough, I could pretend that love, that life, was an endeavor a person could undertake with only a reasonable amount of risk.

In short, I was trying to science the shit out of my love life.

And of all of my theories, metrics, and madnesses, none messed me up more than my experiments in Scullymulderism.

"JERSEY DEVIL," Season 1, Episode 5

MULDER: Ever hear of something called the Jersey Devil?
SCULLY: . . . Kind of like an East Coast Bigfoot. . . . Is the autopsy report in here? . . . Mulder, it's the same story I've heard since I was a kid. It's a folktale, a myth.
MULDER: I heard the same story when I was a kid, too. Funny thing is, I believed it.

The year my friends Liv and Meg asked me to officiate their wedding, I was in a relationship that was about to self-destruct due to Scullymulderism. I was ignoring the inevitability of this breakup, even though it was obvious to everyone around me, including, I'm pretty sure, Joey, who responded to the news of my officiation at this wedding by letting me know he would not be able to get time off to attend.

A breakup, at this point in my life, was a terribly familiar story, and I was sick to death of it. I didn't want to do it again. I didn't want to tell people again. I didn't want to feel those feelings and ask myself a series of painful existential questions again. Not that a person gets much choice in the matter, it turns out.

I also didn't want it to end with Joey because I had tried so hard to make it work. And a very truly huge amount of work was required in this relationship because we were such wildly different people. To communicate at all, beyond the physical, was a feat. But I was convinced that it was the fact of our differences that made us perfect for each other.

My role model for this was Special Agent Dana Scully.

I have been an avid viewer of *The X-Files* since the first moment I arrived at my cousin's house in New Jersey and found him watching it on a little TV in his sunroom. Onscreen, an entire train car full of alien corpses was about to be confiscated by the CIA (probably) because they didn't want anyone to know the truth (or did they . . .). Since then, I have seen *The X-Files,* in its entirety, four times. Some seasons, some episodes, so many more times than that.

The first time through, I watched on television. My friend Tahereh and I were what the early internet called "shippers," which is to say weirdos who watched less for the governmental conspiracies and more for the MSR (Mulder Scully Relation-*ship*). We watched every Sunday night for ages. And when she moved away to New Hampshire, we called each other on the phone, watching long-distance, gasping and cackling, debriefing and theorizing during the commercial breaks.

Years later, living in France, whenever I ran out of money to go dancing or out to dinner, I satisfied myself by watching pirated episodes of what we called Les Ex-Feels *avec sous-titres* with my friends JP and Thibault, all three of us in pajamas, taking regular breaks so JP and I could go smoke Gauloises downstairs.

In college I was so desperate to watch the show again my friend Kristin ordered bootleg DVDs from China, which arrived with Val Kilmer's face on the discs, presumably because the makers believed most Hollywood white men to be interchangeable with David Duchovny, a mistake for which I salute them. Every evening we would sit on our futon, eating scrambled eggs for dinner, retching as a flukeworm man splashed through the sewers. "We've got to stop watching this while we're eating," we told each other, but we never learned.

The last full re-watch I did on my own, when the series came to Netflix. I was fresh off a breakup and elbow deep in another love postmortem at the time, which is perhaps why I became convinced that this was what had gone wrong in my last relationship: I had been a Scully dating a Scully. Autopsy rules dictated, therefore, that what I needed, this time, was a Mulder.

Here's the Mulder/Scully dynamic:

Mulder believes in everything and Scully believes in nothing. Or rather, Mulder is all feeling and instinct and trauma-legacy and Scully is all facts and reasoning and medical degree (with a pinch of Catholicism). Mulder says: It's aliens! A flying saucer! And Scully says: There have been twelve known incidents of swamp gas mistaken for aliens in this town alone.

Mulder has a mattress and a fish tank of mostly dead fish in apartment number 42 (the meaning of life) and Scully lives in a well-lit apartment with a white couch, like a competent adult woman with mixed feelings about having no children.

And they want to bone. And they do bone. And I could write you a dissertation about the tension and the boning and the thesis of that dissertation would be that when Mulder calls Scully he just says, "Scully, it's me," and when Scully calls Mulder she just says, "Mulder, it's me," and if that isn't peak everything I don't know what is but that's beside the point. The point is that Scully is Science and Mulder is Blind Belief. Scully is Evidence-Required and Mulder is Anecdotes from the Early Internet. Mulder is the one who knows that there's a monster living in the lake, and Scully is the one who says there must be a plausible explanation for all this moments before her Pomeranian gets eaten by said monster. Mulder is the one who makes things happen, and Scully is the one who gets things done (if you're confused about the difference you should take a good hard look at yourself). Mulder is the one who shouts, "I've gotta go!" without explaining his hunches and Scully is the one left behind weighing the stomach contents of dead teenagers she refuses to accept were killed by vampires.

Because Scully is the one who does the autopsies.

Both characters change along the way, and both characters absolutely need each other. And so, what Chris Carter taught me about love (Mr. Carter, please find, herewith, my therapy bills) is that the very best, and sexiest, and truest kind of boning there is, is the kind where two very different kinds of people find a mode of working together—of loving each other because their *differences* make it an active process of perpetual growth! And excitement! And spiciness! Which is to say not boring in all the ways I have always feared adult relationships might be boring. This pathologizing of dynamic difference is what I mean when I say Scullymulderism. And Scullymulderism was why I had worked so hard at my relationship with Joey, who was nothing like me. Who would dump me only a few weeks after Liv and Meg's wedding.

BAD BLOOD, Season 5, Episode 12

SCULLY: Four fifty-four p.m., begin autopsy
    on white male, age sixty, who is arguably
    having a worse time in Texas than I am . . .
    although not by much. [She holds a scalpel in
    her hand] I'll begin with the "y" incision.
    [The blade falls to the floor] Yee-haw. [Very
    unenthusiastically]

*LATER [Scully plunks his heart into a scale tray
        and looks up at the readout]*

Here's how Liv and Meg asked me to officiate their wedding:

I got a packet in the mail. Inside I found Feist's *The Reminder* on vinyl, a packet of fresh guitar strings for my Seagull acoustic, and a two-page letter written extra-large, in marker, on pink construction paper. The letter reminded me that the first time Liv and I had hung out was during Thanksgiving at my parents' house. My sister and I had both brought our roommates home. Liv and my sister were dorm mates at Connecticut College. In addition to living together, my roommate Adam and I worked together at Camp Broadway, which meant we had the bad fortune to be working the Macy's Thanksgiving Day Parade. We had spent the morning wrangling children into singing a horrifically grating song called "Making Magic" on national television and then getting them back to their parents, after which we took the train up to Connecticut to eat Thanksgiving dinner with my folks. Liv and Adam took to each other immediately and, as they were both queer, branded the occasion Gay Orphans Thanksgiving.

The four of us made my aging grandparents laugh and played that Feist album, which had just come out, and watched *Home Alone* in a heap on the couch and all called my mom Boo as she flapped about the kitchen refusing help and demanding we get out of her no-fly zone.

Liv and Meg's letter asked me if I'd wanted to maybe get ordained and come to Maine that October to officiate their long-awaited wedding.

Now, because they are horrible liars, the students in my writing workshops will tell you that I hate happy endings and especially weddings. I *love* a happy ending, and I *love* a wedding; I just think that most happy endings—and most weddings—are full of shit. The rare happy ending I appreciate is one that makes room for the whole painful fact of the world at the same time it offers the reader some joy. I love, for example, the part of Jewish weddings where the glass gets stomped and someone tells us it's supposed to remind us of the larger suffering of the world even as we celebrate our more proximate joys. That is a gorgeous philosophy to embrace, in both fiction and in life.

There is one notable exception to my students' claim.

"The only happy ending Professor Hauser likes," a student once said, "is a gay wedding."

It's true. I don't even need anyone to step on a glass.

So, did I want to be a part of Liv and Meg's wedding?

I drew a little sign that said YES I WILL MARRY YOU in big marker letters. I propped the sign on my dog's fluffy haunches and sent Liv and Meg a picture.

Then I started panicking.

Perhaps, in part, because the state of my own relationship was such that I was getting close to having to acknowledge, yet again, that I was very bad at relationships. And didn't that make me an unlucky sort of person to have at the helm of a wedding?

Not to mention, the last wedding I was supposed to be a part of was . . . my own. And I'd failed to show up.

I didn't get married, in no small part, because I was suddenly stricken by a deep uncertainty about what it meant to get married, and how a person knew when they should do it. I had found myself feeling like *Well, of course I'm getting married, this is what people do, look at us, we look like people who would be getting married. We have the invitations and the photos and the rings, and sure, some things aren't going that well but all relationships are a struggle, right? All relationships are work? That's not a good reason to not get married, is it?*

And then my brain would swap, reverse itself completely, and say, *No, that is not what marriage is for, marriage is for insane, life-bending passion and certainty only. It is for end-of-the-line love, and that's not what this is, so get out, now.*

There are so many moments like this on *The X-Files*.

Moments when the certainty of the world Scully used to unquestioningly accept gets upended and suddenly she looks around her and doesn't know what's real, what's a lie, whom to trust. *The X-Files* is a show about how the only way most of us truck along every day is by accepting certain facts to be enduringly true so we can get on with our life. But when, every day, you're starting from scratch in terms of what you do or don't believe, the world can feel like a pretty terrifying place.

It's a show about how a person can become disoriented in their relationship to the truth.

Or maybe that's just me.

Because when it comes to love, that's how I feel. Every day, when I wake up in the morning, it's like *Let's start this whole process of knowing over again. Take it from the top!*

Every. Single. Day.

When I flung myself back and forth and ultimately decided not to get married it wasn't because I had finally achieved some state of wisdom. It wasn't because I had resolved my beliefs. It was just that I'd reached a kind of peak misery that I needed to make stop, and so I did, by exiting the equation.

I walked out of the problem I was living in, but that didn't mean I had answers to my questions. I didn't have any more certainty about what marriage was or who it was for or why a person might do it. And I'm pretty sure most normal, happy people have fewer questions than this. Are more certain, and more practical, and more lovely to be around, because they are not forever scrawling on cocktail napkins about Muppets, or finding themselves in crises they need to talk through, or rushing out the door in search of some kind of larger truth.

I was very sure that these kinds of people were infinitely better choices as wedding officiants. Because shouldn't a person who is officiating a wedding in some way be competent in love? Knowledgeable about it? Shouldn't they exude a great sense of certainty?

I did not fit this bill.

Who would ask such a person to marry them?

"MILAGRO," Season 6, Episode 18

SCULLY: These are, uh . . . these are my autopsy
    reports from the second victim. As you can see,
    the heart was removed in the same manner as the
    previous victim. No incisions, no scope marks,
    no cutting of any kind. . . .
MULDER: And yet, you still refuse to believe my
    theory—that what this is is psychic surgery?
SCULLY: Mulder, psychic surgery is some man
    dipping his hand in a bucket of chicken guts
    and pretending to remove tumors from the sick
    and gullible.

And yet, I set about getting ordained.

As I was filling out my form, there was a space for my title,
and I asked myself whether it was possible to be ordained as
Special Agent Dana Scully and still have this wedding be legally
binding in the state of Maine. I texted Liv and Meg.

SO, IT LOOKS LIKE I CAN MAKE MY TITLE ANYTHING I
WANT. LIKE, IN THE SLOT WHERE IT NORMALLY SAYS
REVEREND, I GET TO FILL THAT IN? SO LIKE, I CAN BE
GRAND KHALEESI OF LOVE OR ANYTHING AT ALL THAT
WOULD MAKE YOU HAPPY? WHO WOULD YOU LIKE TO BE
MARRIED BY?

We determined that what I wrote would, in fact, be printed
on their legal marriage certificate. So, two weeks later, when I
got my wallet-size card in the mail, blue, with doves on it, and a
one-year expiration date, it declared me Professor CJ Hauser.
And so I was.

Drunk with power, I walked around the house declaring that my tape dispenser and stapler were now married. I officiated a brief ceremony between my dog and his stuffed Lamb Chop toy. I threatened my students.

"Be good," I said, "or else I will marry you to each other."

"That's not how that works, is it?" they said.

"Look," I said, and I flashed them my Universal Life Church card, flipping open my wallet the way Scully does when someone doubts her credibility and she needs to show them that she is an FBI agent. She is the authority on something.

Liv and Meg and I planned a weekend at my sister's house that summer to hang out and talk about the ceremony. I interviewed them together. I interviewed them separately. We were often laughing as they teased each other lovingly. Often laughing, like kids who could not believe we were in charge of scripting from scratch such a very real thing as a wedding.

At one point, I said, *"Do you want me to tell you to kiss or would that be like a real-life version of the meme with the giant gawky face pushing two stick figures together shouting, 'NOW KISS'?"*

"You should definitely tell us to kiss," they said. *"We will be too awkward to know when to do it if you don't tell us."*

I asked them what sorts of words were important to them. I asked them about love languages. I asked what they valued about their life together. I asked what they wanted their community to hear and know, and what each wanted the other to hear and know. I said I would interview their friends and family. Meg was naturally inclined toward sweet rituals like this and it was immediately clear she would write something perfect. Liv was forbidden from performing a tight five in lieu of vows. They cried and I cried multiple times because they said beautiful, adoring things about each other and, for a person who often finds herself short on certainty, it was so clear, so very intensely clear, that yes, these women were in love, and yes, they should be getting married.

This is what makes a good wedding so good. That feeling of true belief in the thing you're gathered to witness and celebrate.

When we left that weekend, I told Liv and Meg to text me lots as they kept thinking about things. "Keep me in the loop," I said.

A week after our hangout I got a video text from Liv.

The video pans across their adorable deck, which is strung with twinkly lights. It is summer and it is evening.

"Meg is making this," Liv says in the video, and pans to Meg, in a cute exercise outfit, assembling an Adirondack chair. Meg looks up briefly, then returns to her work. "And I made this . . ." Liv says, and pans to a pitcher of sangria, a glass in her hand, an orange wedge floating amid the ice. Liv pans back to Meg and says, "Watching Meg build things is my love language."

Truly, the hardest part of writing the ceremony was keeping it short. There were too many wonderful things to include. But, in retrospect, some of the ceremony I had written flirted with Scullymulderism. It was about how Liv and Meg complemented each other so perfectly. It was about how Meg built the chair and Liv built the cocktails. It was about how different they were and how much they loved each other for those differences. I had a nagging feeling, though, that the ceremony wasn't complete yet.

Four days before the wedding, as I was packing my bags and printing out the script I'd written for the ceremony, I worried there was some part of their relationship I had failed to capture. Then I realized there had been, let us say, an oversight.

UM SO WE DID NOT MAKE A PART OF THE CEREMONY WHERE

YOU SAY "I DO," I texted in a panic. IS IT FAIR TO ASSUME YOU WANT TO SAY "I DO" TO EACH OTHER?

YES, they said, THAT WOULD PROBABLY BE GOOD.

OKAY I AM GOING TO WRITE IN A PART WITH "I DOS" NOW. I AM SORRY I ALMOST FORGOT TO MAKE SURE YOU ACTUALLY GOT MARRIED.

That must have been the reason for the something's-missing feeling, I told myself, as I revised and printed out my script again. I put it in a charming floral clipboard that in my mind matched both the blue of Liv's suit and the lace of Meg's dress.

I thought I had found it. I thought I was done.

"MULDER AND SCULLY MEET THE WERE-MONSTER,"
Season 10, Episode 3

MULDER: It shot blood at me. From out its eyeball, Scully. I think. It was hard for me to see, because I had blood in my eyes.

SCULLY: I haven't done the blood analysis yet, but it's probably residue from the prior attack on this victim. And—animals don't shoot blood out of their eyeballs.

MULDER: Oh, no? Well, tell that to the horned lizard. Which shoots blood out its eyeball, Scully, yes. It's a defense mechanism. Scientific fact!

SCULLY: Mulder, the internet is not good for you. . . .

MULDER: You're really enjoying yourself, aren't you, Scully?

SCULLY: Yeah. I am. I forgot how much fun these

cases could be. It's been a long day, Mulder.
Why don't you go back to the hotel and get some
sleep? And try not to dream about monsters.

There's a recurring dream I used to have as a little girl. In it,
I'm walking down this long white hallway that goes on forever.
The hallway is lined with white doors, and the handles to the
doors are all these elaborate brass knobs shaped like different
creatures. I walk down the hall for a long time before I get tired
of walking and decide I want to leave. So I try a door. When I
touch the handle, though—say, one shaped like a squirrel—it
comes alive, and tries to bite me. I draw back. Then, the brass
animal leaps down and starts chasing me. I try another door
handle to escape, but then that one, a bird, comes to life and
starts attacking me, too. I run down the hallway, trying to get
away from these monsters I've brought to life, but they pursue
me. I know that the only way out is to open more doors, but
also that every door I try will add to the pack. I always wake up
before I get out of the hallway.

Every relationship I autopsied, every resulting postmortem
theory I came up with, every new belief system I tried, it was
only ever another doorknob I turned. A new monster to be
afraid of as I kept searching for a way out. And I was the one
doing it. I was the one who kept making the monsters.

It has, perhaps, occurred to you by now, if you have been
reading this book in order, if you are an *X-Files* fan, that my
most crucial mistake (and vanity) was in misidentifying myself
as a Scully in the first place.

It was probably already very clear to you: I'm a little spooky.
I'm a Mulder.

No matter how many autopsy rules I came up with, I was not a scientist. I was not seeking rational truth. I was not about to crack the case.

I was Fox Mulder in a basement office with my feet up on the desk, eating sunflower seeds, feeling, if we're honest, a little too smug about my own vibe, my own trench coat, my own renegade personality, getting off a little too much on the fact that I was sure it was me, only me, who could see the real truth and horror of the world out there.

I was tending my archived files of horror, poring over them again and again, instead of heading out into the world, into the light.

Mulder, it's me.

"NISEI," Season 3, Episode 9

SCULLY: What are you watching? . . .
. . .
MULDER: According to the magazine ad I answered,
   it's an alien autopsy. Guaranteed authentic.
   [Scully looks at the screen. It is the alien
   autopsy that was being conducted before. The
   view of the camera obstructs the view of the
   body, the doctors standing in the way.]
SCULLY: You spent money for this?
MULDER: Twenty-nine ninety-five, plus
   shipping. . . .
   But it . . . it does look authentic. [He
   walks over to the television and stands next
   to her, carrying a remote control] I mean,

the setting and the procedures. I mean, it
does look as if an actual autopsy is being
performed, doesn't it?

The night before Liv and Meg's wedding, I was out at a restaurant with Liv's half of the wedding party. We were going
around the table and saying things that we liked or admired
about Liv. Her impeccable hair was mentioned many times.
When it was my turn, I started to tell a story about her humor,
about the hardest Liv had ever made me laugh, with a story
about her and Meg running away from a rogue praying mantis.
I thought I was telling the story because it showed how funny
Liv was . . . but halfway through, I said, "I think this might
actually be a story about how amazing Meg is?"

"Yes," the table said. "She's ride or die."

But I was already busy mumbling, "Next person, go,"
and downing my spicy tequila drink while scribbling in my
notebook.

The next morning, the morning, to be clear, of the day on
which Meg and Liv were getting married, I woke up and immediately started revising the wedding ceremony to include the
story from the night before. A story called the Mantis Shuffle.

Was it appropriate to tell a funny story about a praying
mantis during a wedding? I wasn't sure. But I knew that it
was the best thing I could think of to say about Liv and Meg's
love. I knew it meant I had been wrong to focus so much on
Scullymulderism.

Liv and Meg are goals for so many reasons. But the Mantis
Shuffle had shown me the truth, which was that Mulder and
Scully were still perfect, but not for the reasons I'd thought. I

had misunderstood the nature of their dynamic, Liv and Meg's, and Mulder and Scully's. This whole time, I kept trying to find a complicated reason that their love worked, that two very different people fit together so well. But it wasn't so complicated, after all.

The story I wound up telling, on an insanely glowy autumn day, on which Liv and Meg were surrounded by their friends and their family and also a lot of decorative gourds and scenic barnscapes, the day on which I had the honor of pronouncing them married, was a monster-of-the-week episode:

X-Files theme plays*

One day, Liv and Meg were headed out to the communal hot tub in their condo complex. They were about to slide open their plate-glass door to the outside, when they saw *something*. On the other side of the glass.

It was a gangly, prehistoric-ass, mandible-chomping praying mantis.

"What was he doing there?" I asked Liv.

"Shuffling around," Liv said. "Being disgusting. Ruining my night."

And then he waved. The mantis waved! Through the glass.

Liv immediately advocated for murder. "I *know* he's going to wind up in the house," she told Meg. "I realize this makes me evil. But I don't do bugs—especially not bugs of that stature, with heads that swivel in a way that suggests the thoughts inside it are plotting."

Meg advocated for peace ("because she's kind and they're endangered or something," Liv said) and peace won out.

They went to the hot tub and left the mantis behind.

Or so they thought.

Later that night, Liv wanted to open the sliding glass door and pull the screen so they could get some air. But she was worried about the opportunity that this would present. There would be a millisecond in which neither the screen nor the glass door was closed, and Liv told Meg she was afraid to do it. She was afraid *he* was out there, waiting. As Liv monologued by the door, Meg was sitting on the couch ("likely ignoring me," Liv said) when, as quickly as she could, Liv slid the door open and pulled the screen.

Liv then felt, on her head, the shuffling of mantis feet.

"I immediately knew what it was," Liv said. "My fears had been justified. *He had been waiting for me.* There is no other explanation aside from premeditation."

When she tells this story, Liv creates a small mantis out of a pinched hand she holds above her head. "I could feel him," she says, "shuffling around up there," and with this, she will dance her fingers. "He was doing the Mantis Shuffle."

Liv screamed, and batted at her head.

"Run!" Liv yelled. "Get to the bedroom, right now." Meg jumped up from the couch and grabbed Liv's hand and they ran to the bedroom and closed the door. Liv locked it to be sure.

They were both out of breath by now, leaning against the slammed door. Meg turned to Liv. "What are we running from?" Meg asked.

"You didn't see it?" Liv said.

"My contacts are out," Meg said. "I can't see anything."

Liv started laughing. "Wait, but then what were you running from?"

"I was following you!" Meg said. "You said to run!"

Please take a moment here, and appreciate Meg.

Because, like, yes, as the wedding party squad correctly identified the night before, this story shows that Meg is ride or die. But there's more to it than that.

The Mantis Shuffle, the way I see it, is the ultimate love story.

Because love is believing in your person's reality.

It's their invisible world becoming real to you.

It's the poster on Fox Mulder's wall that says I WANT TO BELIEVE.

It's running when a person you love says run because, like, there really might be a mantis shuffling around somewhere. But the mantis is not the point. The point is that you trust your person. You believe them. Without facts or files. Without hesitating.

In the whole, insane cosmology of *The X-Files, this* is at the center of everything.

When the world is on fire, and bees want to give you small-pox, and aliens are rummaging around your womb, sometimes there is one person who you can come to trust completely.

And that's the thing I've never had. Not because I keep dating people who don't like Muppets or the beach, but because I won't let myself trust anyone that way. Since that first, mythical time I fell in love, I have never trusted a person that same way.

Everyone gets their trust broken but most people find ways to do it again. This is an everyday sort of miracle.

I'm just so bad at it.

I am afraid. I am afraid by nature and I am afraid for reasons. I have trusted badly before. I have been held hostage by other people's fantasies. I am constantly held hostage to my own. No matter how reassuring a new relationship is, I find myself panicking, going full-on Season One Scully. *"Is this real?"* I say. *"Are you sure it wasn't swamp gas?"*

"Trust No One" is one of the *The X-Files*'s tag lines. But that doesn't apply to Mulder and Scully. "Trust No One" means everyone else. Because over the course of the show, even though the world seems scarier and scarier, even though more and more monsters reveal themselves to be real, Scully comes to trust Mulder. She becomes a person who, when he says run, *runs* instead of asking for proof.

Literal blind trust—to get to a place where I can someday do what Meg did—is the work of my lifetime.

"BORN AGAIN," Season 1, Episode 22

DET. LAZARD: Excuse me. Could I talk to you for a second?
SCULLY: I just started the autopsy.
DET. LAZARD: Yeah. Um, I don't think he's going anywhere.

The most upsetting *X-Files* episodes, for me, are the ones in which Scully is unable to reason her way to safety. Where she is vulnerable and no amount of rational rightness can save her. Because for a long time I thought pretending to be a Scully would save me. But even Scully gets abducted by aliens. Even Scully gets kidnapped by men who love her for the wrong reasons. Even Scully can't protect her sister. Even Scully lives in uncertainty and stress and misery and sometimes wonders if continually going back to Mulder in any and all capacities is good for her. Even Scully wears a cross. Even Scully sees an angel.

I wasn't a Scully looking for a Mulder, I was a person seeking some sort of mutual trust. I was a person who wanted to believe that two people with wildly different ways of being in the world, which is, let's be honest, most any two people of any genders, could come to trust each other as a matter of pure instinct. That you didn't need to believe all the same things, or have lived the same lives, in order for trust to be possible. That difference is just difference. It's just human. It doesn't need to activate into some perfect complementary cycle. It doesn't need to be pathologized. You just have to believe the other person's things are real and valid, too. You just need to know that if you called them, they would pick up the phone. That it would almost be beside the point to say, *It's me,* because they would know.

— III —

But this is a story you are telling yourself, I said, a story that will make you unhappy . . . There's nothing inevitable about it, it's a choice you've made, you can choose a different story.

—GARTH GREENWELL, *CLEANNESS*

Nights We Didn't

When we were undergrads at Georgetown, I fell for a girl I'll call Maggie while I was dating a boy I'll call Sam.

I wasn't out, but I'd always felt a little queer. At thirteen, I taped a magazine picture of Liv Tyler to my closet door in which she was holding a tiger cub, and the pull quote read "My hands are bigger than most men's," and I longed for Liv Tyler and those hands just as much as I longed for the gentle tattooed boys and their guitars I taped below her. At fourteen, I was illustrating favorite poems on my parents' driveway in chalk and somehow these dusty tableaux always managed to be full of naked women, which stopped dog-walking neighbors in their tracks. I drew La Belle Dame Sans Merci on her horse, rendering her tits in exquisite detail even as I neglected to draw her face, a woman that powerful still partially impossible to imagine. At seventeen I conspired with a girl from my art class to let me take pictures of her naked with various fruit for our senior art project. Cantaloupes and tits. Watermelons and hips. Unspeakable papayas. And I wanted to make this art but I also hoped, that maybe, once she was naked, something, anything, might happen between us.

These days I say bisexual, I say pansexual. But back then?

What did all these scraps of feeling, impulse, wondering, amount to? There was no story to tell about them, I would have said. These days I say queer, but in college? I said nothing.

Sometimes I play this game I call Time Travel.

In Time Travel, I take myself back to the places where I caused a hurt. And in my mind, *I fix it*. I undo what I did. If only I knew myself the way I do now, I wouldn't make such a mess of things, I tell myself. The scope of my time travel is vast. I return to queer moments, sure, but also moments of not understanding my own fears, my own traumas, my own needs, my own self.

What an unhealthy pleasure it is, to play this game. Even as it hurts to time-travel to these moments, to rake myself over the coals of my wrongness again and again, it also feels like relief. Penance, even.

And when I play Time Travel, more often than not, I return to the night Maggie and I didn't go to the Black Cat.

You'll remember I've told you part of this story before. That Maggie and I were meant to go out dancing in a group of women. Brit Pop Night at the Black Cat club. We were wearing an inordinate amount of eye makeup. I'd ripped my own stockings with razor blades. We had made these plans happen, she and I, because we wanted to dance together. Or maybe I should speak only for myself. I wanted to dance with Maggie.

I told you just the easy part before. The fun part. The funny part. The rest is harder to tell.

It had snowed, and this was Washington, DC, where snow debilitates the city, and so we never made it to the club. The night seemingly sapped of its opportunities, we wound up smoking on the balcony of yet another tedious apartment party as the snow accumulated in the parking lot below, where the shuttle buses' brakes exhaled loudly.

I saw Maggie across the balcony and she looked at me meaningfully and gathered up her shirt in her fist. I was the only one looking and she lifted the hem to reveal what she'd written across her stomach, in red lipstick: I'D RATHER BE AT THE BLACK CAT. And I died. I still die, when I think of this. She pressed herself against me as she went inside, her hand sliding, briefly, between my legs. And then she was gone.

That week, I broke up with Sam without explaining why, and this was horrible of me.

The first time Maggie and I kissed we were walking home, holding hands, on those crooked cobblestone streets it was impossible not to trip on. We paused in front of one of Georgetown's secret fenced gardens, a town house with flowers strangling a wrought-iron gate, a Vespa the color of eggshells inside. We leaned in to look at it, that little world beyond the gate, and then turned to each other, as if to see what we were thinking. We were thinking about kissing. We kissed. I died. I still die.

We started seeing each other and didn't tell anyone, drinking bourbon in my room and blasting music and tumbling in bed. It was good for the hot minute it lasted.

Then everything went sideways.

Sam was hurt beyond hurt from our breakup. *And of course he was.* A chaplain from our Catholic university came to tell me that I had done a lot of emotional harm to Sam and that she was worried. And I was devastated, and panicked. Sam didn't even know about Maggie yet, and the chaplain was already in the loop?

I am not Catholic, and my parents had left behind their Catholicism before I was born, but there is a certain amount of cultural Catholicism that, it turns out, does not release its hold so easily. Did the chaplain actually come to me, or did someone just tell me what she'd said about me? In my mind I can see her, but it's possible that I only heard it secondhand. That she looms so large in my memory, that I can see her approaching me on the little dorm quad bench, because I think of her so often. Because an adult in a position of power wanted me to know I'd been an agent of pain. And honestly, in the hierarchy of bad guys in this story, I rank myself as the chief bad guy, maybe the only bad guy, but that chaplain has a not-insignificant ranking on my shit list, whether she came to me in person, or only in her words. Because I cannot tell you the number of times in my life I have remembered, and re-remembered, what that felt like. The shame and guilt of official personnel telling me how responsible I was for someone else's pain.

And I *was* responsible. But sometimes, when I'm playing Time Travel, that chaplain almost breaks my game. My game, which is meant to be about punishing myself. Because when I see her, I think that what I was supposed to learn from that moment, but didn't, was that sometimes you do cause pain. Because you make mistakes. You fuck up. Or just because you don't want to date someone anymore. Because you make choices that make you happier and other people sadder. And you have to sit with that responsibility, and bear it, and understand which parts were and were not within your power to make better. All that would have been a healthy thing to learn as a college student. If I had learned that, in fact, I would not be here, playing Time Travel.

Instead, what I learned back then was: You did what you wanted and now bad things are happening. And you could fix it. You could make someone stop hurting, if you were less selfish.

So I put an end to things with Maggie, this relationship I wanted, as if giving her up would expunge my guilt instead of adding to it. And Maggie was hurt beyond hurt. *And of course she was.*

Listen, I am not an officially elected delegate of bi-kids-who-were-not-yet-out-in-college-who-messed-you-around, but I will offer a statement on our behalf to whoever needs to hear it anyway: That was so, so fucked up of us. We are so, so sorry. We were trying our best or maybe we didn't know how to try our best yet, but it doesn't matter. You deserved so much better. I am so sorry to Maggie. I am so sorry to Sam. I am so sorry to whoever you are reading this who recognizes yourself in this kind of story.

And then, things got messy. At a party, Maggie came on to Sam, who still didn't know she and I had been together, and after they'd had sex she whispered to him what *we'd* done in bed (does it go without saying that we were theater kids?) and Sam was beyond devastated. *And of course he was.*

Sam came to me, and told me what had happened, and we talked and talked and talked it out, on the banks of the Potomac, on a day so full of the possibilities of mid-Atlantic spring that we both got sunburned. And eventually Sam said we should get back together and I said yes, as if this would make things right. As if, by getting back together, I could go back in time to before I'd made such a mess of things. As if this would make me less culpable for every mistake I'd managed to make with both of them.

At night, I would leave the nine-person house I lived in with the other theater kids and walk across the street to the performing-arts high school there: the Duke Ellington School for the Arts. On their lawn was the Big Green Chair—a fourteen-foot-high Adirondack painted mint green—a DC landmark. I would climb up into the lap of that larger-than-life chair, and stare at my own house, across the street, and chain-smoke, and cry. I was shaken by how much emotional damage I'd managed to do in such a short amount of time. I was guilt-stricken and horrified by myself. I would have tried anything to alleviate the pain I'd caused.

When Sam and I got back together, a lot of the gay boys we were friends with were furious about it. They were his friends, really, and they hated my guts for what I'd done. *And of course they did.*

They said, *Dump her. She doesn't know what she wants.* They said, *Don't trust her—this was her first stop on the train to gayville.*

On the one hand, the boys had *seen* me. Had affirmed my queerness. But it didn't feel good. Because in the same breath they were saying that my being queer meant I was unsure of myself and what I wanted. Were saying my nascent queerness made me dangerous. That, in my lack of certainty, I would hurt people.

The train to gayville.

The boys were just sharpening their teeth on me, the way we all did back then. And I don't blame them. But it was their saying these things that hurt the most. So I decided I didn't want the boys to be right that I was going to hurt Sam again. That I was a person who hurt people. And so I stayed with him until I graduated. I would prove I wasn't an agent of pain. I wouldn't explore being queer anymore, if that's what it took. If that was the price.

When news of the whole gossipy saga traveled through our theater-kid community, my friends asked me about Maggie, how it had been, earnestly trying to be supportive, to understand whether I was coming out or not.

"How was it?" they asked, meaning, being with Maggie. And I lied.

I said, "It was confusing—too many boobs." And by saying this I made my friends laugh.

What a fucking betrayal that was.

It was not too many boobs, and I wasn't confused about anything other than how I could possibly ever kiss a girl again now that I had made such a mess of things. I told myself I would graduate soon. I would leave. And then I would move to Brooklyn and kiss whoever I pleased.

Fifteen years later, and this story should have released its hold on me, but instead, I time-travel to it again and again, performing a penance that serves no one. I agonize over the pain I caused. I yell at myself: Just know yourself better. Just be less confused. Just be always already fully aware of who you are and what you want.

I did move to Brooklyn and I kissed some people I pleased, but not many. If I'm honest, I felt like the Black Cat had blocked me. Things had gone so badly before I could ever be with Maggie properly that the experience never became the coming-out story it might have been for me. Instead, it was a story I couldn't tell to anyone. Even tell to myself. The shame of it was too much.

I held back from speaking out loud who I was, and that lack of speaking out loud meant, that for a long time, more often than not, I wound up kissing men. Because who had heard I wanted anything else? A while ago, on a date with a woman I'd had a crush on for a long time, she said she hadn't been sure if I was queer or not. We had both been flirting with each other at a wedding two years prior, but neither of us had been bold enough to kiss the other, and it was this not-knowing, more than anything else, that had stood in our way.

Standing at the counter of a jazz bar in DC, I made excuses. "I mean, my friends know I'm bi," I said. "My parents know." She shrugged and smiled.

I was still being so quiet. I was still not saying things out loud. It had prevented us from recognizing what we wanted at that wedding. Prevented our kissing, which finally arrived, in that jazz bar, on a night when so many people had turned out to play that the room was more musicians than listeners, more music than talk, and I understood that, if this was what my quiet had been drowning out, I should probably get loud.

I think it's important to own the pain we cause. I take responsibility for mine. But maybe the self-flagellation can stop. Maybe it's okay to look at the pain we caused before we knew ourselves, and to learn from it, but also forgive it. Because I think it is possible that when I play Time Travel, the pain I am trying to avoid causing might not just be for Maggie and Sam. I think I am also trying to save myself. I travel to visit the girl smoking in that giant Adirondack chair, and this time, instead of prickling with shame about what a mess she is, how much hurt she's caused, instead of thinking of her, of me, as some enormous and powerful agent of pain, I see someone figuring out who she is. And in that Big Green Chair on the Duke Ellington lawn, that girl looks so small.

· · ·

There's another reason the story of the Black Cat blocked me for so long. And it's because the story of what happened with Maggie was in so many ways the story of what *didn't* happen with Maggie. How we *didn't* go to the Black Cat. How we *didn't* wind up together. How it *didn't* last but a minute. How I *didn't* give it a fair chance.

So it *didn't* become a story I could tell myself about who I was.

Like the rest of the ephemeral archive of my queerness, like my magazine picture of Liv Tyler and her tigers, like La Belle Dame Sans Merci's tits chalked on the family driveway, like the girl from school who I asked to take off her clothes "for art," the Black Cat was a *non-event*. The *absence* of a story. A time *nothing* managed, after all, to happen.

A group of new friends recently changed the way I think of this story.

It was summer in Tennessee, and we were at writer camp. We lingered at our lunch table, had stayed up too late the night before, playing guitar and reading one another's tarot and listening to the Brood X cicadas screaming about their changes in the trees. We were debating going for a swim in the lake, where the water was so silty everyone floating in it glowed the color of strong tea. How did we start talking about the girls we didn't kiss? Maybe it was Heather, who talked about a camping trip where she slept in a tent with a girl she had a crush on. "I slept like this," she said, and froze her body into a hot dog, arms pinned to her sides. "I stayed so still all night so that I wouldn't touch her," she said, "because I wanted to touch her so much." By now we were already laughing so hard we had almost peed ourselves, but maybe it was when Kat talked about the time her ice-skating choreography called for her to hold hands with an older girl on her team she had such a crush on and how, when they held hands, she thought to herself, *Oh my god, oh my god, we're holding hands, we're in love!* Maybe it was when I told the story about the girl in my art class. How she had taken off her clothes in my parents' rec room because I'd asked her to, how it was too bright in there, but she was still so fucking beautiful. How she shivered as I sliced the cantaloupes between photographs, a triptych of a melon progressively opening. How I scooped out the seeds and put melon slices on her body. And I took the photos. And nothing happened. And even as I told *this* story I was tempted to play Time Travel, to go back to the rec room and apologize to this girl, or to kiss her, or both. But as I was telling this story, my new friends had their heads on the table, which trembled as they shook with laughter. They were laughing not at the girl, of course, but at me. At all of us.

"But did you have a crush on her?" my friend Bea said.

"Of course I did!" I said, and realized it was true. "I think I thought that once she was naked, and the cantaloupes were happening, it would just become obvious what should happen next."

"Oh," my new friend Darcy said, out of breath with laughter, full of tenderness, "I love queer beginnings."

"But how is it the beginning," I asked them, "when nothing happened?"

Darcy looked at me, not unkindly, but like I had missed the point.

I had always thought of the night Maggie and I never made it to the Black Cat as a failed beginning. A beginning, because she touched me and I died. I still die. A failure, because it never went anywhere.

But a beginning is yours. Heather sleeping so still in her tent, Kat holding hands in the rink, me, optimistically slicing cantaloupes and hoping for something I couldn't even articulate to happen. The first time you felt a way. The first time you tried to be the way you felt. These are stories, too. These nights you didn't. You're allowed to call them beginnings.

One time, Maggie and I talked about Time Travel.

It was after I had broken up with Sam, when we'd started flirting in earnest, over AOL Instant Messenger, mostly. We talked about how we'd had such crushes on each other from the very start of the school year. The first time we'd met in the theater office. How each of us had thought the other probably wouldn't be interested. How each of us thought it would be too embarrassing to ask, to see, to try.

The night we didn't go to the Black Cat had never been our beginning.

It had always been this one afternoon, so many months before. When we had sat on the couch in the theater office together. Had both felt something, and done nothing.

On AIM, one of us typed to the other: I WISH WE COULD GO BACK IN TIME AND JUST ASK EACH OTHER OUT.

Maggie said goodnight, and when she put up her away message, I remember it was a blue hyperlink whose string of text revealed nothing about where it might lead.

And I clicked on it.

And there was this diagram. There were these instructions. The link led to a webpage where some generous internet soul had offered up to us their elaborate plans for building a time machine.

Act Three: Dulcinea Quits

The last time you talk to the boy you are in your thirties, and you are planning a wedding. You are unhappy but don't know why yet, so you are letting the momentum of the life choices you've made carry you along, reassuringly enough.

So when your phone lights up with the Los Angeles area code, even though you told the boy he could call, you are terrified. Your first feeling is an absolute certainty that if you talk to the boy, if you hear his voice, you will throw any good thing you have built for yourself out the window. Immediately. Enthusiastically. That much power is still there. Just in his name.

But he's texted to ask if he can call, and you know why. You haven't talked in years, but he has posted to Facebook to say that his longtime NA sponsor has died. He has written a lovely thing about what the sponsor meant to him in recovery and then a bit more about how not okay he's felt since hearing he was gone. You understand the gravity of the loss of a sponsor. And so whatever part of you that knows you shouldn't get back in touch is immediately overwritten by the part of you that knows This Is One of Those Times You Pick Up the Phone.

You pick up the phone.

To hear his voice is, at once, terrifying and like coming home. You talk about his grief for his sponsor. You talk about your lives. He is still the funniest, sweetest, weirdest boy on Earth. One who has never been afraid to be tender and peculiar. Sensitive, and affectionate, and interested in sensitivity and affection. He has a gorgeous voice. Always has. This is a thing you're a sucker for because you were raised to the sound of stories read aloud by your grandfather, the radioman. The boy's voice has a deep, warm, purring register and he knows what he's doing with it. You feel yourself relaxing into the conversation, letting yourself believe that maybe you can be in each other's lives again now that you're older.

You walk right up to the edge of this seawall, and look down, all the ways you've ever felt for him crashing against the rocks beneath you, and it is so fucking beautiful, more intense than anything else you know. And you tell yourself you've been so good for so long, maybe you've earned a self-destructive plunge?

But then the reason for the call comes out.

He talked about you with his sponsor, he says. Like, a lot. They decided, years ago, that, someday, when he got sober, the two of you could start your relationship over again. That it would be a kind of quest for him. And whenever the boy doubted why he was doing this, his recovery journey, he would tell himself that he was becoming a man who was worthy of being with you again. Who was ready for that. And this, he said, worked. The sponsor told him not to contact you these past years. Forbade it. That would ruin the quest, he said, and it wasn't fair to bring this struggle back into your life before he was ready to be good to you.

But now his sponsor is dead. So he's reaching out. Because there's no one to tell him not to. And he's reaching out because he's ready. He is sober and stable and a good man worthy of love. The quest is complete. It is time for the two of you to begin your relationship again.

You start scratching at your wrists. You have been contracted into this arrangement without knowing it, but your first feeling is that you have no choice but to go along with the bargain he and his sponsor made. About you. Whether or not you want to is immaterial. You scratch and breathe too fast, a too-small animal. Nothing makes you more panicky than feeling irrevocably trapped by other people's choices.

You say maybe you could talk on the phone sometimes and try to be friends—you don't say friends *again,* because you and he had never been friends, not even when you were seventeen. Not because you were fucking but because you were so impossibly in love with each other. With him you have always felt that something in you could see something in him and vice versa. Have always felt that whatever weird frequency you vibrated on in this life he was on it, too. And whatever you call that, you have never felt it again with anyone else. You stopped looking for it years ago. Because, it turned out, it wasn't fucking good for you. *I am special. I am special!*

So you tell the boy perhaps you can try to be friends, for the first time. And of course this is disappointing. He is grieving, and what he has left of his sponsor is the way he showed him to fight to get better. Which is great. Except the way he taught the boy to do that is through you.

"We could get to know each other," you suggest. "I mean, we don't even really know each other anymore."

"Don't we?" he says.

And then he describes you. The person he's been fighting to get better for. To be worthy of.

And of course she's not you.

Or she is.

She's your own ghost.

It's you at seventeen. You as a virgin. You, still fresh and relatively unmarked by the world. A peach with maybe just one artful bruise on it.

Who were you back then, anyway?

As you remember, you were badly dressed but skinny, with gravity-defying tits and an ass the boys sometimes slapped at school, even if you were wearing something patently unsexy like those striped train-conductor overalls you loved. You were frizzy-haired and plain-faced and privileged and sweet and moody. You were tediously Pollyannaish about anything to do with social justice and performatively contrarian about everything else. You kept a shrine to John Lennon in your bedroom at the center of which was this satisfyingly heavy biography you'd never read but in front of which you lit flying-fairy Chinatown incense. You liked to say you were "born at the wrong time." You preferred animals and children to anyone else. You had no idea what to do with your body but you were always already a hedonistic little ball of senses and you understood pleasure. You loved music and food and the smell of the boy's armpits and being touched. You had enormous eyes and enormous ears and you were just cripplingly earnest, but, having been raised by fast-talking New Yorkers and having consumed too much art, sometimes disarmingly adult banter came dropping from your mouth and the contrast must have been alarming. You were happiest alone in the woods or with a book. You cried over things like the fact that flowers didn't bloom for that long.

That they had to die. Seriously, literally, you cried about this. You had just turned seventeen and the facts of the world were pressing in on you for the first time with a sort of tedious, metaphysical, white-girl sadness that felt too much to bear. And he was the first one who said to you, *Hey, people have like, written poems about that stuff, you know? And songs. Do you know Keats? David Byrne?* He showed you how to find yourself in this way. Introduced you to the sacred texts of the terminally sensitive.

This is how you remember it, anyway. This is more or less the girl he conjures. How odd it is to hear this girl spoken of, and to recognize her. How strange to notice that the girl's most defining feature is how very different she is from the woman you are now.

These days, you're a mechanical, not a lover.

You're an Act Two kind of Fantastick.

He is describing his Dulcinea, but you are Aldonza.

Don Quixote, as you know, is a man who has read so many books about knights, about chivalry and quests, that it has muddled his brain. He becomes convinced he is a knight errant who will sally forth in search of good deeds to do, wrongs to right, and ladies to save. And the lady he is doing all this for, he decides, is Dulcinea del Toboso. A woman whom, if she exists, he has never actually met. But it does not matter that she's imaginary—she still motivates his noble quest.

What is a knight without a lady to do it all for?

In *Man of La Mancha,* the 1965 musical based on Cervantes's novel, there is a song Quixote sings to the woman he has decided is his Dulcinea (in reality her name is Aldonza, and she is a barmaid and prostitute at the local inn, which he mistakes for a castle). She is dirty, and cross-looking, and sad.

DON QUIXOTE

[Enters the inn]

Sweet lady . . . fair virgin . . .

[Don Quixote averts his eyes worshipfully]

I dare not gaze full upon thy countenance
Lest I be blinded by beauty. But I implore
Thee—speak once thy name.

ALDONZA

Aldonza.

DON QUIXOTE

My lady jests.

ALDONZA

Aldonza!

DON QUIXOTE

The name of a kitchen-scullion . . . or perhaps my
lady's serving-maid?

ALDONZA

I told you my name! Now get out of the way.

[She clears past him to the table]

. . .

DON QUIXOTE

I have dreamed thee too long,
Never seen thee or touched thee.
But known thee with all of my heart.
Half a prayer, half a song,
Thou hast always been with me,
Though we have been always apart.

Here's the thing that kills you: even as Quixote sings to Aldonza? She never, never *stops working*. Her whole performance is delivered at the same time she cleans, and brings food, and beats back the other men who snicker and proposition her.

The innkeepers worry whether Quixote, mad as he is, will have money to pay for his stay. One decides, "When has a poor man ever found time to run mad? Of course he has money."

Here is a thing you sometimes want to shout: When has a woman ever found time for a quest?

And still, you understand how a quest might save your life. A quest was what the sponsor used to help the boy find his sobriety. And maybe recovery is a by-any-means-necessary sort of bag. But the day the boy calls you and tells you about his quest, you panic. Because you can't meet up with him and see what might be possible. You are engaged, for one thing. You have a whole life you've built. And buckets of other doubts besides.

You can't be his Dulcinea.

But winning the lady is the final stage of his quest. And he has done the work. So now, if that doesn't happen, it's going to blow the foundations out of his narrative. He tells you as much. And you don't want to do that. You don't you don't you don't. But why has his sponsor built him such a fragile house to live in?

There is no one to ask. There is no one to blame. And this only makes things worse.

A man is on a quest. And he is singing about it.

You just keep saying what it is you *can* give him—your actual thirty-three-year-old self as a friend. But you can tell it isn't enough. The person he needs is a fiction to whom so much real-life consequence had been tied that her failure to manifest is disastrous. But you cannot summon her, this ghost of your seventeen-year-old self. She is gone. And when you hang up the phone that day, in addition to all the guilt and confusion you feel, you are also mourning.

Because, that girl, how did you let her get away? You miss her, too.

For years, you feel guilty and ashamed about your inability to be the boy's Dulcinea. It haunts you. Painfully. Loudly. Still. You try to tell yourself that even if you had offered more, offered to run away with him, offered love and sex and a new relationship, it would not have been enough. Because when you arrived on his doorstep you still would have been Aldonza.

The last time you hear the boy's voice it is in a voice mail, a few years later, saying he is on the East Coast. Somewhere near Albany. He thinks he remembers that you live in this part of the world and are perhaps nearby. He has something to ask you. The voice mail has the outdoor sounds of wind in the background, cold wind on a cold night, and this upsets you. You feel like maybe he is in trouble and you should call him back. Instead you call a friend.

Your friend says: "Don't call."

"He might be in trouble," you say.

"Listen to yourself," she says.

You listen. But you feel sick with guilt.

This is not an ending. It's just the last entry in the record of times you still haven't been over the boy. An incomplete taxonomy of all the different ways you'll never be over him.

It is easy to forget that the musical *Man of La Mancha* is not actually set in the fields of windmills and tavern rooms you remember best, but in a prison.

The whole show is a spectacle being put on by Peter O'Toole's Cervantes, slipping on a fake beard, and trying to distract himself and his fellow prisoners from the reality of their own choices.

Years later, you are at home, watching *Man of La Mancha* with a man you're dating, and you point out the rotund little man next to Quixote.

"That's Sancho Panza," you tell him. "I almost named my dog Sancho Panza."

You gesture to your roly-poly dog on the floor. He is belly-up, one useless fang exposed, and he googles his eye at you, as if to say he is wearied by your infinite human folly.

Onscreen, Sancho Panza is huffing and puffing, trying to convince Quixote not to attack the windmill he's mistaken for a giant.

"Tell me that man isn't my dog in human form," you say, shaking your head. "I should have done it."

"Naw, because that makes *you* Quixote," he says, pointing out what he perceives as a flaw in the plan. There is a shout and you both look back to the screen. O'Toole is rolling on the ground, having tumbled from the windmill. He begins raving about something he once read in a book.

"Oh," the man you are dating says.

It's all well and good to say it was the boy who made a quixotic fantasy of your love, who turned you into something you weren't, but then again, here you are, staging this play in three acts, still performing the story of who the two of you used to be.

The Second Mrs. de Winter

*The sexiness of [Rebecca] is maybe the most
unsettling part, since it centers on the narrator's being
simultaneously attracted to and repulsed by the memory
and the mystery of her new husband's dead wife.*

—EMILY ALFORD, *JEZEBEL*

Rebecca had good taste—or maybe she just had the same taste as me, and that's why I thought it was good. She loved a particular shade of vintage, minty turquoise. The kitchen cabinets were all this color. As were the plates inside. The cups and bowls were white with dainty black dots on them. Not polka dots—a smaller, more charming print.

I loved them. I might have picked them out myself. It made me feel sick that I loved them.

I imagined Rebecca had picked out these cups and plates when she moved into this house, but the cupboards I was investigating, and the very lovely dishes inside them, now belonged to her ex-husband, my boyfriend. Rebecca lived fifteen minutes away.

Of course, her name wasn't really Rebecca. But grant me a theme. We'll call him Maxim.

. . .

Every once in a while, a book will pass through my writers' group, all of us swept up in reading the same novel. In the early days of my dating Maxim, that book was Daphne du Maurier's *Rebecca*. My friend Emily was rereading it to write an essay for *Jezebel* called "The Nihilistic Horniness of a Good Gothic Read: Ranking the Genre's Sexiest and Scariest Secrets." *Rebecca* ranks number one. Emily's love for the novel was so persuasive the rest of us soon joined in.

The basic premise of *Rebecca* is that our narrator, a naïve young woman, marries an older, brooding widower and goes to live in his strange and beautiful house, where it rapidly becomes clear that the legacy of his dead wife, the titular Rebecca, is . . . potent. The narrator constantly worries over whether she can run the house as well as Rebecca did.

At one point, Emily was in the bathtub with a Scotch and the novel and somehow still had enough hands to live-text us: THIS WOMAN'S ONLY PROBLEM IS THAT THE SERVANTS ARE MEAN TO HER AND I WANT THAT LIFE.

The servants do not like the narrator for the very good reason that she is Not Rebecca. Beyond the servants, of course, the narrator is also concerned that she'll never live up to Rebecca in Maxim's heart. That in the wake of his great and tragic love, she stands no chance.

Again, from Emily's bath: EVEN THE DOGS DON'T LIKE HER.

I had never read *Rebecca* before. About fifty pages in, I felt remiss because I hadn't retained the narrator's name. I flipped back through the opening and still couldn't find it. Maxim was the husband. Rebecca was his dead wife. Mrs. Danvers was the housekeeper. Jasper was the dog.

WTF, I texted Emily. THE DOG HAS A NAME BUT NOT THE NARRATOR?

HE'S A VERY GOOD DOG, Emily said.

For 410 pages, the narrator of *Rebecca* is only ever known to us as the Second Mrs. de Winter, and isn't that just the whole story?

CAN I TELL YOU SOMETHING HORRIBLE? I asked Emily.

OF COURSE

I'VE BEEN FEELING A LOT LIKE TSMDW LATELY

OH GIRL

The little white house in New York where my Maxim lived was no Manderley, but like Manderley, the house was an issue. The house with Rebecca's lovely dishes in the cupboard. The house with art on the walls no man would ever have picked. The red calico curtains, which Maxim eventually took down because, despite having sewn them himself, he had never liked the print Rebecca picked (I did), and after that there were no curtains at all. The kitchen, where I cooked us dinner and accidentally used a special salt Rebecca had favored, but left behind, which made Maxim look up from his meal and ask, "What did you put in here?"

One afternoon I was working at a desk in the office and, playing with the drawer, found inside Rebecca's birth certificate. I'd already known we were born a week apart because on our second date Maxim had asked my birthday and blanched when I'd said October.

More than once Maxim returned an article of women's clothing to me that was not mine.

There were notes in Rebecca's handwriting on the fridge

and photos of her in the house, and this was right and good, because she and Maxim had a daughter, an eight-year-old girl who was funny and sweet and whom I was very lucky to know for those almost two years. I must leave her out of this—she is a still-becoming person—but of course she remains an invisible source of gravity in this story. There were photos of them at Disney World. Photos of them holding their daughter the day she was born.

All of which is to say that Rebecca was everywhere. In the house, and beyond it as well.

Once, playing music in the car, I put on one of my favorite albums, and Maxim grabbed for the dial to turn it off. I had accidentally played the song to which he and Rebecca had walked down the aisle at their wedding. We had eerily similar taste in music.

None of this was Maxim's fault. I must have felt like a haunting to him. It must have been uncomfortable. I came to recognize and dread the look and silence that came over him in those moments when I accidentally assumed a Rebecca-like posture. I felt guilty, though didn't know precisely for what.

In the most excruciating scene in *Rebecca*, TSMdW throws a costume ball in an effort to be the kind of hostess and charmer Rebecca once was. She decides she will dress like a relative of Maxim's, Caroline de Winter, whose portrait hangs prominently in the house and who TSMdW refers to as "the girl in white." She prattles, extensively, tediously, about what a big secret her costume is and how bowled over everyone will be when they see it. She orders a wig that will curl just so. She orders a white dress. She means this to be a surprise for Maxim.

TSMdW waits till the party is under way to make her entrance and then appears at the top of the stairs, completely transformed into the woman in the painting. "They all stared at me like dumb things," she says. "Beatrice uttered a little cry and put her hand to her mouth. I went on smiling, I put one hand on the banister."

And then: "Maxim had not moved. He stared up at me, his glass in his hand. There was no colour in his face. It was ashen white. . . . 'What the hell do you think you're doing?' he said. . . . 'What is it?' I said. 'What have I done?'"

We come to understand that Rebecca once had this very same idea for a costume. "It was what Rebecca did at the last fancy dress ball at Manderley. Identical," sister-in-law Beatrice says.

Seeing her at the top of the stairs, Maxim believes TSMdW to be the ghost of Rebecca. He believed this to be a haunting.

Of all of this, the bit that sickens and thrills me most is when, just as everyone else sees she has blundered into a pantomime of Rebecca, TSMdW remains ignorant and *continues smiling*. She still thinks she is herself. She still believes she is unique.

This doesn't last for long. As the novel goes on, TSMdW becomes desperate and horrible as she tries to outpace her predecessor's shadow—but readers have little reason to believe she will succeed. The Second Mrs. de Winter believes she is narrating the story of her own life but, little does she know, *the book in our hands is called* Rebecca.

Often, when we went to restaurants, or on hikes, or to concerts, this would prompt stories of past times Maxim had been to those places. He had lived his whole life in this part of the country, and so of course many of those stories had Rebecca in them or implied her around the margins. I came to feel like a verdict had already been passed on every song I might sing, every dish I might cook, every date we might go on—because Rebecca had already sung them and cooked them and been to these places before. I felt trapped in a rerun of someone else's life, and I didn't know how to fix it.

Of course, the only way Maxim could tell me about his life was with these stories, and I couldn't know and love him if I censored his past. So why did it hurt so much to move through these recently vacated spaces? Why did I feel like every date we went on had been *used up* because he had been there for the first time with someone else? Why could I not get over the feeling that this made our experiences somehow redundant, lesser?

That I felt this way betrays deep insecurity and narcissism in the same instance. Worse, it betrays a belief that to be a first love, or a great love, is the only way to be.

When I confessed to my boyfriend that I felt this way, he said a smart and beautiful thing.

He said: "Who says the first time is always the best time?"

I loved him so much when he said that. And I promised myself I'd stop seeing his past as an intrusion on our present. But knowing you're being stupid seldom alleviates the stupidity—it only adds a blanketing layer of shame.

Why *was* I so obsessed with being first?

Have you ever watched one of those ensemble-cast-of-friends shows where they try to introduce new characters several seasons in? Chachi, on *Happy Days,* is the most famous example and I am still not over *Buffy the Vampire Slayer*'s Dawn Summers retcon. But the most memorably painful of these late-stage introductions was Tori Scott on *Saved by the Bell.* After five seasons of one stable gang, Kelly and Jessie were disappeared from Bayside High without comment. The sixth season opened with an episode called "The New Girl," in which new-to-the-school motorcycle chick Tori takes Zach's parking spot, resulting in a presexual squabble. When Tori agrees to help Lisa organize the Fall Ball, Lisa, full of gratitude, exclaims: "You're my new best friend!" She starts to walk away, and then, in a strangely meta moment, as if remembering the existence of Jessie and Kelly, turns back to Tori with a face of absolute horror. "You're . . . my *only* best friend?" The show seemed to hope we would forget about Jessie and Kelly, forget about the past, and while there was nothing implicitly wrong with Tori, I felt like: *Let's not pretend we don't know who the main characters of this show really are. Let's not pretend we don't know who counts.* I was terrified I would never have enough gravitas to earn a permanent place in Maxim's life, because I was afraid I had arrived too late to count. I was obsessed with being first because I didn't want to be a Tori or TSMdW. Because, in my mind, the original cast are always the main characters—everyone else is *expendable.* I found the very existence of Rebecca threatening because of who it implied I was in this love story. And for more reasons than that besides.

I have a low threshold for surprises. Life is mostly surprises, to be fair, but I specifically mean the You Didn't Know This New Large Feeling Was Scheduled for Today sort. The *Today is the day you are meeting my ex-wife, she'll be here in an hour, is that okay* kind of surprise. The *Oh, these five people you are currently shaking hands with at a dance recital are my former in-laws* kind of surprise. All of which is to say, eventually I met Rebecca. In most ways it was uneventful. I found her beautiful. Blond where I was dark. Quiet where I rambled. Remarkably little passed between us.

On this occasion, I behaved fine on the outside, but on the inside, I thought, *I am not good at this.* It was silly, but I felt I hadn't prepared adequately for our meeting.

I suspect you'll make the same understandable mistake Maxim made: he thought I was anxious about these meetings because of the usual bouts of awkwardness entailed in meeting a person's ex, even if (especially if?) that person is the mother of your boyfriend's child. And sure, it was a little bit that. But that's not what I wished I'd prepared for.

I had to prepare myself not to understand Rebecca too much.

I am a person who always chooses the woman. Prefers the company of a woman. I suffer from a myopia that prevents me, in all but the most extreme circumstances, from seeing any hetero breakup as the fault of the woman.

I was very afraid that I was going to like Rebecca.

You'll think I'm a misandrist or humble-bragging, and both are probably true. But what I'm trying to tell you is this: in my warped mind, the flip side of the coin that read *Liking Rebecca* was: *Disliking My Boyfriend.* I couldn't conceive of any gray area.

I didn't want to meet Rebecca, because if I did, I might see a glimpse of another version of the story of her and Maxim's marriage, and I was unprepared to know anything at all that might make me doubt the way he had treated a woman.

We are all of us flawed, we have all of us behaved badly—and to expect someone in their thirties to have an immaculate history is unreasonable, I know this. But this was the first time I'd fallen in love with someone who used to be married. Who'd gone through a painful divorce. And in my desire to think of my boyfriend in the particular rosy way love encourages, in the story of his past, I wanted to see him as the good guy and her as the bad. I thought this was the only way I could be a good partner to a person who'd gone through a divorce. I thought this was the only way I could trust him.

A readerly confession: during every scene of *Rebecca* where TSMdW and Maxim hash out their relationship and life at Manderley, I found myself impatient, wondering, *But could you say more about Rebecca?* Because TSMdW is a drag and Rebecca is fascinating. Rebecca kept up a nautical sex-cabin in which to have affairs. Rebecca took the sailboat out to sea, even in storms. Rebecca organized inspired dinners and parties. She was loud, unruly, sexual, powerful, and charming. Rebecca wasn't a "good person," per se, but who cares! She was deeply fucking interesting in ways TSMdW could never be and, more important, she got there first.

On Valentine's Day, in an effort to avoid celebrating someplace Maxim had once gone with Rebecca, and to avoid too many grand expectations of romance, I suggested we get drunk at the mall and visit the Mirror Maze, a curtained storefront with a glittering proscenium.

The mall, I swear to god, is called Destiny.

The maze was janky but beautiful. We were given loose, crinkly plastic gloves to wear, so when we inevitably touched a mirror, mistaking it for a doorway, we would not smudge the glass. The wide mirrors' frames had slivers of neon color around their edges. Inside there were zones of multicolored lights and zones of blacklights. We were reflected everywhere, ridiculous and clinical-looking in our gloves. It was a bit like a carnival's hall of mirrors, except it was a back-channel mall outlet, swaddled in black cloth. Ambient mall noise trickled in despite the canned pop they played, echoing weirdly through the passages.

We'd had a beer or two before entering and were laughing a lot as we traveled the maze. We held hands until it became clear we'd hurt ourselves if we kept it up. We separated, then. I went down a hallway, which dead-ended, and then tried to get back to where I'd been. I saw Maxim, walked toward him, and banged into a mirror.

I was legitimately shocked. It's the sort of thing that you think won't happen if you know the trick. We were adults, and the maze was a game, but the maze could still fool us. At first, I felt delighted. Then Maxim's reflection disappeared. I tried to find a way out of the hallway I'd walked down but clunked into pane after pane of glass. Be reasonable, I thought, even as I panicked. Maxim was nowhere to be seen and I was multiplied everywhere. I willed my own reflection to open up for me, to transform into a door.

In the fourth grade, I used to sneak away with other girls to do Bloody Mary in a small mirror that hung in the teacher's supply closet. The room smelled of construction paper and tempera paint. The lighting was dim and the mirror very smudged. We chanted and chanted at that supply-closet mirror, and I was scared, but I also really wanted to see something. But it was only ever my own scrawny face I saw in the mirror, overfull with desire, wishing something remarkable would happen. I frightened myself.

Eventually Maxim called out to me that he'd found the exit to the maze. I followed his voice and left behind the tunnel of my own reflections.

We went back to the beer hall and had another drink and soon were in the middle of an enormous fight.

We had found out, earlier that week, that Rebecca was going to have a baby with her new boyfriend. I'd asked Maxim if he wanted to talk about this, and he'd said no. I'd pressed, and he'd demurred, and so I'd left it. But now, four beers deep, still a little dizzy from the hall of mirrors, still inside the Destiny mall, on Valentine's Day, he brought it up. Suddenly he was talking about how our plans to move in together, to buy a new house and leave Manderley behind, would need to be indefinitely postponed until Rebecca had the baby, until Rebecca decided where to live with the baby. We didn't know, couldn't know, the how or when of any of this. We would just have to wait until Rebecca had made her choices about where to live, Maxim said, and then we could make our own, in response to hers.

And this was hard for Maxim—of course it was—but the logistics of it all? Putting our plans on hold in this way? It unhinged me. I couldn't see anything else.

I cried. I shouted a stupidly elaborate metaphor about being the rattled caboose of a driverless train. I made all of my first-rush feelings known instead of understanding that this was not the moment for my feelings. But I was too drunk to access the fine-motor skills of emotional control. On the cab ride back to his place I raked my nails along my own forearms, leaving long trailing welts, as if to persuade myself the pain wasn't all inside my head.

I felt like I couldn't even have one night where I wasn't asked to stand behind her in line. Like all the important decisions about our life were being decided by Maxim *and Rebecca,* instead of Maxim and me. Like I was a mall-mirror reflection of a reflection of a girlfriend. A thing diluted beyond meaning. What was the point of me?

I hated feeling this way. I hated reacting this way. But I also hated Maxim telling me that his hands were tied.

I needed to get out of the maze, get out of the mall, get out of Manderley, get out of this other woman's story. I didn't want to live inside a book named for someone else. I knew this. And yet, in the morning, I would wake up, and apologize. I would tell myself, again, that I couldn't blame Maxim. That this was all Rebecca's fault.

The secret in du Maurier's novel is, of course, that Maxim has murdered Rebecca. A body, soon to be revealed as hers, is discovered in a wrecked little boat two-thirds of the way through the book, and this is what prompts Maxim to come clean to his new wife. His confession comes as a surprise to very few readers, I am sure, seeing as Maxim behaves like a petulant schoolboy sociopath for the entire first half of the book and always looks funny when people mention *the cove*.

What's interesting, though, narratively, is that his confession is a misdirection.

The real surprise is still two beats away, and this is Du Maurier's genius.

After Maxim confesses the murder to TSMdW, the reader relaxes into his horrific but expected revelation . . . only to then be jump-scared by the thing they could not have seen coming, which is *how gleefully TSMdW responds to the news that her husband is a murderer:*

> I held his hands against my heart. I did not care about his shame. None of the things he had told me mattered to me at all. I clung to one thing only, and repeated it to myself, over and over again. Maxim did not love Rebecca. He had never loved her, never, never. They had never known one moment's happiness together. Maxim was talking and I listened to him, but his words meant nothing to me. I did not really care.

TSMdW does *not really care* that Maxim is a murderer. She is ecstatic, romantically aroused by the news. The second Mrs. de Winter is *relieved* Maxim murdered Rebecca because this means he did not love her. *Never, never.* Which means that she, and not Rebecca (who let me remind you, is dead), comes first in Maxim's affections.

She is preceded by no one.

What a fucking takeaway.

The murder as a literal act means nothing to TSMdW—but the murder as a metaphor for erasing the past, for expunging her visions of Maxim and Rebecca's happy history together, means everything.

It's so deliciously fucked up.

And I kind of understood it.

Because *I* was trying to erase my boyfriend's Rebecca. I was afraid of her. Afraid of her primacy, and the sway she held over my life, sure. But more than that, I was afraid of knowing her, liking her, allowing for the possibility that she was a good person who was part of a divorce that was, as is literally always the case, to do with two people and not one. I wanted to erase all that from the record. In a warped contradiction, I wanted to keep loving my wonderful, complicated boyfriend, *who was who he was because of his past,* but I wanted to expunge that past, too. Pretend it had no power over us. I wanted to pretend we could have the kind of blank-slate love affair I was convinced lived at the top of the hierarchy of romance.

It's only ever been you.

What a stupid thing to want.

God, I wanted it so much.

Most people read *Rebecca* for the suspense. Probably only a very troubled person would learn things of a personal or moral nature from Du Maurier. But I did. Du Maurier showed me that promising a new partner that they will eclipse our past is an act of violence against the meaningful loves that existed before. It's a fucking bloodbath, and we are the murderers, and we forgive ourselves for it, every time.

When we love more than once in this life, this kind of murder can feel necessary, even virtuous. That's the idea the Second Mrs. de Winter embraces when Maxim confesses. She is all too happy to become complicit in Rebecca's murder. Helping Maxim get away with it is their most bonding act as a couple. It's the whole last third of the book. But the thing is, once I got to that part, I wasn't rooting for them. I didn't want them to get away with it. I didn't want to believe in this kind of murder anymore. I recognized myself in TSMdW's relief, and it was horrible. I didn't want to be anything like her. And the way to do that, I realized, wasn't to insist on being first, on being Rebecca—it was to find a way to live alongside her.

Rebecca had also kissed my boyfriend, had also irritated him with a love of Americana songs, had also loved him, and *that* was why, when I kept slipping into her postures, I got scared. Because she had also loved my boyfriend, and then she had stopped. Because I was there loving him, and I never wanted to stop.

I used to think I saw Rebecca's ghost reflected everywhere, but of course it was only my own face, full of want. I'd been frightened by the mirror maze's reflections, kept turning from what I saw in them and chasing Maxim's voice instead. As if it were him who could show me a way out, and not the woman I kept turning from, in whose reflection, somewhere, was an opening.

Months passed, and Rebecca finally bought a house and settled herself, and we began talking, again, about him leaving Manderley. About a new house where we might live together. It was finally happening.

That weekend, I drove to Maxim's house, full of possibilities.

I turned my key in the door and found myself in the middle of a construction site.

The wall that used to exist between the downstairs office and living room was gone. Or, not gone, but blown through. Maxim had sledgehammered the Sheetrock between the struts. As I walked around the mostly empty space, a fine white plaster dust powdering the floor, I felt like TSMdW descending the stairs. Still moving forward, even as I had the prickling sense that something was wrong.

Maxim appeared, freshly showered, smelling wonderful, finger-combing his hair.

He told me he was making the downstairs office into his master bedroom. It would suit him better. Had been inspired late the night before and just taken his sledgehammer and gone to it.

My friend Emily's essay, the one ranking gothic houses' sexy secrets, turned out marvelously. And it taught me that the tension in so many gothic stories comes from the lingering of the past in a present space.

Do you know what thrills me in so many of those gothic novels? When a woman sets fire to a house. Sometimes a house feels *too* haunted, *too* complicated, to live in anymore. Imagine the cleansing relief of burning the whole thing down.

And sure, burning a house down is powerful on the page because in real life it's almost never the answer. Eventually you need to find a new house to live in, and all houses have their ghosts. I am done being scared of ghosts, done being scared of women. I am getting better at letting the past hover next to the present without flicking its ears and getting a rise out of it.

But I still have the arsonist's urge.

Because no one should have to live at Manderley.

Listen: if you find yourself learning how *to take care of* a haunted house? If you find yourself the lady in charge of its maintenance and upkeep? If you are *managing* the haunted-ass property in question?

That is not your house, girl.

Burn that house all the way down.

Sometimes the trouble is the structures you're living inside.

Sometimes you are living inside someone else's trauma.

It wasn't Rebecca Maxim wasn't finished with. It was his own pain. The story of his life he was telling himself. And he was *remodeling it*. He did not *want* to leave Manderley.

I did so much work to fit myself into Maxim's life. But he was never going to make room for me there. And once I realized that, I spent a lot of nights spinning a lighter in my hands. Thumbing the wheel. Sparking blue.

In October, Maxim took me to a Jenny Lewis concert for my birthday. Jenny Lewis has sung to me in ways I needed in every era of my life. If I am lucky, she will keep singing me through the rest of it. This was a perfect gift.

I should not have been surprised when it soon became clear Rebecca would also be at the concert. After all, our birthdays were a week apart. She also loved Jenny Lewis. Her mother had got her tickets.

"We probably won't even see each other," Maxim said.

We saw each other when we first arrived, in the merch line.

We saw each other again in the ladies' room.

We saw each other again in the beer line.

And honestly, it was fine.

Maybe it was fine because I had by now finished reading *Rebecca* and resolved to never let myself become TSMdW. Maybe it was because the idea of the two of us circling each other on our birthdays in a concert hall was the sort of thing that would make for a good Jenny Lewis song. Maybe it was because we were in an amphitheater of people who all loved the same music, and I'd given up the teenage idea that other people loving the same band I did threatened my love of the band.

Or maybe it was because Rebecca's mother came to say hello to me. She said she'd read an essay I'd written and related to it. So many of us had the same story, we agreed.

I went back to my seat. I brought my boyfriend an over-priced beer. I whispered that I'd talked with Rebecca's mother and it was nice. He squeezed me.

The seats in the amphitheater were narrow, and Maxim was leaning over into my seat, so I didn't quite have enough room to drink my beer. It wasn't his fault—he was so tall—and yet, it occurred to me, he could have leaned the other way a little. This whole time, if he wanted to, he could have made a little more room for me.

Onstage, Jenny Lewis, in a golden gown, her hair unbeliev-ably high, picked up a neon-pink telephone and answered a call that had been a long time ringing.

The Two-Thousand-Pound Bee

From the sixties into the eighties, my grandparents owned a house on Martha's Vineyard. In Menemsha, if that matters to you, which was considered the artsy part, the Jewish part, the active fishing part, of the island. It matters to me because my grandparents sold the house before I was born. It was a gray saltbox on a lake with a barn and a rowboat. It's still there. I know, because in 2019 I went to Martha's Vineyard looking for John Belushi's grave and I did a drive-by. More: I left the car running and walked as far up the driveway as I felt I could get without someone calling the cops on me.

The house matters to me because it is the setting for all the happiest and most beautiful photographs of the older generations of my family. In these pictures my family are young and tan and at ease. Everyone's hair is wild from the salt spray, everyone is barefoot, everyone is reading fat, trashy novels and is catching bluefish and cleaning bluefish and eating bluefish and eventually my mother is pregnant, so I suppose I was there, in that house, but only in utero, accessing a great quantity of bluefish, but missing out on those paradise summers, which gives me ruinous feelings of envy.

I'd always imagined that some version of my family's life, a story like their stories, was available to me. That I would someday find myself in a story like my grandparents'—a love so inevitable it began on the stage of the Blackfriars Guild theater and lasted more than sixty years. Or that, someday, I would, surely, be in a story where there would be pictures of me, triumphantly young and pregnant by the sea, like those of my mother, wearing her black one-piece and rubber Swatch watch.

But I am no longer young and the story of my life so far doesn't resemble anything like the lives they lived. The kind of story I imagined would have unfolded on that paradisiacal deck on the Vineyard. The kind of life I don't even really want anymore, except for out of habit. A habit that's been hard to break.

What I'm trying to tell you is that when I stood in the driveway of what was no longer my family's house, car still running, I recognized it from my fantasy of my family and a story I used to tell myself about what my life might be. A story, it seemed, I wasn't quite done mourning yet.

———

I will tell you the anecdote that sets this whole thing off, but you should know, before I tell it to you, that my mother is an impressionist when it comes to the truth.

When my mother was a little girl she went to the Vineyard with her brother and her parents. Her godparents, Penn and Janet Kimball, also spent summers on the island. The adults were all journalists.

Penn was bereft when Janet died and she was buried in the Chilmark cemetery because she loved the Vineyard more than any other place. The way my mother tells it, Penn was at Janet's gravesite regularly, weeping and bringing flowers.

"And then," my mother says, "John Belushi died and it all went to hell."

John Belushi, as you probably know, was a comedian, a *Saturday Night Live* star, the lead of *Animal House,* and *Blues Brothers,* a raucous seventies white-boy party icon.

My mother says, "So he was buried right next to Janet, and there's Penn trying to mourn his wife, and the Belushi fans keep showing up to party."

"What do you mean 'party'?"

This is the split screen my mother paints: Penn, an aging, WASPy journalist crying to the left. A gaggle of *Animal House* extras celebrating to the right. Topless, drunk, living fast and dying young. Tequila poured on the grave, broken bottles, people having sex and "always leaving their underwear behind."

At this point, the story already seems improbable. But my mother goes on.

"So he had him exhumed," she says.

"What?"

"Exhumed! Penn was so mad he got them to dig up Belushi's body and they moved him to some real estate on the other side of the cemetery so Penn could grieve in peace."

"Were there still parties over there?" I ask. "Was his family mad?"

"I think they put him somewhere that no one could find him," my mother says.

"That doesn't sound right."

"Except his wife, of course."

"Of course."

The thing about my mother's Belushi story is that it's not true. Or maybe it's more accurate to say that her story is wrong in its details but right about what it's trying to communicate.

When I first told my mother I wanted to look into her story about Belushi, she seemed concerned. That night I got a text from her, dictated to Siri, arriving in all caps:

HI SWEETIE MAYBE IT WASN'T RIGHT NEXT TO JANET'S GRAVE BUT IT WAS DEFINITELY IN CHILMARK ABELS HILL CEMETERY A-B-E-L-S LOOK IT UP OKAY LOVE LOVE LOVE

I wrote back: BOO DON'T WORRY IF THE STORY IS DIFFERENT. I'M JUST CURIOUS.

She responded, I'M GLAD I SERVE ONE PURPOSE

This is a family shorthand.

"I'm glad I serve one purpose" is a thing my mother says when she has told a story so delightfully and conspicuously false that the family crumples with laughter and then calls her on it. "I'm glad I serve one purpose," she says, meaning: to be teased, to be picked on. Also meaning: to be the one who keeps things interesting around here. Meaning: what would you all do without me.

I had no stake in proving my mother's story wrong. It was the idea of incompatible griefs that had struck me—two people being mourned so differently on the same plot of land.

I was interested in their mourning because we don't have any rituals for the dead in my family. Our lack of rituals is not to imply we haven't lost anyone, that we haven't had to contend with our dead. It's just that we don't know what to do with them.

UNAUTHORIZED OBITUARY FOR MY GRANDMOTHER

Maureen Joyce was born in 1928. Maureen Joyce grew up in New Bedford, Mass., where boys clubbed frost fish in the Cape

Cod Canal. Maureen Joyce was French Canadian and Irish and probably English, too, but we don't talk about that. Maureen Joyce never lost her Massachusetts accent and pahked the cah at Hahvad Yahd. Maureen Joyce told her granddaughters not to pick up any sailors when she left them alone at the mall. Maureen Joyce was fully capable of picking up sailors.

———

Even a little research reveals that Belushi was, in fact, exhumed, but despite sharing a cemetery, definitely not because his mourners were offensive to my mother's godmother's spirit.

It was Judith Jacklin, Belushi's wife, who decided to move the grave, and I was relieved no one in my family orbit was responsible for any exhumations.

There *was* a lot of action around Belushi's grave. I haven't found any evidence that people were "always leaving their underwear behind," but it seems possible, given that *Time* magazine lists Belushi's headstone as a "Top 10 Celebrity Grave Site." The piece reads: "When Belushi's tombstone gets trashed in the name of rock 'n' roll, there may be issues. After fans repeatedly littered the area around Belushi's grave, funeral workers at the Martha's Vineyard, Mass., cemetery where he's buried moved Belushi's body at his wife's request to an unmarked plot some distance away from the tombstone. Now the *Saturday Night Live* funnyman can rest in peace."

Of course Belushi's family didn't want to mourn in a place that was regularly trashed, but I like the idea of a tombstone becoming a cluttered archaeological site—look how busy, how messy, how alive.

Here's what I don't like. Someone who died tragically young

being referred to as a "funnyman." Of course he was funny. But he also overdosed on heroin and cocaine. I imagine him as a raucously joyful person on the outside, but heavyhearted on the inside, a kind of figure I have a soft spot for, though it's possible I'm projecting. Funnyman. I am projecting because I'm a little bit like this myself and if, someday, someone carves the word FUNNYMAN on my tombstone, I will come back from the dead just to flip them the bird, just to tell them, "You have missed the point. Even in death. Especially in death."

And so there are two gravesites for John Belushi. One, a public headstone with a toothy skull and crossbones, that says: HERE LIES BURIED THE BODY OF JOHN BELUSHI // I MAY BE GONE BUT ROCK AND ROLL LIVES ON, and then a secret one, unmarked, known only to his family. He was buried twice in that cemetery. Or rather, there are two versions of Belushi and each of them was buried. He was a man who required doubling in death. Perhaps life required this of him, too. Perhaps that was painful.

———

My mother's story of incompatible mourners forced to share a graveyard obsesses me even, and especially, after it starts to unravel.

So I book a ferry ticket to spend a few days on the Vineyard. I ask two of my Amigas Sin Fronteras, Marta and Monica, if they want to come with me and look for Belushi. They say they would love to come and eat good seafood and that they are sure I will find them on the beach when I get back from my time in the cemetery.

———

UNAUTHORIZED OBITUARY

Maureen Joyce was a props mistress at the Blackfriars Guild and a secretary at Paramount Films. Maureen Joyce worked for a number of newspapers. Maureen Joyce claims she is responsible for the Rockettes going on strike for health care. Maureen Joyce claims she invented CPR for dogs and once resuscitated a bulldog named Chauncy with voluminous jowls who had choked on a chicken bone. Maureen Joyce learned to cook Chinese food in Beijing and to do ikebana in Tokyo and to dance well in Haiti and to ride a horse in the Santa Ynez Valley, and these were the places she loved best. Maureen Joyce once killed a venomous copperhead with a rake and kept him in the freezer. Maureen Joyce showed her granddaughters the mating tarantulas who danced in a sex parade in the backyard, and told them they were beautiful. Maureen Joyce boiled chicken carcasses for the buzzards who circled her backyard, fed them regularly, and in lieu of a picture of her family, kept on her desk a framed photo of those buzzards. Her "Big Boys," she called them.

———

When I told my mother I'd booked a ferry ticket to the Vineyard, she said, "Oh, good, you can scatter your grandparents' ashes while you're there."

Listen: writing about taking a journey to scatter someone's ashes is a fucking cliché.

I once considered making a list of plots my students were forbidden to write stories about and A Whimsical Journey to Scatter Someone's Ashes in Which the Scatterer Learns to Live Again would have been a top-five contender.

But these ashes hijacked my Belushi mission. If I'd had it my way, I would have written about other people's dead and then gone to the beach.

I'm sure the last thing you want to hear is another story about ashes, but the truth is that there are too many stories about ashes because too many people have died. That we keep losing and losing the people we love, and so this trope isn't going anywhere unless we all agree to have our cremains fired out of circus cannons like Hunter S. Thompson, an initiative I would wholeheartedly support.

And honestly?

The only thing worse than reading a story about someone on a journey to scatter ashes is to be an actual human person toting around the cremains of people you love. A person who is wrecked, who is grieving, who is angry, but who also now feels like a fucking cliché. As if there is something tired and redundant about her sadness, which is no less heavy for its being common.

I had young grandparents. They were barely fifty when I was born, and they helped to raise me. The summer I went looking for John Belushi's body, they had been dead for one and five years.

My grandparents had both been cremated but we'd done nothing with them. I worried it was wrong for me to perform this ritual on my own.

"Isn't this a thing we should do, like, as a family?" I ask my mother.

"Everyone will be thrilled if you do it," my mother says. "It would be like a favor."

"Call Randy," I say. Her brother, the son of the cremains. "Ask Leslie," I say, my sister.

"It's fine," my mother says. "No one will mind."

"Holy shit," I say, "I am not doing this unless you call everyone and they agree."

I realize this may sound strange to you. But my uncle lives abroad. My sister had just had a baby. My mother and father had just spent three painful years providing 24/7 care for my grandmother as her Alzheimer's took hold and her body weakened, and they did this with levels of patience and grace that were something close to saintly. Everyone in my family was very busy with their own families, except me. My other family *was* Marta and Monica, but we were not perceived as a family.

I call my mother a few days later and learn that not only is my uncle okay with this plan, he has made me a ranked list of optimal beaches for ash-scattering.

"What's 'optimal'?" I ask.

My uncle's list of viable beaches is weighted according to two factors. Factor number one is how much my grandparents liked the beach. Factor number two is how likely I am to be arrested for scattering human remains on said beach.

We're a ha-ha-funny kind of family. I played my role well at the time, but I'll admit that later I felt a little sad, a little angry, to have been asked to do this. I'd hoped I wouldn't have to figure out how to grieve alone. I had believed that, if my biological family did this together, it would not have been so hard, that I would not have felt so ill equipped.

But there was nothing to be done about it. So I decided, instead, that this was fine. It was funny, even. In the thick of our feelings, we are a family who cracks a joke and hopes for the best.

See, it's okay. We can laugh about it.

Put me in syndication. I'm ready. I've had a lot of practice.

In a zany twist, Funnyman brings her grandparents' ashes on vacation! Hilarity ensues when Funnyman's mother puts the ashes in a beribboned gift bag. Funnyman puts her hands on her hips and says, Is this really appropriate? *[Cue the laugh track. Roll again.] Tonight. In a Very Special Episode, Funnyman remembers her last boyfriend cheated on her not long after her grandfather died, and was it because she was too sad to have sex for a week? [Sad Trombone Effect. Roll again.] Funnyman gets sick on the ferry after eating too much cranberry fudge! [Roll again.] A rerun of last season's finale. Funnyman's next boyfriend doesn't understand why her grandmother dying is such a big deal. He blows up her phone with texts about his own anxiety over attending a wedding as she sits by her grandmother's bedside. [Canned Laughter. Roll again.] Funnyman cries in a rocky beach inlet full of seagulls. [Canned Laughter.] Funnyman wonders if her grandparents would really have wanted this. [Canned Laughter.] Funnyman says:* How do we know what to with our dead? *[Cue the laugh track. Don't mind the footage. Cue the laugh track and it will all be okay.]*

Every complicated family has its jester, and I can hang with the best of them.

Funnyman is a clown who keeps the peace with humor because so long as everyone is laughing, Funnyman is safe. Funnyman will crack her own ribs open so you can see what a ridiculous thumping thing she is inside, just for the gag, just for a laugh.

Don't try telling me it doesn't have to be this way.

It's too late. I am already in love with my own bells.

The way the press described Belushi in death was horrible. The *Los Angeles Times* published a piece that read: "the hefty, hard-living star of television's *Saturday Night Live* . . . was found dead Friday, his nude body curled on a bed in a $200-a-day Hollywood hotel bungalow."

"Curled" is good writing. It's intrusively descriptive. There's a sense that Belushi's body is no longer his own in these lines, and perhaps when his gravesite was so hard-used, it felt that way again to his family. That to move the grave was to hide his physical body away from strangers who thought they had some claim to him. In a 1984 *Rolling Stone* article by Lynn Hirschberg about the controversy over *Wired,* Bob Woodward's sensationalistic Belushi biography, Jacklin says: "People claim it's all facts. . . . It's not all facts. It's a bunch of people's opinions and memories put forth as facts. . . . [W]e're talking about my life here. I was there. He may have it that way in his notes, but it's wrong."

Jacklin moved John's body to a new site, but left the original grave standing. And ironically, this public gravesite stresses the physical nature of the burial:

HERE LIES BURIED
THE BODY OF
JOHN BELUSHI

It's a lie, a misdirection, not only because the earth beneath the stone is empty, but because the part of Belushi that Jacklin was willing to give the public, in the form of this doubled gravestone, was not his body, was not even his real self as his family knew him; it was a grave for the idea of him. A fantasy place for us strangers to mourn every ephemeral, conjured part of the Belushi we thought we knew.

———

I have been asking my mother to give me the ashes for days and eventually she admits she does not have them.

"Where are they?" I ask.

"The funeral home," she says, which means my grandmother's ashes have been at the funeral home for nearly a year.

"They're commingling her, with your grandad."

"Can you tell me something?" I ask. "I thought Grandad was scattered in the mountains. I thought the Rancheros took him out for One Last Trail Ride."

The Rancheros are a sort of cowboy fraternity my grandfather joined when he moved to the Santa Ynez Valley in California. They did things like sneak into one another's barns at night and paint one another's horses in primary colors, even though they were in their seventies and everyone in the county owned a gun. My grandmother had been part of their sister group, who, I swear to god, were called the Fillies. It was my understanding that there was a spot along their annual trail ride in the mountains where fallen Rancheros could be scattered, and this was what I thought had become of my grandfather's ashes.

My mother shakes her head. "They only scattered one scoop of him," she says.

"A scoop of . . ."

"Your grandmother said she'd mail them his ashes but then she thought she might want them to be together so she only took one detergent scoop of his ashes and mailed it off to the Rancheros in a Jiffy bag."

"A Jiffy bag?"

She nods, solemnly. "The rest she kept because she wanted to be commingled with him. They did it already. I just have to go pick them up and I keep forgetting. I've been a little busy."

"Just don't get weird and forget on purpose to give me the ashes," I say. "I'll be home again next week."

"Just remind me if it looks like I'm forgetting," she says.

I leave early the next morning and before I do I try to think of what I could possibly write on a scrap of paper to remind my mother to pick up her parents' commingled ashes that won't feel like waking up to a Post-it that says: DON'T FORGET BOTH YOUR PARENTS ARE DEAD! I go to the laundry room and find the scoop for the detergent.

I write, DON'T FORGET! on a scrap of paper and put it in the scoop. I leave it on the kitchen counter.

I am two hours into my drive when my phone dings.

My father's text reads: OH MY GOD.

My phone dings again.

My mother's says: I'M ON IT!

———

When I consider scattering my grandparents' ashes I feel a relief that we will, at last, have done this. Because the ashes of these people who lived such epic lives should not be hoarded in a closet, probably. But also I want my family to show me how to be in grief. How to mourn. How to experience this loss. "Who are we? Who am I? How do I do this?" I want to ask of them.

I am terrified thinking I will have to learn to do this alone.

And perhaps the idea of a ritual that is, yes, for them in absentia, but is, really, only for me, in practice, is terrifying as well. What sort of goodbye will *I* give these epic people *I* love? From me? For me? How could I possibly know?

——————

It is summer and Marta and Monica and I are sitting on my patio. My dog is circling and attempting to wedge his snout under their arms. I have made strong, limey gin and tonics in blue Mason jars, and I wait for them to finish their drinks before I tell them about this update to our "vacation." It is one thing to enlist as good company for a mission to a celebrity gravesite. It is another to cart someone else's dead to the beach. I am convinced they will make excuses and back out.

"Of course we will help," Marta says.

"My family is very good at illegally scattering remains," Monica says. The story that follows involves a busy Staten Island Ferry.

I am so relieved.

——————

BEST OF BELUSHI
SATURDAY NIGHT LIVE, SEASON 3,
EPISODE 13, 03/11/78
"SCHILLER'S REEL: DON'T LOOK BACK IN ANGER"

[Film opens on an elderly John Belushi sitting in a train car]

JOHN BELUSHI: I guess this is my stop.

[Cut to John walking through a cemetery on a cold winter's day]

JOHN BELUSHI: Yeah . . . they all thought I'd be the first one to go. I was one of those "Live Fast, Die Young, Leave a Good-Looking Corpse" types, you know? But I guess they were wrong. [Points his cane to the tombstone] There they are—all my friends. This is the Not Ready for Prime Time Cemetery. Come on up.

[John struggles up the snow-covered hill]

Well . . . here's Gilda Radner. Ah . . . she had her own show on Canadian television for years and years. *The Gilda Radner Show*. [Moment of silence] Well, at least now I can see her on reruns. She was a button, God bless her. . . .

This is Garrett Morris. Now, Garrett . . . Garrett left the show, and then worked in the Black theater for years. Then he died of an overdose of heroin. [Laugh track swells]

Here's Bill Murray. He lived the longest—thirty-eight years. Ah . . . he was happy when he died, though—he'd just grown his mustache back. It's probably still growing.

Over here is Chevy Chase. He died right after his first movie with Goldie Hawn.

Over here is Danny Aykroyd. I guess he loved his Harley too much. They clocked him at a hundred and seventy-five miles an hour before the crash. It was a blur. I had to be called in to identify his body. I recognized him by his webbed toes.

[Drops flowers on Aykroyd's grave]

The *Saturday Night* show was the best experience of my
    life. And now, they're all gone. And I miss every one of
    them. Why me? Why did I live so long? They're all dead.
    [Reflective] I'll tell you why . . . Because I'm a dancer!

[Music plays, and John drops his cane and dances among the graves]

[Zoom out, fade to black]

Marta and Monica and I drive my car onto the ferry.

There is a way the wind whips and the engine hums and the
spray kicks up that pleasantly eradicates a person on a ferry-
boat. I always ride outside. I always lean too close to the edge.
I let my hair become a situation.

The island grows large to meet us, and we arrive and drive
off the ferry and into the traffic from the dock to our bed-and-
breakfast. The cars barely crawl in what feels like a proces-
sional. Bumper-to-bumper vacation. Every car plays music,
our windows rolled down. We are a parade conquering the
streets to announce that we are here for a good time. I wear a
strand of my grandmother's white china beads decorated with
blue ink. They hang low on my chest.

Four years after Belushi dropped flowers on Danny Aykroyd's
imaginary grave, Aykroyd would ride his Harley, at something
slightly less than 175 miles an hour, in Belushi's funeral procession on Martha's Vineyard. The cars would wind slowly through
the dusty roads. Aykroyd wore a leather vest and an American
flag bandanna. If you want to have your heart broken, look up

the pictures of Aykroyd riding his Harley in this procession. Look up the pictures of Aykroyd carrying the casket.

The Killer Bees were the first characters to ever recur on *SNL*. According to Lorne Michaels, the network told him to cut the sketch after their first appearance, because, essentially, it was too dumb ever to be aired again. Out of stubbornness, or a desire to flaunt his control, Michaels instead committed to making the bees a recurring skit. In episode after episode, Belushi and the cast put on stripy bee jumpsuits that look like they've been made by a loving but untalented parent. The bees wear sproingy antennae with little balls attached. Their antennae wobble hypnotically during the skits, which seldom have plots more complex than Bees Want Your Pollen. Some of the skits are very racist—bees as Mexican bandits. A truly astounding number of bee puns get made.

In one skit, Belushi creeps in the set window and over to a living room couch where Gilda Radner is reading. Belushi holds a knife to Gilda Radner's throat and she mugs for effect. A radio on a nearby table crackles. The announcer warns people to be on the lookout for the killer bees. "The bees are overweight!" the announcer says. Belushi's little belly is accentuated by his striped suit.

A bee skit drags on forever. Every time, it feels like the skit will never end.

"I hate the fucking bees," Belushi once said, reportedly because it was a group gag, with no room for him to take center stage.

But if it were me? It would have been about more than that.

Some days you resent the role you've been given in this life.

Some days it feels hard or embarrassing to be a bee.

Sometimes you don't like the casting.

We open on Funnyman pulling on her leotard. It is too tight! *Funnyman says.* Who was this leotard made for anyway? *[Cue the laugh track] Funnyman finds herself outside her grandparents' old house on Martha's Vineyard and starts climbing in the window. She is carrying the gift bag of her grandparents' ashes. Funnyman tumbles into the living room, almost dropping the bag in an antic juggle. [Cue the laugh track] Gilda Radner is on the couch, and she startles. Funnyman and Gilda stare at each other for one long beat. Funnyman's bee antennae are bobbling.* I belong here! *Funnyman shouts.* I belong here? *Gilda Radner looks dubious. The man on the radio says,* There is an almost-forty-year-old woman on the loose and she thinks she's about to start a family in this house. *Gilda screams. [Cue the laugh track] Dan Aykroyd enters, stage left, shaking his head disapprovingly. [Cue the laugh track]* I am going to live in this house! *Funnyman says.* My babies and I will eat bluefish on the deck! *Gilda Radner screams again. Funnyman hugs the gift bag of ashes closer, her leotard pulsing with her too-fast breath. Dan Aykroyd points to the bag.* Put those down, for crissake—this isn't your house. But it could be, *Funnyman says.* Someday. *[Cue the laugh track]* No, *Aykroyd says, and he takes the bag of ashes from Funnyman.* Just because it was theirs doesn't mean it's yours, *he says, and walks off set. [Confused laughter][Cut to black]*

Being a person who goes through the motions of dating and "trying" and "putting myself out there" and talking about some imaginary someday when I'll get married and have children and . . . performing my belief in all that? Performing my increasingly shaky certainty that I *even want it*?

That's my bee skit.

The first time I trundled out onstage in my bee suit I think

I just accepted that this script was a thing I wanted because it was the thing people in my family did. The thing people I knew did.

No one made me perform the skit the first time. I just assumed it was my role to play.

But now, years later, I'm still here, doing the bee skits. It's Funnyman's longest-recurring gag. And I find myself wondering: But *will I* ever celebrate my sixtieth wedding anniversary like my grandparents? Will I ever be young and beautiful and pregnant by the sea?

I will not, I will not, I will not.

Many futures are possible but these particular ones have already been precluded by time.

And I know this, and yet, it feels impossible to stop hoarding the ashes of this life story that will never be mine. Especially, perhaps, because I keep performing my bee skit for other people. Because I keep acting like maybe someday it will become real.

And the longer the skit goes on, the more uncomfortable it becomes. Here I am, dating in my thirties! Here I am, turning it all into funny anecdotes! See how bad I am at love, at the sort of life I thought I was meant to be living? See how badly this leotard fits?

Can I just peel this thing off?

Who is this skit for?

————

The bee skits are likely one of the reasons that, one day, when Belushi and Aykroyd took John's Jeep to the beach, and listened to the tape of a band called The Ventures, and heard a song called "The 2,000 Pound Bee," they howled with laughter. It's a deliciously fuzzy, distorted surf-rock instrumental with proto-punk vibes. It's a little ridiculous, but it's also fucking great. According to Woodward's biography, after they laughed their way through the song, Aykroyd said: "'You got to promise me something. . . . If I die before you do, you have to play this tape at my funeral. . . . Because it's . . .' And he lost control with laughter, then continued: 'Wouldn't it be great to lay this noisy, heavy tape on a church full of people!' 'Sure,' John said. 'And you do the same for me.' He was serious: A perfect message—'The 2,000-Pound Bee.' 'Absolutely,' Aykroyd promised. 'Absolutely.'"

———

Monica and Marta and I arrive at our Menemsha B&B and unpack our things.

The car is empty except for the gift bag, inside of which is a box, inside of which are my grandparents' ashes. I am unsure whether it's weird to bring the bag inside and so I just stand there in the parking lot of crushed clamshells.

"Should we invite your grandparents inside?" Marta says. "It seems rude not to."

It is determined my grandparents will reside next to the mini-fridge.

That evening, we head off to the beach. We lay out a blanket.

The beach at Menemsha is small and rocky. At the far end of the sandy stretch, there are great black rocks, against which waves crash. Tidepools form and birds feed. There are also rocks in the tide, thousands of wave-smooth stones the size of peas and the size of tangerines: brick red and eyeball white and moss green, all tossing together in the water.

I consider myself a scientifically minded person, but will

cop to also being schmaltzy and whimsical as fuck. Maybe this is why it appeals to me that, after death, all the atoms in a body go on to become parts of other things. I mean this in a way that would sound better if Carl Sagan were saying, *Matter can be neither created nor destroyed,* as a triumphant seventies *Cosmos* score played over it.

I watch those multicolored rocks tumbling in the surf, and say to my friends, "This is the spot." It is not my uncle's top-ranked beach, but I know it is right. Then I doubt myself. As I confer with the family group text about whether or not this beach is acceptable, more people come and lay out blankets next to us.

WHATEVER SEEMS RIGHT, SWEETIE, my father, the family spokesperson, writes, after a very long pause.

I look up from my phone. The beach is crowded.

I think this is right. *I* know this is right. At least, for me.

"Have you ever been," Marta says, "to one of those beaches where people clap for the sun when it sets?"

"This is absolutely that kind of beach," Monica says. We laugh, because the assumption is that we are not "the kind of people" who clap for sunsets. We watch the sun grow lower. Everyone on the beach is talking quietly and the mood is lovely and communal. If my mother were here, she would say, "time to watch the ball drop." I wish my mother were here. It is okay that she isn't.

The sun ducks beneath the tide line in one last orange snap and we clap for it. For the fucking sun. We are those people. And who isn't, really. We've got one more lap in, after all. We should be so lucky.

On our way back from the beach, I gather stones, and

because I am thinking of my mother, I choose her favorite ones, the kind she calls lucky rocks. There is a particular kind of dark-gray stone that can sometimes be found with a perfect ring of white traveling around it. It's the ring that makes them lucky, my mother says—it holds in the power. I find three lucky rocks on the beach, and every time I stoop to pick one up, my grandmother's beads clack around my neck.

We've left the beach not long after sunset, but it gets dark more quickly than we anticipated. We walk through the reeds and over the dunes and arrive at the back end of the B&B property's long, shrubby lawn in darkness. Everything smells of dune dust and salt stickiness and orchard grass.

And then we smell skunk.

We move in a pack, lighting up a phone flashlight. We brush against something skunklike in the dark and scream, running ungracefully, yoked to our flashlight beam. Like if we move fast enough, we can outrun the inevitable.

———

Three days after Dan Aykroyd rode his Harley, three days after they buried Belushi on the Vineyard, there was a memorial service in New York.

Peter Kaplan's 1982 write-up of the memorial for *The Washington Post* is called "Belushi, Exit, Laughing." Kaplan opens: "Under the 110-foot soft gray Indiana limestone arches of the Cathedral of St. John the Divine, about 1,000 of John Belushi's friends and family mourned today as they thought he would have had it, if he were in town instead of away."

The first time I read that line, I cried. It's the kind of gentle deflection people like my family trade in. "If he were in town instead of away" lives next door to honesty. It's a laundry scoop on the kitchen counter.

Aykroyd spoke at the funeral, and he made good on his promise. Kaplan writes:

> Aykroyd opened his blue knapsack, and pulled out a tinny tape recorder and held it next to the microphone. "And so, here's a little instrumental by the Ventures, 'The 2,000-Pound Bee.'" The Ventures' guitars in their bee patterns filled the Cathedral of St. John the Divine, reached nooks and naves that probably hadn't been checked out before.
>
> Hundreds of people sat, stunned at first, and then began to rock and laugh. Their laughter took over, the real thing, the authentic laugh of new comedy that ambushes an audience, that Aykroyd and Belushi made raw and mean and yet somehow affectionate. There wasn't a person in the cathedral who didn't understand the joke, and it was the tribute to John Belushi that there probably wouldn't have been a person under 35 in America who wouldn't have.
>
> When the great-bad music and the laughter finally stopped, Aykroyd looked out and said, "So there, Johnny, and you can be sure that I'll have my antennae out for the paranatural and the spiritual, and believe me, if there's any contact with him," he looked out to the audience, "I'll let you know."

The day we visit my grandparents' old house, there is a heavy-duty lawn-mowing crew parked in the driveway. I look around, consider the fantasy of the house, but then a mower revs and I startle and run back to the car, where Marta and Monica are waiting for me. We sit there for a moment. They agree it is a shame this house is not in our possession. Maybe one of us will serendipitously become very rich and buy the house back.

I had wished for my family to be here. To teach me how to grieve my grandparents. How to grieve the sort of life my grandparents lived, which I once thought I would live. For them to tell me I was allowed to let this life go.

But this wasn't what *they* needed. It was what *I* needed.

And here are Monica and Marta.

Sometimes it's your Danny Aykroyd, your Bill Murray, who get you through the days. Sometimes, your Not Ready for Prime Time family pulls through for you.

Like these women, helping me speculate about whether, when we make our millions and buy back the now-terrifically-expensive house, we will have to get a rowboat for the pond, or whether the rowboat will be included. For a million dollars it should be included, we reason, frugal even in our millionaire fantasies; for a million dollars they should throw in one lousy rowboat. And was rowing a boat like paddling a canoe, which we knew how to do, or was it different? Wasn't the location good? Weren't we very close to that good sandwich shop? Which sandwich shop? The one where we saw Tony Shalhoub wearing flip-flops and were proud of ourselves for "playing it cool" over this celebrity sighting? Would we be friends with Tony Shalhoub, we wondered, when we bought back the house and lived on the Vineyard year-round? We might be. What was not possible in our new, imagined life together?

None of this was likely to happen. But it was no *less* likely than my bee-skit premises. And it felt powerful to laugh about the world as we liked to imagine we could live in it.

In the driveway of the old house, I released my biological family from my unreasonable expectations of how much we could possibly be to one another. How much I expected them to teach me. Do for me. And this freed them to be what they actually are to me. Which is plenty.

———

UNAUTHORIZED OBITUARY

Maureen Joyce was addicted to internet Tetris. She had a borderline erotic online relationship with an ornamental-carp specialist in Japan, whom she messaged at all hours of the night about rare koi colorations. Maureen Joyce favored hot-pink lipstick and wedge sandals and referred to the hairstyle she wore for thirty years as her Perfect Wave. Maureen Joyce said the day she could no longer do her own eyeliner perfectly was the day we should come and "take care of things" with a smothering pillow, and in this, we failed her. Maureen Joyce once saw Marilyn Monroe in a restaurant and said she had bigger feet than you would have thought. Maureen Joyce smuggled rare plant cuttings across international borders in her hatband. Maureen Joyce had a foul mouth and cursed exquisitely. Toward the end, she was forgetting things, but she was always squeezing her granddaughters' hands and telling them, "Whatever you do, live an interesting fucking life."

The last thing we ever told Maureen Joyce was that we loved her.

After that, for good measure, we told her not to pick up any sailors.

———

On the one hand I want to be done with bee skits, done performing my false belief in a fantasy future that my life likely won't ever resemble—one I'm not even sure I want anymore.

But on the other hand, here I am, writing my grandmother's obituary for you.

And this obituary is absolutely a performance. It is full of beautiful lies.

When is a performance a lie and when is it a celebration? When does performing make a person feel expansive and generous and when does it make you feel full of shit?

———

Marta and Monica and I go to the beach very early in the morning so as to avoid scattering human remains proximate to swimmers. We have forgotten that children are also people who wake up early, and we are alarmed to see two tiny people in floaties swimming near the shore. We walk as far down the beach as we possibly can, and then pause ten feet from the rocks where I plan to do the scattering.

"Do you want us to come with you?" Marta and Monica say.

I am so grateful they are here, and mean to say yes. But this morning in Menemsha it seems clear that a person can only be walked so far down the beach. There are permutations of grief and of love you can only carry for yourself. No one can tell you when to release them. No one can tell you what it will feel like to live without them.

Only you, a first-person person, a tired little bee, can do that.

Marta and Monica remain on lookout duty as I carry the box of my grandparents the last bit of the way down the beach.

I arrive at a rocky, shallow, seaweedy spot next to a jetty, where no one would want to swim. All of this is delusion, of course, because once my grandparents are in the water they will be everywhere, not just this one spot, but I can't worry about that now.

I crouch, in my sneakers, on a large rock above the water, which is lapping and splashing. I can see all the multicolored pebbles in the clear shallows, and this is good, I tell myself. This is correct.

I have gathered stones along the beach, and I make a small pile of them on the rock next to me. One for each person in my family I'm here to represent.

I open the box.

I find a hermetically sealed plastic bag inside.

"Jesus Fucking Christ," I say.

I unclip my keys from my shorts and slice the bag open with the jagged edge of the key to my house.

It wasn't always the case that my grandparents' ashes would be scattered on the Vineyard.

My grandmother was not very kind to my mother during the time she was caring for her. Her Alzheimer's had crept up on her quickly. She was understandably scared and frustrated and she took this out on the person closest to her. The person she could say any horrible thing to and know they would not leave. *Glad I serve one purpose.* It was around this time we thought we should confirm with my grandmother that she wanted to be commingled with the remainder of her husband's cremains and scattered by the Rancheros, to which she said, "No! Absolutely not!" and "Where did you get that idea?"

And this was troubling, because we'd gotten the idea from her, but the thing about losing track of your memories is that you forget having made up your mind. This makes it very difficult to honor a person's wishes, because which one of these versions of my grandmother and her wishes was the one she wanted last? The one she wanted most?

We chose the Vineyard because of a conversation she had with my mother, very close to the end.

"So tell me again," my mother asked. "Where do you want to be scattered?"

My grandmother thought about it. She paused. Then she said, sounding annoyed, "Well, where are *you* going to be?"

My mother was surprised. She thought about it.

The truth is it was my mother who said she wanted to be scattered on the Vineyard.

"Then that's where I want to be," my grandmother said.

It was such a *her* gesture. She was claiming for her own some good thing belonging to my mother. Calling dibs on it.

But also she was saying she didn't want to lose her daughter, who spent most of every day with her in a sick-smelling semi-hospital that sang out death, death, death in every room. Her daughter, whom she called on the phone about six times a day on purpose and three more by accident. Her daughter, who fed her and cleaned her. She was saying that for their bodies to ever exist in separate places was a thing she could not bear. She was saying, *Where I want to be is with you.*

———

I pour my grandparents' ashes into the water slowly. I thought that the water would carry them away, but the ashes linger in a cloud above the multicolored rocks for longer than I anticipated. From my squat on the rock, I watch the cloud, unsure of what to do.

So I talk to them.

It is good to talk to our dead.

Here is what I say when I talk to the lingering cloud of my grandparents:

We talk about you all the time. We are always remembering you.

If my grandparents can hear me, it is the thing I think they'll be the most pleased to know.

I tell them: *The Vineyard house is gone, and I am never going to live a life that looks like your life, but I promise I am trying to live an "interesting fucking life." I promise that the only kind of pretending I'm going to do is when I am performing your best stories, the ones you loved most, the ones you held up over and over again, especially as you got older, about who you were or wished you might be—I promise we are all always putting on a show for you, about you. I promise that we are completely full of shit, and it is lovely.*

I watch as my grandparents' ashes linger, and linger, and it goes on for way too long, and maybe the too-long is what's funny about it. How excruciatingly long it takes to get to the point, and how, once you get to the point, you realize the buildup, the stalling, was the whole gag. After that, all that's left is a punchline, and the punchline, it turns out, is: cut to black.

———

It is the hottest day of the summer when I finally bike to Abel's Hill. I lean my blue bicycle against a split-rail fence that sets apart a small part of the cemetery.

The area has an open entrance and I realize this is it, Belushi's public gravesite. It's the first thing you see.

There is a large natural rock on one end, into which the name BELUSHI is carved in a tall, traditional serif font. In the middle, there is a bench to sit on. On the other side is the grave marker. The dark-gray headstone with the skull and crossbones that bears the assurance that there is a body buried here (there is not) and that rock and roll goes on.

The dates: January 24, 1949, to March 5, 1982.

Someone has planted a small American flag next to the headstone. Someone has left a lucky heads-up penny. Someone has kissed the upper-right-hand corner of the grave and left a fat lipstick print. In front of the grave is a pile of stones with clover coming up in between. On one flat stone someone has written, WHEN THE GERMANS BOMBED PEARL HARBOR, a quote from *Animal House*.

I sit on the bench and spend a little while in the space. I have, in my backpack, the lucky rocks I collected for my mother. When I get up, I leave two as an offering. One, beneath the grave, another on the big rock with BELUSHI engraved in it. I know the big rock isn't the real second gravesite, but it feels right to double up.

The cemetery is big enough to have wide, dusty paths between neighborhoods of graves, and I decide it's okay to bike along them, if I go slowly, bike respectfully.

Fifteen minutes later and I have not found anyone I am looking for.

Instead I find two flat, square stones in the ground. A husband and wife. The dates imply that she was buried here in 2014 but he is still alive, seventy-seven years old.

Beneath her name it says: PLEASE WATER THE PLANTS.

Beneath his it says: YES, DEAR.

I am resting, staring at these stones, when three ladies on horseback approach, a slow, gamboling walk. One of the horses is a paint, splattered in an irregular pattern, tan on white, very much like a horse my grandmother used to ride named JR. I think about the one scoop of my grandfather his riding buddies scattered in the mountains. I think about my grandparents' tack, each of their favorite bridles, which hang in my house, and which I have not soaped up in too long. I think about the walkie-talkies my grandfather and I carried with us when we rode into the Santa Ynez Mountains, so we could radio home to my grandmother and check on dinner, the corn-and-green-chili casserole she always had in the oven. Our walkie-talkie names were Lewis and Clark . . . *Jerry Lee and Petula, that is,* my grandfather would say. I often wish for some kind of long-distance walkie-talkie signal from them, a crackle from over the mountains, where they are, because, goddamn, I miss them, but maybe these horseback women with their easy seats, their faces crinkled and tan beneath their hats, are good enough. I am glad to see them.

"It's too hot to be out here," one says.

"You should be drinking water," another says.

"Do you know about the cemetery at all?" I ask, but they don't.

"Sorry, honey," they say.

———

I am out of breath and straddling my bike by the entrance again, about to give up and leave Abel's Hill, when two women arrive at Belushi's gravesite, whispering. Tourists in floppy hats and sandals.

They stand there silently for a minute and then one says, "Crazy right?" She takes a picture.

"You have to put those in your album," the other says.

"I think a lot of people put things here for sobriety purposes."

"I put my one-year AA chip on my dad's grave. All my friends came with me."

"That's nice."

They get back into their car and drive away.

I didn't consider the grave as a sober pilgrimage site. I thought about my mother's stories of partiers. All this time, I'd been thinking of the empty tomb as a lie. But in this moment I am floored by the generosity of offering it up to people. For this, or whatever they might need it to be for them. Not a lie, just another kind of truth.

And aren't I here, too, crying in the heat, making Belushi all about me?

———

A confession: when my grandmother was dying, her perfect wave gone flat, her hair braided into pigtails by her daughter, no eye makeup at all, I told her lies.

We were sitting with her in the hospital the night before she died. We cried together, and we sat near to her.

At some point, that didn't feel like enough, so I started telling stories.

It's what we do in my family.

The stories were about her: Maureen Joyce. The ones she told us about herself, which we repeated over and over. And, goddamn, I am sure none but half of those are true. But I told them to her so she'd know how much we knew about her. How much we would keep knowing, and would remember, and tell out loud again and again.

"Grammy," I said, "do you remember that you helped the Rockettes go on strike?"

"Grammy," I said, "do you remember that you were the first woman to ever perform CPR on a dog?"

I swear to god she laughed.

My family laughed then, too, even though we were all crying our fucking eyes out, because we hadn't been totally sure she could hear us. But it was clear in that moment that she was listening to us tell her stories about who she was.

All of which is to say: on the last night on this planet we spent with Maureen Joyce, we performed her life for her. And our performance was wrong in its details, but right about what it was trying to communicate.

———

Funnyman wants us to party at the Belushi gravesite.

Funnyman wants to get drunk and scream rock and roll.

Funnyman wants to offer up our tokens and hope we stay sober.

Funnyman wants that place to give us whatever we need.

Funnyman promises to stop biking around cemeteries.

Funnyman concedes that fact and fiction got commingled in the cardboard box she brought home from the funeral parlor.

Funnyman admits that maybe it's not that funny that her grandparents, plural, are now her grandparents, singular, one pile of ashes.

Imagine: Funnyman scrabbles onto the rock at the far end

of Menemsha Beach and combs through the box with her bare hands, sorting the ashes into two piles. *You are the truth and you are the lie?* Funnyman says. *You are my grandmother and you are my grandfather?* But Funnyman is gonna leave those mixed-up ashes alone. She is ready to empty the whole thing out into the sea.

Please don't play the laugh track over this?

Funnyman promises to stop hoarding ashes.

Funnyman admits that the kind of life her grandparents lived is never going to be hers.

Funnyman pronounces her long-expired fantasy DOA.

Funnyman knows that offering herself up as a joke in a bee suit will get her only so far.

Funnyman does not regret to inform you that the bee skits have been permanently canceled.

Funnyman tosses her head back, not a laugh track, *laughing*, and she is thinking, *But wouldn't it be great to lay this noisy, heavy tape on them?*

———

The stupid, obvious truth that it has taken me this long to know is this: it's not about fantasy versus facts . . . it's about living in both. Both at once. Both simultaneously. One tomb a place for public performance, for skits, and shows, and generously offering yourself to others. And another that does not compromise. A first-person sort of tomb. One just for you, and the people who love you honestly.

It's about how one allows the other.

It's two fucking tombstones, all of the time.

— IV —

*There is no logic that can be superimposed on the city;
people make it, and it is to them, not buildings, that we
must fit our plans.*

—JANE JACOBS, "DOWNTOWN IS FOR PEOPLE"

– VI –

Unwalling Jackson's Castle

M y sister has made it very clear she would like me to stop insinuating that her baby is the reincarnation of Shirley Jackson. But also:

SOME REASONS WHY MY NIECE IS PROBABLY THE REINCARNATION OF SHIRLEY JACKSON

My niece is eight months old. She was born into Shirley Jackson's old house in Westport, Connecticut, which my sister and brother-in-law bought when they wanted to start a family. Do you know who Shirley Jackson is? I'm sure you do, but if not, what I need you to know is that Shirley Jackson was an author who most famously wrote about two things: 1) children 2) haunted houses.

My sister and brother-in-law claim the name Theodora just "came to them," but when I think of the name Theodora, I think of Theodora Crain, arguably the most badass character in Jackson's most famous novel, *The Haunting of Hill House*. Jackson gives Theodora all the best lines ("Whose hand was I holding?") and all of the most daring moves. So if you were the ghost of Shirley Jackson and intended to be reborn, if a lady got pregnant in your old house, wouldn't the name you once gave your coolest character be the name you gave yourself?

If you were me, wouldn't you look into my niece's endless black eyes and fat, knowing face, and wonder?

If you can, imagine the look on my beautiful, exhausted sister's face when, an hour after she gave birth, I arrived in her hospital room and declared this theory out loud.

"No," she said.

"Hello, tiny Shirley," I whispered to the perfect changeling in the plexiglass bassinet.

Eleanor looked up, surprised; the little girl was sliding back in her chair, sullenly refusing her milk. . . .

"Her little cup," the mother was explaining. . . . "It has stars in the bottom, and she always drinks her milk from it at home. . . . You'll have your milk from your cup of stars tonight when we get home. But just for now, just to be a very good little girl, will you take a little milk from this glass?"

Don't do it, Eleanor told the little girl; insist on your cup of stars; once they have trapped you into being like everyone else you will never see your cup of stars again . . . the little girl . . . smiled a little subtle, dimpling, wholly comprehending smile, and shook her head stubbornly at the glass. Brave girl, Eleanor thought; wise, brave girl.

—SHIRLEY JACKSON, *THE HAUNTING OF HILL HOUSE*

The house in *The Haunting of Hill House* is haunted because of what's gone wrong between Eleanor and her dead mother. The book figures the feminine care that passes between daughter and mother as a kind of ouroboros succubus. Mothers caring for children, children caring for mothers, both winding up alone and with nothing more to give.

This is how a Jackson house becomes haunted. It becomes a physical representation of the domestic sphere. A house carries inside it the power of women's disappointment and anger and fear and violence.

During her life, Jackson was celebrated for her work, but she was seen primarily as a genre writer—a horror writer. Shirley Jackson wrote about haunted houses, in part, because the house was the structure that held, and embodied, the domestic life. It wasn't until later that readers and critics came to recognize Jackson's haunted house as an *unreal trope* that could communicate the *emotional reality* of female care and motherhood in 1959. What does it mean for the structure of your life to feel menacing? To be imprisoned within it? To feel like it might kill you?

Jackson asks us: How could a mother and daughter possibly live in a house and avoid its becoming haunted?

> *No live organism can continue for long to exist sanely under conditions of absolute reality; even larks and katydids are supposed, by some, to dream.*

—SHIRLEY JACKSON, *THE HAUNTING OF HILL HOUSE*

When my sister and brother-in-law returned from the West Coast to start a family, they wanted a modern house. Everything they own is stylishly smooth and/or crisply well tailored. So when they told me they were buying an oddball historic Victorian with a legitimate turret and a wraparound porch, I was surprised. But they'd fallen in love with the place.

Jackson's time in the house was brief, but eventful. Jackson and her husband, Stanley Edgar Hyman, a critic at *The New Yorker,* lived in Westport with their four children from 1949, just after "The Lottery" was published, until just after 1950, when their eight-year-old son Laurence was hit by a car and injured, just beyond the driveway of the home, while riding his bike. After the accident, the Jackson-Hymans sued the city of Westport. According to Judy Oppenheimer, one of Jackson's biographers, the accident "turned Shirley against Westport for good," and the family returned to Vermont not long after.

But it wasn't all bad. Jackson loved motherhood, according to later biographer Ruth Franklin, and the house was sprawling and had room for the family of six and the rotating cast of visitors who stayed there. The family hosted Ralph Ellison, who purportedly completed *Invisible Man* in the house's third-story turret—this is now Theodora's reading nook. J. D. Salinger (who it seems was only ever called a recluse by people who never visited Connecticut in those years) is said to have played catch with the Jackson boys out front—from Theodora's nursery window you can see the even green of neatly mowed lawn between the hedgerows.

The Jackson-Hymans were a literary power couple. They hosted parties on the house's enormous wraparound porch, and among the attendees was the poet Dylan Thomas. Oppenheimer writes that after "liquor and smoke and endless rhetoric," Jackson and Thomas "met alone outside on the enormous porch that wound around the house . . . [Jackson] confided to me that, yes, she was one of those women Dylan Thomas screwed on the back porch." These days, hanging on the porch, is a fake historical placard. It was created, in the same style as the authentic placard on the front porch from the Westport Historical Society, by my mischievous uncle. His false placard

reads: IN 1949 SHIRLEY JACKSON HAD A LITERARY ENCOUN-
TER WITH DYLAN THOMAS ON THIS PORCH. My sister keeps
a rocking chair on that porch and sometimes sits in it to feed
the baby.

These days, Jackson's house is the place where my sister is
making her family. And when I visit, I can't stop myself from
wondering: If Shirley Jackson's spirit returned to this house,
in the form of my niece, was it because she was haunting the
place, or because she'd been happy there?

I must admit that, at first, my sister's house made me afraid.

*We moved together very slowly toward the house, trying to
understand its ugliness and ruin and shame.*

—SHIRLEY JACKSON, *WE HAVE ALWAYS LIVED IN THE CASTLE*

I wasn't afraid because I thought the house was haunted.
And I wasn't afraid my sister would be unhappy in the house,
either. She and my brother-in-law are beautiful, hilarious people who have made a beautiful, hilarious baby.

I was afraid because, like so many writers, I am a narcissist,
and so I was worried about what this all meant for me.

The Haunting of Hill House has never been my favorite Jackson. Jackson's book I most love is *We Have Always Lived in the
Castle,* which is a haunted house from a different angle: one to
do with sisters. The Blackwood sisters' family has been murdered over dinner; only the two of them and an elderly uncle
survived the poisoned sugar bowl. In the aftermath of the
murders, Merricat and Constance live alone inside their family
home, the "castle" of the title, with just an ailing uncle for company. They live together because they love each other. Merri-

cat is particularly and ravenously in love with Constance, and Constance, for her part, cares for Merricat despite her being strange and feral. They live together because they have seen horrors in their family that only the other understands (the murders, but also one can read between the lines of Merricat's relationship with her father and see the specter of abuse). Who, from outside, beyond the castle walls, could understand these things? Their isolated feminine happiness is threatened when a man comes to romance Constance (in service of stealing the family money). Love is what splits the sisters' affections for each other. A man is what ruins their odd domestic paradise. Things go off the rails once he moves in, as Merricat desperately tries to find a way to drive him out of her sister's affections and their home.

In the end, the man is removed and the sisters literally barricade the house against him, and their neighbors. They lock their doors. They live alone, together again, walled inside their castle.

I wonder if I am the only reader who cheers when they do this. Who thinks that, as Shirley Jackson stories go, this amounts to a kind of happy ending.

The way I read it, the Blackwoods' house shows us that a castle can be a structure that isolates and imprisons you, but can also be a kind of protection from having to face people who don't understand you.

When my sister got married and moved into Shirley Jackson's house and had a baby there was a part of me who felt: but *we* are the ones who have lived in the castle. Who feared that she would now live behind walls with her new, lovely family and I would be a strange little Merricat left out in the cold.

"Fear," the doctor said, "is the relinquishment of logic, the willing relinquishing of reasonable patterns. We yield to it or we fight it, but we cannot meet it halfway."

—SHIRLEY JACKSON, *THE HAUNTING OF HILL HOUSE*

The week my sister brought her baby home, I realized how wrong I was. "My boobs are about to be out," she said, and settled into a cushioned rocker. She looked like a glowy Renaissance painting of motherhood even as a string of profanity and shushes and opinions came out of her mouth. "Could you wash this and bring me a new one?" she said, handing me a nipple shield. "Here, I've got it," my brother-in-law said.

I could have cried, I was so happy. I was still inside the castle.

When my sister went back to work and my brother-in-law took over daytime parenting, I moved in for a week to help. I have always held that I won the brother-in-law lottery; he is one of my favorite people. We changed diapers and bounced Theodora and discussed whatever debacle was on CNN that moment and our favorite adult cartoons. It was a lovely, quiet week. After I left, he told my sister I could pop in and out like family—I didn't need to be invited over like a guest.

And so now I linger in my sister's house whenever I can. I make food in the kitchen. I taunt the dog. I squeeze the baby. I ask about the state of affairs vis-à-vis nipples. Even now, I feel like a weird little vampire who has been lucky enough to be invited over the threshold. I don't know why I so feared I wouldn't be.

Or I do. Because of the stories I have read. Stories that tell us that families must be protected from outsiders with walls and secrets. Stories that describe motherhood, especially, as a walled place.

I think the reason I want my niece to be Shirley Jackson so badly is that I want to believe that women, especially mothers, don't need stories about haunted houses anymore. That we are less trapped by the domestic and less silent about what goes on inside our walls. I want to believe that we can find a new governing metaphor. And I know this isn't quite true, or that it isn't true yet, but maybe we are just close enough in range to such a time to know to hope for it. After all, here is my sister, living in Shirley Jackson's house, in an unwalled state of motherhood.

I want my niece to be Shirley Jackson so she can see that.

I read Theodora stories in the turret where Ellison finished *Invisible Man*. I roll a plastic ball to her on the lawn where Salinger once played catch. I sit with her in a rocking chair on the porch where Jackson wooed Dylan Thomas. From that porch, we can look behind us, and see her house, but we can also look out and see cups of stars above the lawn and cups of stars above the unlocked garden gate.

The Fox Farm

———

I was never a little girl who dreamed of weddings. What I dreamed of were houses.

I drew these houses. I drew secret passageways behind spinning bookshelves. I drew windows made of prisms so there would always be rainbows. I drew an entire room of trampolines. I drew unexplored hallways full of old-growth forest, where the carpet was made of moss and the lamps set to dusk. I am pretty sure I never drew a house that didn't have at least one fireman's pole between floors, and these usually terminated in subterranean rooms filled with pillows, or possibly marshmallows, or possibly Angora rabbits. I drew bedrooms for every person I'd ever loved. I drew rooms for horses and rooms for dogs and rooms for giraffes and rooms for elephants and all of these had door flaps (of varying sizes) so the animals could roam outside, because mine would be a house of free movement and no one would have to stay who didn't want to. The trick was that my house would be so magnificent you'd never want to leave, even though the door was always open.

I drew no husband, no wife, no children. Just an infinite collective of friends and animals.

How disappointing to grow older and find I do not live in this house.

How heartbreaking that my friends have scattered themselves across the country, the world, so we not only do not live together, but do not even share the same weather, the same time.

How sad I was, in early adulthood, to find I had very little money and could afford no house at all.

I have lived in any number of places in my life, and only two have ever come close to *feeling* the way my childhood dream houses were meant to feel. The first was a bungalow I rented for three years in Tallahassee, Florida. The second was a house of my own on the top of a street called Johnnycake Hill in a tiny town surrounded by the bounteous farmland of central New York. A johnnycake is an unbearable sort of cornmeal pancake, but the name made people laugh when I recited the address, and this was its own kind of gift. "A woman must have money and a room of her own if she is to write fiction," Virginia Woolf says in *A Room of One's Own*. And I wrote a book in that house. I made some money of my own. I made the house more beautiful. I did not make it fancy. There were no firemen's poles or indoor forests. But it was mine. I lived in not just a room, but a *whole house* of my own, and I was writing my books. But—forgive me, Virginia—this essay is about how I came to fuck that all up.

VIENNA, AGE TWELVE

*I imagine my house to be made out of wood, and to be very
cozy, with a huge backyard, blooming garden, and a forest near
it. I would live with my best friend, Autumn, who wants to
be an engineer and horse rider when she grows up. She would
have three horses, I would have thirty ducks, I would have my*

writing office, and she would have her engineering studio. We
would share a bedroom but have separate beds.

"I hate sharing space with men," I told my friend Brynn.

I told her this because at age thirty-six I had made the horrible mistake of falling in love again and seemed to have purchased a new house in which to live with the man for whom I had fallen.

Sharing a house with a man is a horrible fate. Most men's houses are unlovely and scattered with mysterious items that never seem to move, a stray sock in a corner, a nail clipper on the coffee table, stacks of unopened mail. These objects persist in their nonsense spots as the months wear on, attesting to a way of existing in space that I personally cannot fathom.

"Why am I doing this! Talk me out of it!" I screamed at Brynn as our dogs gamboled about her garden. We were sitting on the front porch of her log cabin, inside of which everything is very clean and cozy and good art hangs on the walls. I had brought over a delicious bottle of cold wine and she had brought out some beautiful glasses for us to drink it from.

Brynn shook her head. "Women know how to live," she said.

ELI, AGE THREE

I will sleep on an apple.

The week I signed the paperwork for my new house, which my enormous, gentle dog and I would share with this man I'd inconveniently fallen in love with, and his very lovely daughter,

Lydia, age eight, whom I had also fallen in love with, and their Chihuahua, Princess Diva, whom I had distinctly not fallen in love with, I frantically texted all my friends who had gotten married and made families.

"Is this a horrible idea?" I asked them. "Is a family in a house a good thing?"

"What?" they said. "Slow down."

"I mean, shouldn't I perhaps get three more dogs and keep my own wonderful house as it is now forever? Which is to say within my control? Shouldn't I become a dog-nun?" I said. "Isn't that a better plan?"

"I think being a dog-nun seems great," my best friend, Cora, said. We were video-chatting. Then she held her perfect, fuzzy-headed baby up to the screen.

"Goddamn it," I said.

Her son entered the frame, curious. He is three.

"Eli," I said. "Eli, when you grow up, what will your house be like?"

Eli didn't have much to say on the subject besides the fact that he would sleep on an apple.

This was around when I became obsessed with asking children about houses. Wondering if they had the same utopian visions of freedom and creation and animals and play that I'd had.

"Tell me about your dream house," I kept asking children.

As if they might teach me how best to live.

I asked adults about their childhood imaginings, too. You'd be surprised how many people have an answer at the ready. We do not forget these first dreams of the spaces we wish to call ours.

NORA, AGE SEVEN

Nora has drawn a house in brown marker. A large palm tree grows nearby, bending over the house protectively, full of orderly rows of orange fruit. She has drawn the sun incredibly large. It is so much bigger than anything else in the picture that it makes a person think that if they lived in Nora's house it would be full of sunshine, of light and of warmth, all the time.

I will tell you about the first time I ever cohabitated with a man. It did not end well. It didn't even begin well, if I am honest.

I cannot explain why I moved in with Bob when I was twenty-four except to say that my biological family felt a little shaky back then and I was eager to invent a new family of my own so that it might feel less disastrous if my biological one imploded on me.

At that time, I did not possess the creativity required to consider ways of doing this besides dating-as-a-conduit-to-marriage.

The Brooklyn apartment we found was too expensive for us, but Bob convinced me we could swing the rent. The first night we moved in, it felt so open and empty, there on the second floor above Park Slope's Seventh Avenue, a place that seemed impossibly adult to me.

That night, Bob asked to take naked pictures of me. This was a thing I had never done before and have never done since. But it was dark in the apartment, we had no lamps yet, and there were these blue curtains the old tenants had left behind that obscured us just enough, I thought, that it might be okay.

And so I stood naked in front of the window, backlit by the busy avenue underneath, the glow of the Key Foods and the church, and I let him take some pictures of me with his camera, just a silhouette in front of those glowing curtains. And then we went to bed. Lying on our mattress, on the floor, I felt I might never be able to sleep again.

I don't know what sense of spiritual rightness or celebration I expected of our first night in our new place, but it did not come. Instead, there was a fearful gonging in my heart that said this was wrong, wrong, wrong.

And sure enough it was. Sure enough, I had to work four jobs, on top of going to grad school, just to pay my half of the rent on the place that was indeed too expensive for us. Sure enough, I was shocked to learn that Bob's parents were paying his half of the rent, though not as shocked as perhaps I should have been.

I was hardly ever home as a result of my four jobs. Soon, I stopped eating. I suppose we could call this anorexia but it had less to do with my body and control and more to do with the fact that I kept going from job to job and there was never time to eat and, when I got home, I was so unhappy to be there that I sort of felt like *Why eat?* It is possible I was trying to disappear myself out of the life in that apartment I'd made and now felt stuck in forever.

There were a lot of reasons I decided I had to leave that apartment. It was Bob, but mostly it was also the way he made me feel about myself. Like I was always doing things wrong. Like I was young and dumb and understood nothing of the world. Like I was embarrassing to him, to myself. Eventually I decided I would rather be embarrassing on my own with no one around to notice, so I packed up my pet chinchilla and a backpack of my most necessary things, which included three books.

It was almost midnight when I left, and I sobbed on the subway with my chinchilla, in his carrier, in my lap. The 2 train had only a few people in it and, like good New Yorkers, they ignored my crying.

Just one man did a double take as he passed me.

It was now past midnight, and I thought he was going to comment on my sobbing. Instead he said, "Yo, is that a chinchilla? That's fresh!"

I stopped crying for a moment and nodded. Then I laughed. I hadn't been laughing very much lately, I realized. I hadn't been doing any of the things that made me happy for fear that they would seem young and dumb and embarrassing. But some people didn't even think it was embarrassing if you were crying on the subway with a chinchilla in the middle of the night. Some people thought it was fucking fresh. I wanted to live in that midnight subway car with my chinchilla forever. I never wanted to be trapped in another space that forced me to be other than I was ever again. Never wanted any man or any house to try to reform me.

The man on the 2 train smiled and made his way down the rest of the aisle, opening the heavy door at the end and stepping into the windy space between the cars of the moving train, hopping from one to the next. It was the first time I'd ever seen someone do this. It had never even occurred to me that a person could open those doors, could move between spaces even as the subway was barreling along.

BEATA, AGE ELEVEN

House Requirements [abridged]
- *Room converted to be a ballet studio*

- *A piano*
- *Doors that close properly*
- *I do not want to live in an area prone to any natural disasters, such as hurricanes, earthquakes, typhoons, cyclones, floods, mudslides, or avalanches.*
- *Moving on to the topic of people, there are a few things I would like to mention:*
  - *I do not wish to be married. I do not need people trying to change my way of life. I feel that if I was married they would want too much to be "normal." This is not something I wish to be.*
  - *I am fine with children but rules would apply. I would rather adopt children than have my own. I am not sure if the children would enjoy having me as a parent, for I would have many rules for my children.*
  - *I want to live in a neighbourhood of lovely people. I want to get along with my neighbours and know each and every one of them.*

The first home I ever truly called my own was a little white bungalow in Tallahassee. I moved into it, sight unseen, the year I turned thirty. My friend Kilby had told me it was lovely, and I had asked the price, and been sent some phone pictures taken while the current tenant was in the process of setting her soon-to-be-ex-husband's clothes on fire in the barbecue on the front lawn. After Kilby, this woman would become my first true Tallahassee friend.

I said I would take it.

I arrived in August, a time of year when Florida is hard to love. And yet.

The windows to the house were slightly fogged when I arrived in late morning, condensation rolling down the panes like fat tears. I went immediately to the office. A whole room, just for writing, with a door that shut. It had been given a fresh coat of paint, which could not quite contain the smell of the thousand cigarettes the last tenant had smoked in there. I had told myself I was going to quit smoking, again, once I moved, and this would not help.

There was a bedroom and a bathroom and a laundry annex that might as well have been a greenhouse for all the ferns pressed against the glass and lizards who lived in there, green anoles with flaring orange gullets who streaked into the house whenever you opened the door. There was a fireplace, which it would get cold enough to use exactly one month of the year. There was exceedingly ugly floral wallpaper in almost every room.

The yard was full of fire ants and there was an enormous oak tree from which Spanish moss full of biting bugs drifted down upon the yard, which was canted at such an angle that to mow it was to always be in danger of falling into the busy road. Across from the house was an empty lot full of tall grasses and trash where people met up to buy drugs. Around the corner was a cemetery of old, crooked stones. A family lived across the street, and the cops came screaming into their driveway at least once a month, and I never really knew why. The man who lived there never wore a shirt and had a long scar across his belly and rode his bicycle in infinite loops around the block even on the hottest days. He always said *Hello* or *Good morning* or *Good evening* or *Storm coming.*

Everything about that Tallahassee house was perfect.

The landlords were something of a mystery. Meredith was

the one I talked to on the phone and Bill was the one who came in person, even though Meredith owned the house.

The day I signed the lease, which was only for one year, Bill said, "We're going to sell the house next year, you know."

"Oh, okay," I said, already sick about losing this house I hadn't even lived in yet.

The bungalow had been Meredith's before she married Bill and moved across the state line to Georgia, where they had two kids. I know this because when I asked Meredith, over the phone, if she would mind if I put up new wallpaper, she said: "Oh, but those flowers. I remember picking out those flowers . . ." She reminisced awhile. She had been so young in this house, she said. Single, and living her own life in her own space for the first time.

Those ugly flowers were a portal to that time. I understood.

"Okay," I said. "Don't worry. I'll leave them alone."

I lived in the bungalow for three years. And every year Bill would say they were going to sell the house and every year they wouldn't.

I'd call Meredith to ask if I needed to renew the lease or not, and she'd say, "Honey, don't worry about it. I bought your book! It just thrills me to think of you living there."

"I love this house," I said.

"I did, too," she said. "I think of it as my single house. I was so happy there."

I had no doubt Meredith was happy now, too. She talked about her boys with such love. She tried to pretend she got annoyed with Bill but there was never any edge to it. It was healthy, recreational complaining. Since we'd still never met, I tried to imagine what she might look like. What she'd looked like when she lived in the bungalow. The second time we tacitly renewed my lease Bill said, "Meredith is never going to sell this place," and sighed. "We could make a killing."

He was right. The house was near the university and there was a shortage of housing for students. Developers were sniffing around.

"Why won't she?" I asked.

"She needs a place to go in case I don't work out," he said, and laughed.

Their kids were in the car, six and eight.

SIMON, AGE SIX (VIDEO TRANSCRIPT)

[Simon has built his house out of cardboard boxes and art supplies on his apartment balcony]

   Simon: This is the door to the house and this is the handle to the door.

   Simon's dad: What animal is the handle?

   Simon: It's a DEER. [He squeezes it affectionately, then swings the door open] *And if I go inside* [Crawls though the door] *there's pictures* [Simon has made art of rainbows and flowers and it hangs from the walls by clothespins] *and walls and here's a little hole that I can see people going through.* [Peers through cardboard tube spyglass to outside world] *And this is a steering wheel.* [Deploys a small rubber wheel taped to wall] *And this is the aquarium. I putted a sting ray in there.* [All I can say of the aquarium is that it is glorious] *And this is the pillow where you can lay down and read.* [Simon flops on the pillow, considering the possibilities of its comfort] *And this is a water thing that if water goes in, it will come down.* [A tape and cardboard system is rigged to collect rainwater and make an indoor waterfall]

When I got a teaching job in upstate New York, the time had come to leave my bungalow behind. My boyfriend Nick proposed, and we took a trip to New York to buy a house together, an endeavor that felt both impossibly stressful and impossibly exciting. We counted bedrooms as we toured the properties, making sure there were enough for the children we thought we might have.

I was going to cohabitate again.

I let the landlords know.

"Perfect time to sell the house," Bill said.

Meredith asked if I knew of any grad students who might want to rent the place.

A week or two before I moved out, I pulled into my driveway and saw Bill's truck, but it wasn't Bill. A beautiful woman had a ladder up against the house. She was power-washing the vinyl siding. It had gone a little green over the years—plant life will grow on just about anything in the Panhandle; it is the most *alive* place I have ever lived. In fact, it got pretty close to my childhood dream-house fantasies of having the outside *inside*.

The woman power-washing the bungalow looked strong. She was wearing a blue one-piece bathing suit and black sport shorts. Her thick brown hair was tied back in a ponytail. She was very tan. The breeze turned, and for a moment a curtain of spray hung in the air, then blew back on her. She shook her head and the silvery hoops she wore flashed in the sun.

"Goddamn it," she said, as the washer jammed. She shook its wand.

"Meredith?" I said.

"Oh!" She said, "I'm sorry. It's just . . ." She shook the wand again. "It's so good to finally meet you!" she said. "It's so strange that now I guess we're saying goodbye?"

"I know," I said.

She was maybe ten years older than I was, a little less. Enough to feel like she was just one phase of life ahead of me. Like she was here from my future or back here tidying up her past. She gestured to the clean white siding where she'd washed.

"I just want it to look nice for the next girl," she said.

We didn't know who would rent the place yet, but I liked that she already knew it would be a girl. It was, in so many ways, a single woman's house.

"I kind of thought you might sell it," I said. "Bill is always saying you're going to."

"Yeah," she said. "We should. We could make some money."

She climbed down from the ladder. She was spangled with spray.

"I was just so happy here. And I'm happy now. But I think one of the reasons I *can* be happy now is that I know this house exists. I know that there's this place and it's in my name, and I own it myself and if for some reason I'm at home and suddenly the kids are driving me nuts or I'm mad at Bill, I have this place, and it's just mine, and I could come here. And then I feel better because I know I *could* do that and the kids don't seem so bad and I look at Bill a little different." She shook her head, water flying away. "Is that crazy?" she said, and then she looked at me like she'd forgotten whom she was talking to.

I laughed. "No, I know what you mean," I said.

We went inside and she took down two glasses from my cabinet and filled them from the tap. We drank the water.

"I'm sad to leave this place," I said. "I mean, I'm excited to move in with my fiancé, but this was a really special time for me."

She nodded. "How many bedrooms in your new place?"

"Three," I said. "Upstate is cheap."

"Good," she said. "Make one of those rooms your room."

ANDY, AGE SIX

For his house, Andy draws a space station in which there is one room absolutely full of golden retrievers. There are one hundred golden retrievers in it. [HE HASN'T DRAWN THEM ALL, HE SAYS, BUT ENOUGH TO MAKE THE POINT.] *And of course they are in zero g. So they float, their golden coats weightless as you hover among them in this perfect space.*

On the first night of my second cohabitation, on Johnnycake Hill, in upstate New York, I also immediately knew something was wrong.

Nick and I were sleeping on a mattress on the floor, and as we lay there that night, I was so euphorically overwhelmed by the fact of this *whole house* that was now *our house,* which *we had bought.*

"It feels so generous," I said, in the darkness of our new room. "I hope it always feels like this much. I hope we never get used to how amazing it is."

Nick didn't say anything. Then he reminded me that we had to investigate the drain in the garage. And then he fell asleep.

When he and I split up less than a year later, he moved back to Ohio and I bought him out of our mortgage.

After the emotional dust had settled enough for me to think the most basic kinds of thoughts, what I thought was this: I should sell this house.

It was absurd, I told myself, for one woman plus one very large dog to live in a three-bedroom house by themselves. What had already felt like *so much* for us to start a family in was certainly too much for just me. The house's very form spoke to the creation of a family. There was simply too much for one person to reasonably have to herself.

But my tiny town had limited rentals, most of which weren't much cheaper than my mortgage, and having bought out my ex, I was now in debt.

And I was tired. I had just bought a house, moved the length of the East Coast, halfway planned my wedding to Nick. The idea of selling and buying another house and moving all over again was unbearable. I'll stay for the rest of the school year, I told myself. And then I'll sell it.

The feeling persisted that I was living the wrong kind of life for a house like mine, and I was not the only one who felt this way.

When people came over, they often said, *Oh, you live here by yourself?*

Oh, are you renting or did you buy?

And when it became clear that, yes, I owned the house and, yes, I lived there by myself, they were surprised, alarmed, even.

But what will you do with all this space? people said.

At first what I did with all that space was that I cried in it. I cried in every goddamn room of that house.

With half its furniture gone, it felt very empty. I divided my secondhand bungalow furniture between the rooms, as if trying to warrant their existence. But every space reminded me of the life I was supposed to be living, the family I had meant to be building in the house, and how I was coming up short.

Sometimes, when people I didn't know very well said, *You don't mean you live here by yourself?* I blurted out the whole story, as if to excuse or explain my owning such a space. To apologize for it. And as it turned out, a relative stranger telling them about her called-off wedding was less galling to most people than the idea that she lived in the house, by herself, *on purpose.*

JOE, AGE THIRTY-EIGHT

[JOE, FATHER OF ANDY, AGE SIX, HAS FOUND FAMILIAL-ARCHIVAL DRAWINGS OF HIS DREAM HOUSE.]

Much like Andy, I used to draw highly elaborate spaceships, like this triple-decker space shuttle. The part that looks like part of someone's colon is the warp drive. There are the redundant controls on each level of the shuttle house. I think that might be so that I could drive, but so that my two brothers could also drive. Because if there weren't three controls, I don't think they would have let me take a turn.

I desperately needed just one room in my house to feel okay, and I couldn't bear the master bedroom, so I moved into a small, warrenlike room on the second floor. I set up the old wrought-iron bed I had slept in during my single-bungalow days. I dragged the dog's bed upstairs and hung on the wall the pages of an old calendar, which had pencil illustrations of rabbits paired with song lyrics. A squat dwarf lop bunny with a curious-looking eye had Smog lyrics: YOU ARE A FIGHTER, YOU ARE A FIGHTER. A pair of elegant wild rabbits had Seger:

ALL I KNOW IS THAT I'M YOUNG AND YOUR RULES THEY
ARE OLD.

A few weeks after my ex cleared out his things, my friends
Emily and Olivia rushed up to stay. "We are coming," they
said, a statement. There is no nicer thing a person could have
done for me. We went to the winter farmers' market and tried
natural deodorants that smelled incredible and did not work.
We watched our favorite show about drag queens on the little
love seat in the living room even though it wasn't big enough
for three people and one of us had to sit on the floor and lean
against the others' legs. I built us fires and we drank too much
and gossiped in front of the fireplace.

Having people I loved in the house made it feel better, it
seemed.

So I threw kind of a lot of parties.

There was a dinner party we called Maestranza Feast for
people grieving after Trump's election. We took "Maestranza"
to mean the people alongside whom one struggles in good
work, and decorated with branches and stumps and leaves we
dragged indoors so our friends would know how wild we were
and how much we loved them. The dinner table was so long it
sprawled through three rooms. There was a Halloween party
so good adults got drunk and kissed strangers in disguises
while dancing in my kitchen. I hosted a baby shower for scientist friends at which there were no fewer than two kegs. For my
annual white-elephant party I made enough pomegranate cake
and spiked cider for thirty-five people, most of whom wound
up wearing a unicorn onesie at some point in the evening.

Since having people I loved in the house made it feel better,
I decided I might try love again. I let myself fall for a funny,
handsome man I'd had a crush on for many years, since the first

moment I saw him, really, even though I knew he lived abroad. I went and found him in Paris and we climbed all the steps of Montmartre to hang out in Moroccan bars, and eavesdrop on the singing inside the Lapin Agile, and to sit outside the Metro station sipping beers, watching the tides of people coming and going. When he came to stay with me in my house it was mid-winter, and it snowed so hard there was nothing for us to do, and I worried about how my house was not as good as Paris. But the snow bucketed down and we played guitar and had sex all day and it was perfect. And then my house was a house where I had feelings again, where I had sex again. And after he left, I cried, but a house where you have cried over multiple heartbreaks is infinitely better than a house where you've only cried over one, defining, bad thing.

Once, a friend had surgery and recuperated in my house while I was away, and when I returned she had left the freezer full of dinner rolls she'd made from scratch, stuffed with pesto and sundried tomatoes. Once, I came home to find friends I was meant to meet up with later already in my house—eating snacks in the kitchen. "The bar was closed," one said. "You never lock your door," said another. Once, a beloved student who often dog-sat for me had a horrible time with a midterm and texted me in tears at nine p.m. and said she thought she might feel better if she could just hug my giant dog. I wouldn't be home for another hour, I said, but the door was unlocked. When I arrived home I found her and my dog sitting on the floor, the dog's fat paws draped across her lap as he happily did heavy breathing in her face. "Do you feel a little better?" I asked. "Yes," she said.

I started dating again. A new boyfriend, Maxim, had a

charming daughter and we staged epic Nerf battles in my house, which, having ample hallways and peekaboo corners, was ideal for such a thing. That little girl laughed so perfectly when she popped out of the stairwell to attack her father and me with a hail of Nerf darts. Even after they were no longer in my life, every once in a while I found rogue Nerf darts in the couch cushions or behind the bookshelves. I saved them in a heap, and sometimes I thought about cramming them into an envelope and posting them back . . . one last volley in return.

All of these people—who did not live *with* me, per se—became part of the life being lived in my house. And this was what made it livable for me. Kurt Vonnegut once wrote that whenever a couple is shouting and fighting, what they are actually shouting at each other is *"You are are not enough people."* Because we have deluded ourselves that a human can be happy living alone with one or two other people in this world.

But we need so much more than that.

ANDY, AGE FORTY-THREE

Andy remembers that he and a friend drew a lot of mazes in middle school. Once they drew a maze with a house in the middle. Then they began to draw the house and Andy divided the house into two.

You'll live on this side and I'll live on that side, *he said.*

You know we're not going to live together when we grow up, right? *his friend said.*

Yeah, *Andy said.* I know.

Andy remembers processing this information. That he wouldn't live with his best friend when he grew up. Says he internalized in that moment that he never should have suggested it. Should never even have imagined it. This story breaks my heart.

There was a while, after I called off my wedding, where I caught myself saying "we" even though there was no "we" to speak of anymore (*we pay way too much for snowplowing; we have never been to the planetarium before*). I found these moments humiliating and painful. As if I had drawn attention to a shortcoming I'd hoped others would not notice. "*I* pay too much for snowplowing," I corrected.

I tried to practice speaking only as myself.

But as time went on, and life and living brought people through my house, I found there usually *was* some arrangement of friends or family or colleagues or students involved. Some "we" to speak of, though a stranger would be hardpressed to imagine what collective I might be referring to.

A stranger might mistake my "we" as romantic. But it was better than that.

Perhaps I loved my house so much because it was not unlike the houses I drew as a child, with their infinite rooms and creatures and friends walking in without knocking and everyone always spending the night. Those houses were never meant only for two.

I haven't ever been able to imagine a life of loving one person to the exclusion of others. I am well suited to monogamy of the body, but not the home.

Did I dream of being *in love* when I was young? Oh, yes, all the time. By the time I was twelve I cringily referred to myself as a "hopeless romantic." I have always loved love.

But it is good to remember that as a little girl what I dreamed of were not weddings but houses full of everyone I loved.

Of course, you'll remember the reason I'm writing this essay. You'll remember that I was about to fuck all of this up.

NINA, AGE TWO, INTERVIEWED BY HER MOTHER

So, Nina, if you could live in any kind of house, what kind of house would you live in?
Mama, I am standing on a cloth.
Yes, you are. What would your house smell like?
It would smell like a mummy.
What does a mummy smell like?
Ants.
Hey, what are you doing with that cloth?

I started dating a man called Peter, and, after our first date, he started talking about our moving in together. I was thrilled and terrified. It seemed insane. It felt correct.

But I deflected whenever he brought up the idea of living together, told him to pump the brakes. I was trying to be reasonable. I kept saying, Let's wait a year, at least.

I was trying to protect myself, too. Because no longer seeing Maxim's daughter after he and I split up had almost killed me. And Peter also had a daughter. Lydia was eight, too, and I was afraid to get my heart broken by a cool little girl again. I tried to delay. But then Peter told me about a conversation he'd had with Lydia about houses.

Lydia told Peter that she didn't think she ever wanted to get married.

That's okay, he said. Lots of people don't.

Instead, she said, when she grew up, she wanted to live on a farm with lots of horses and fennec foxes.

SAME GIRL SAME, I said in a text to Peter. I WANT THAT LIFE.

MAYBE, Peter said, WE COULD LIVE ON A FARM AND YOU COULD HAVE HORSES AND FENNEC FOXES BUT LIKE, I COULD BE THERE TOO?

NOPE, I typed.

Because the whole point of this fantasy, which Lydia understood and which I understood, was that if you lived alone with your animals and friends you would be surrounded by joy and ease. Safety, too. This was the kind of living I'd found my way back to on Johnnycake Hill.

But the next time I saw Lydia, she showed me the house she was building in Minecraft. It was our house. The one we said we might all live in together someday. She popped up from behind an enormous computer monitor wearing pink kitten headphones and said, "I'm spawning foxes in our house. Want to see?"

I don't know what I thought Lydia's game was going to look like but when I peeked over her shoulder I laughed.

Our house was absolutely full of foxes.

She was running through the hallways, faster and faster, even though hundreds of chubby, square foxes crowded her way.

"If I bother them too much they'll kill me," Lydia said, "but I still want to spawn, like, so many more."

Soon, I had sold my house on Johnnycake Hill, and bought us a new one.

SABINE, AGE TWO AND THREE-QUARTERS

What color is your house?

Brown!

What color are the trees?

Brown!

Where would you sleep?

In a swing!

You really love the swings—you would swing all day.

Yes!

Do you have a potty?

I have a tall potty—I climb up the ladder and then I go down
   into it and then I kick it in and I say, Bahahahahahaha!

Is that the only place you're allowed to kick things?

Yes.

*Sabine, thank you so much for telling us about your house—it
   sounds really great.*

I . . . I pretend a new house now . . . orange house!

I had met Peter during the COVID pandemic, and at the time
my writer friend Ndinda was living with me. She had been
teaching at our university when the pandemic hit, and by the
time she intended to fly back to Nairobi, all flights had been
suspended. "Come live with me till it's safe to go," I said. The
pandemic had suspended the open-door policy of the Johnnycake house and I was grateful to have the company of a woman
I adored.

We shared a long summer of pandemic isolation from almost
everyone but each other, and Peter, and Lydia. The four of us
learned how to tie-dye, and how to make spring rolls. Ndinda

became obsessed with jigsaw puzzles and showed Lydia how to do them. Lydia taught Ndinda how to play Monopoly like a good American capitalist and Ndinda reinvented the rules to appoint Lydia as her broker, which proved advantageous in real estate dealings with Peter. Ndinda and I developed an entire private language inspired by Tyra Banks and reruns of *America's Next Top Model*.

A few weeks before Peter and Lydia and I were due to move to our new house, Kenya started accepting American flights again and Ndinda booked her way home. We planned a goodbye dinner for the four of us. But when we told Lydia about it, she was so sad and confused.

When we'd talked about living together, she thought that meant Ndinda was coming, too.

And why wouldn't she? We'd been a family.

"Ndinda totally *can* come live with us, you know," Peter said.

And Ndinda had her own life to live, but I loved that he said that.

Because, as I packed my boxes and drew elaborate maps of my perennials to leave behind for the new owners, I felt like Meredith, lovingly power-washing her bungalow, and wondering about the next girl, trying to imagine how whatever came next could be as good as what had come before. But when Peter said that Ndinda could come, too, if she wanted, I felt less scared. I felt like maybe it was possible to have drawn your perfect house, all the rooms and animals and friends, and when there was no more room, to take out a second sheet of paper. To draw a tunnel, linking your old life to the new one. Maybe this new life could expand the one I'd built, with my friends and my families, but not replace it. Maybe good love stories don't crowd out all the other narratives in the room.

Uncoupling

B ack when I first got my tits, in the fifth grade, I had
these ecstatic daydreams in which they were gone. In
these reveries I was running through the tall meadow
grasses of my green yard where wild turkeys noisily exploded
from their cover, and I was wearing my favorite shirt with the
burgundy suns bleach-drizzled across it and it lay completely
flat across my chest and I wore no bra and I was barefoot and
I could move so fast. I knew this was the age when you could
start becoming a version of your future adult self, and *this* was
the version I wanted to be. But the future had already come for
me. The future was a set of double-D tits I have hated since the
day they arrived.

Breasts was never a word that worked for me. And much like
when I realized that I hated being called "Christie" and started
going by my mother's nickname for me, "CJ," I also, at some
point, realized that the indignity of using a word I hated for a
part of my own body was a problem within my control to rem-
edy. And so I have thought of my tits, since that time, as my
tits, because it's a word I like. It's a word I think is full of moxie.

Here are some words other people have used for me or for
my tits that I have not enjoyed. Some of these have been used
by people I love and some by people I don't, but I bear no ill will.

Bazongas. Porno Tits. Sweater Kittens. Boobies. Breasticles. Hooters. Melons. Fun Bags. Jugs. Big Tits Magillicutty or BTM. High Priestess of the Gravity-Defying Breasts, or HPGDB.

Everyone in this essay is going to say *tits*, even though, in reality, they all used different words. Because this is my fucking essay. And I'll tell you right now, if my saying *tits* makes you uncomfortable? We're never going to get out of this essay alive.

———

I could not tell you the number of hours I've spent at my computer looking up reduction surgeries because they are too many to count. I have admired before-and-after pictures and been troubled by them. I have wondered how I could possibly go the necessary amount of time recuperating. I have fixated on the unlikelihood of being able to breastfeed a child post-surgery. I have considered the tiny scars, and people have shown me their own, little trees, little lollipops, around the nipples. I have seen the seamlike trail across the pale underbelly of friends' now fabulously small breasts and I have admired them. I have seen trans friends who were less at home in their bodies than I am get top surgery and I have celebrated their Instagram pictures and felt joy and jealousy as we went to the beach and they appeared in trunks, their new bodies allowing different kinds of visibility and possibility. I have joked with a friend that we will both get surgery and form a lady cult of titless women who wear only overalls, overalls whose straps will lie neatly across our chests, as we do whatever good work we please in our newly unencumbered bodies. I have gotten recommendations and referrals for doctors. But I have never even gotten as far as a phone call. Whenever I get close, I hesitate, and decide to save my tits just a little while longer.

Because, it turns out, there are a lot of imaginary people who I seem to think might need them.

————

I am twelve years old and we, me and four other girls, are sitting on the curb of the parking lot across from the elementary school playground. We are watching some older boys skateboard. We are pretending we are not explicitly here for this reason. The boys come over and I talk to one named Marcus about whether or not he can do a certain trick. He can't yet but he will soon, he says.

We walk back to one of the girls' houses, where we will sleep over. Sometime during this afternoon I get my period. I find pads under my friend's mother's sink and take care of things. Within a year I will have ascended into my double-D tits and I will hate them, but right now, this is new and exciting.

Later, when we are idly playing Truth or Dare, sprawled across a girlish bed with many pillows, in a girlish room, sponge-painted mauve, which smells like raspberry lotion and also the little dish of cinnamon potpourri that one of us once ate, thinking it was Fritos, I want to tell these girls about getting my period but we are listening to Whitney Houston on boom-box repeat and it's very loud and we keep singing and so eventually I have to turn Whitney down and engineer a Truth question so I can tell them about it.

Oh my god! We all yell about my period. *You're a woman,* one says. *Oh my god, you were a woman with MARCUS,* another one says. *You were a woman the whole time he was talking to you and he didn't even know he was the first person you were a woman WITH.*

And we laugh, and I love these girls.

I don't know why it doesn't occur to me that I was a woman

with them before I was a woman with *him.* Why that doesn't count. Why being "a woman" in a bodily way is, always, already, even in this moment, *for someone,* and the someone isn't me. Isn't us. All five of us understand this, intuitively, at twelve, even as we turn Whitney back up, make Whitney louder, as we go back to our games and our singing.

———

I grew up hating dolls and played at being Jane Goodall instead, tending a menagerie of creatures in the imaginary wild. Even so, I have always known I wanted to have children. I have always wanted both to be a mother and to use my body to become a mother. These are different things, and I have understood them as such. I am interested in being a parent full stop. But being pregnant is an experience I've always known my body was interested in having.

In my twenties I used to say I wanted a feral wolf pack of boy children who I'd call inside with a dinner bell when the light started to fade. In my early thirties I used to say I really wanted two kids, please let them be girls. These sub-forty days, I think: One child, and may they be so lucky as to be born in a body that pleases them.

Some days I wonder if I will be able to have a child with my body, and if I do, I wonder how that will happen. It is hard to imagine I will meet a romantic partner and have a child with them at this point in my life. Some days I think that if I do not or cannot have a child with my body, I would like to raise a child some other way. And then, of course, when I think about raising a child without another person who also thinks of the child as their child, I have trouble imagining this, too. Not because there is any shortage of single parents in my life who, by choice or necessity, are doing this exact thing marvelously. But because being in a couple was part of the story I once told myself about my someday-parenthood.

And *some days*? It is summer and I am paddling my kayak around the big lake near my house, and I spend a long time quietly watching dappled fish wend among the underwater plants. Sometimes I bring a beer and a book of poetry out on the kayak and just drift. Sometimes I take my dog out for an ice cream cone with rainbow sprinkles. Sometimes I book a flight to Costa Rica to go to surf camp with my friend Marie-Helene at the last minute and we send each other surf-rock tracks for weeks, in delicious anticipation. Some days I have an abundance of myself to offer to friends and students, and it pleases me to do this. Some days I wonder what it would mean to trade this kind of freedom and mobility for the structures of motherhood.

———

There is a kind of clock of fertility that many women are aware of, and mine is a kind of Schrödinger's clock. It is possible, for example, that my clock has already run out, and it is too late for me to use my body to make a child. Or it is possible my clock is still ticking along. The fact of my not knowing used to be a thing that plunged me into anxiety and urgency and despair. Some days it still does. But mostly, my clock's Schrödingerish quality makes me feel like a happy nihilist, rather que será será about it. Because I have made enough hasty choices in this life to know that the only bad outcome would be to devote myself to this clock at the price of enlisting some person whose presence in my life makes me unhappy.

All of this is to say I have found myself needing to consider which parts of "having children" are the parts I always thought I wanted.

Because it turns out there is more than one choice, more than one concept, melded together in that phrase *having children*.

Most people, as I understand it, never need to consider them separately. But for those of us who find ourselves single, and contending with Schrödinger's clocks, or plenty of other circumstances besides, it can feel rather revelatory to understand the multiplicity of it all. And as I separate out the parts of "having children" that have to do with couplehood, or with wanting to meld genes with a particular beloved, from the parts that have to do with being a parent, from the parts that have to do with being a person whose body makes a life, it seems there are more and different elements to all of this than I'd been led to believe.

I think I might have gone on forever, thinking of all this as one impossibly unified thing, had I not had an absolute breakdown in therapy.

The catalyst for this breakdown, and thus, the uncoupling of these ideas was, of course, my tits.

———

I do a lot of crying in therapy. I love a good cry. But normally it's like there are tears and I am pretending I don't need a tissue and then my therapist gestures to the tissues and this is helpful on multiple levels.

The day I had the meltdown about my tits I was beyond the help of the tissue box.

My relationship with Peter, with whom I thought I was going to have a child, had ended. I had ended it. Had come to know it was not right. That we were good together, but not good enough. Which is a specific kind of tragedy. Because here was this totally lovely man, who, by the way, wanted to have a child with me, but that was not enough for me to stay. This was the second time in five years I had dated a father, planned to have a child with that father, and then had that possibility go away.

And now I was monologuing and weeping about it to my shrink: *I read some article that told me that thirty-five was the point at which a woman should start losing her fucking mind if she wanted to have kids and I helplessly imprinted on that number and now I'm thirty-seven and I feel like, Oh shit, I forgot to have kids!*

In an effort to cheer myself up, I said, *Well, at least I can get rid of my tits now.*

And before my therapist could even ask me what on earth I meant by that, I spun out further: *But what are my tits for? Like what is the point of them? Why have I been carting them around like this for years, if I hate them, and now I'm not even going to use them?*

What do you mean by that? my therapist asked. *"Use" them.*

This was a good question.

I had surprised myself with these words. I tried to explain what my mouth had admitted without my brain even knowing why.

And it turned out that, in my own head, the only reason I still had my tits, which I hated, was because I was going to *offer them to someone.*

To hypothetical tit-appreciating and possibly scar-averse lovers.

To my hypothetical child.

To this hypothetical life I was going to have with this lover and this child.

I have come to understand that not everyone feels this way about their tits.

But I do. I have this whole time. I just didn't realize it until that hypothetical life I'd been saving them for flickered for a moment. Because of the breakup, and my age, I saw it flicker. And in the flicker, the plausibility of me becoming a mother with my body, the plausibility of my sharing my prepregnancy body with a lover, the plausibility of having a romantic partner with whom to share the experience of pregnancy and raising a child . . . all of that no longer seemed *likely*. It definitely no longer seemed *certain*. And when the existences of those imaginary people were threatened? When, for a sobbing therapeutic moment they blinked out of existence and I was left with only my own self?

The first thought I had was: Who are these fucking tits for?

I felt I had been tricked into bearing them (by who? By myself!) for years and years and years, and this had been for nothing.

"You could get surgery now, if that's a thing you decide to do," my therapist told me. "And you could still have a child with your body, and not breastfeed."

"But what about the scars? What if someone didn't like them?"

"Someone?"

"Some partner."

"Do you mind the idea of scars on your body?"

"No, they look like little trees."

"Would you be upset if someone you loved had scars?"

"Of course not," I said.

"Scars from a surgery they'd had that made them happy?"

"Extra not," I said.

"Why would someone not feel this same way toward your body? Why can't you imagine someone accommodating your whole self the way you imagine accommodating someone else?"

Because I wanted to keep my body full of possibilities.

I didn't want to risk defining what it was or wasn't too specifically in case what I made of it wasn't what someone, someday, wanted or needed from me.

These imaginary lovers. These imaginary children.

That my body is for me, is mine, that my body does not have to please others, has been a hard thing to understand. It is a thing I've been working on for a long time. My piercings and tattoos have helped. They are little flags I use to settle the land of my body. To claim it for myself. Mine, I say. I do with you what I please. *Mine,* and I don't care what someone else thinks of this. Someone who sees me tomorrow. Some imaginary someone someday. This has nothing to do with them. I plant a flag. Another. This is mine.

These were the three strands I uncoupled that day:

My body, as it exists for myself.

My desire to be a lover with this body, to have sex, and even fall in love.

My desire to have children, possibly with this body.

What would happen if I thought of these as different things?

It was Nick, my ex-fiancé, who found the lump in my breast. It's not cancer. I am okay. I will tell you that first. I am very lucky and this is not that kind of story and I'm not going to have you sitting around wondering if it is.

The point is, I was messing around with him, I had just turned thirty, and he was grabbing my tits, not unpleasantly, when he popped up to say, *"You have a lump in this tit—did you know that?"* I did not. I appreciated this directness. And he came with me to get the lump checked out and this was very thoughtful and nice of him. There are people in this world who understand that having a lump in your tit is existentially frightening and people who do not. Nick was the former, and this was a blessing to me.

After being mammogrammed to death, which, if you don't know, involves your tit being not unpainfully squished between plate glass on either side, so that what had once been a plump grapefruit is now a vertical splat of flesh under deli glass, the nurses told me: *We have no idea what's going on in there.*

And I said, *Meaning that you're not sure what it is?*

No, the nurses said, *meaning your tits are super dense and full of mysterious objects but we can't see for shit in there so you're going to have to get an ultrasound.*

Like for babies? I said.

Yes, but for your tits, they said.

I see.

Since then, I have had to be a person who fights with hospitals and insurance companies once every six months and locates some oracle to stare into the heart of darkness. I either win the fight and have an ultrasound or lose the fight and have a pointless mammogram, where they realize all over again they can't see for shit in there, and then I get referred to have the ultrasound I always need anyway. Another way of putting this is to say that every six months I have a routine medical procedure where I hear, once again, that my tits are full of mysteries that are probably a benign nothing but are also maybe going to kill me so let's remain in this semiannual cycle of wondering and looking just to be sure.

Schrödinger's tits.

A few weeks after my tits-related therapy breakdown, where I bawled and asked my therapist what they were for, I found a new lump. I had moved recently, and so this time I was referred to a new hospital with a breast health center, where, in the waiting room, everything was covered in pink ribbons and pink flowers and pink-scripted affirmations of strength, and as I sat in this vortex of pink, I had a warped thought, which was: *At least if it's cancer this time my insurance might pay for me to get rid of my tits.* And then I realized how fucked up and disrespectful a thought that was. And I thought of my friends who have had breast cancer and other cancers and in my head I said, *I am sorry I am sorry I am sorry,* to each of them for even thinking the thought.

Eventually I was rescued from the waiting room and led into the ultrasound room and I took off my shirt and my special-order-one-hundred-dollar-bigger-than-DD bra because I was running heavy that year and normal bras from a store would not fit. I waited, in my little blue paper robe, to be seen by the oracle.

The woman who came in to do the ultrasound was very calm and very direct and I was so grateful to her for that. She spread the gel across the curve of my tit gently, moved the wand with even pressure. The report from inside me came up on the little ultrasound screen, black and white and grainy and flickering, and I began to cry.

I am sure the technician thought I was crying because I was scared. But the reality was that I began crying because all of this felt like a movie scene I knew too well. We all do. It's the moment when the woman and her partner go in for an ultrasound and there's the goo and there's the wand and there's the screen and on the screen they see *their baby*. I have imagined myself in this scene before. I have imagined how that might feel.

But this was not *that*.

This saintly technician, who had gooped my tits not unkindly, noticed my crying and she told me she was almost through, and then she complimented the tattoo on my arm. When she was finished she told me she wasn't allowed to say anything but she personally didn't see anything bad in my tits. My doctor would call me when she got my films, but if it were her, this beautiful tit oracle said, she'd want to know that probably everything was going to be okay.

I said thank you for this maybe slightly unethical but deeply appreciated mercy. When she left the room I cried properly. Cried because I was relieved. Cried because she'd treated me like a person. Cried because I was in this bizarre version of a scene from my life I'd always anticipated, but instead of a nurse waving her wand to reveal a baby to me and a person I loved, it was this nurse telling me that the unknowable things inside of me were potentially benign. That they were mysteries, but they would not kill me for being unresolved.

I have been going with my friend Brynn to the fertility clinic. She wants to become a mother. A single mother. She dates men. She has relationships. But she has untethered all that from her desire to be a parent. Because of chance and because of life and because of learning. I go with her because I am excited for her and I am hoping that she'll get knocked up and someday, when I am hanging out with this person Brynn has ushered into being, I will look at them and think of the times Brynn and I went to the clinic together and what scientific fucking magic it all is.

But mostly, Brynn is being generous. She is showing me what this process is like, because she understands I want to learn about its possibilities. I want to see it and understand it and wonder about it, too.

I had always imagined having a child with a partner. When I imagine becoming a mother without another person to do it with, I am not afraid of the work so much as I am afraid to bear the joy of a child alone. Who will be as excited as I am when they do something banal? What would it mean to not have someone right there to turn to, to share that with?

And then I think to myself, You little fool! What about this beautiful friend who is taking you to the clinic with her? Who is already sharing this intimate thing with you? What about the community of family and chosen family and other people in your life who would be in a child's life, too?

And then some fearful part of my lizard brain says: But those people might leave. They would not be forever. They do not have to stick around.

But what makes me think marriage is so much more certain than that?

Why does that ceremony signify so much more stability than these other relationships in my life, these other love stories, which have been so steady, so appearing and disappearing and reappearing, so evolving, these relationships I have tended and have given me so much love and comfort? Why would I not trust this *collective of real people* as much as I would trust this one imaginary co-parent I think might someday arrive?

The way it works is that Brynn drives almost an hour to my house, which is near the clinic. And we drink coffee and shoot the shit and eat cantaloupe with the windows open and the summer morning sounds coming in, and my dog angling to be taken along for a ride. And then we tell my dog that he is not allowed to go to the fertility clinic, and we leave, and Brynn drives us.

This clinic, I should say, is a very, very good and respected clinic. The people in it are good at what they do, and very kind. But also I want you to know that, as she pushes open the door, Brynn says to me, in a low voice, "You're not ready for this."

"For what?" I say.

"It's a vibe in there."

There is a cardboard cutout of the main doctor at this clinic in the entryway, smiling and welcoming us. He has a black V-neck and chain necklaces and silver hair.

A book of his affirmations is on the waiting-room coffee table, which looks like the sort of coffee table a person would do coke off of in a movie about the eighties highlife. There are huge black leather couches and black leather armchairs. An ostentatious chandelier hangs from the ceiling. The gas fireplace has a mantel so tall I can't see myself in the mirror mounted above it. There are smoky-glass baubles and bowls of blooming peonies and huge art of photographed pink peonies on black backgrounds, too. Visual fertility blooming everywhere.

I say quietly, "It reminds me of Vegas."

And Brynn says that this place *is* kind of a numbers game, but it's always given her more of an upscale-chain-steakhouse feeling.

We follow a nurse into the back room, and she, like all the nurses, is wearing a shirt that says BELIEVE.

I give Brynn a look. She gives me a look. Once the nurse leaves, I say, "It would be a nice sentiment, if it wasn't on a T-shirt?"

The nurse returns and lights up an ultrasound screen.

I watch as the nurse investigates Brynn's ovaries with a vaginal ultrasound. The grainy terrain on screen is sloping up and down, over and away, and she starts making little maps with neon green lines on the screen that make a tocking sound as she clicks them. It's hypnotically beautiful to watch.

"You look like the surface of the moon, Brynn," I say.

She laughs and the nurse continues to click and point. She is making a map of the different follicles that are growing inside Brynn, follicles that might become her baby, or might not, this month. We are waiting for one to take the lead. And when one or more does, then "things get barbaric," Brynn tells me. At home, she'll watch a YouTube video explaining how to mix a vial of very-real-seeming drugs, and then she'll give herself a shot in the butt, to trigger ovulation.

The nurse writes down the follicle measurements. She turns off the screen, the map of possibilities. She tells Brynn to come back at the end of the week. Brynn drops me back at home.

"I am rooting for your follicles," I say, as I run up the drive.

———

Who would I fall in love with, who would I *have sex with*, if I wasn't imagining that person as a parent to my someday child? If I took that off the table? Would I have dated the people I dated if I didn't imagine them someday being part of my future life, in which I imagined myself being a parent?

I think the answer might be no.

I can't decide whether this line of thinking is the most obvious thing in the world or if it is truly and deeply unsettling.

If it seems strange to you that I was thinking of the men I was dating as potential fathers, please remember that two of the men I had dated for the past five years of my life, Maxim and Peter, were, in fact, fathers. That these men were fathers was a part of their identities, and their parenthood was a huge part of our lives together. These men were good fathers. And this was a thing I loved about them. When I saw these men with their daughters, I thought, *Oh my god, look at this good man.*

I have never been pregnant, never been any child's primary caretaker, and I am not a mother. But twice in my life, over the course of about five years, I fell in love with a little girl, and then she was gone. This happened because I was their fathers' girlfriend. And I was their fathers' girlfriend, in no small part, because I fell in love with the men *as parents*.

I'm telling you this because, even though I really think I am understanding something important about these different strands of what "having children" means, even though I think separating parenthood from questions of sex and love really is an important thing for me to do, it is distinctly possible that I am full of shit. That I am just trying to protect myself. Because what I actually cannot bear is to again fall in love with a child who then vanishes from my life.

I say falling in love, and I mean it. These were also love stories.

I am a kind of breakup pro at this point. The pain of a breakup is fresh every time, but I have lived it before. I know the arc of it. I know what to do with it. What I did not know how to do, once, and then twice, was accept the disappearance of funny and creative little girls, who I loved very much, from my life, and from my home. There are no movies about this kind of breakup. I have read no books about it. I have a hard time understanding what to do with the pain of growing into a small, but not unreal, role in a child's life, and then, post-breakup, for that part of myself to no longer have a purpose.

Who is this love for? This never-quite-a-stepparent love? I still have it. And I have played my role in these breakups. It is my fault that these little girls are no longer in my life. Still, having my heart broken by little girls is the most confusing pain I have ever felt. The one I feel the least able to understand.

I used to call myself a Bonus Adult. Though that's a kind of armor to wear. It makes my role sound free and easy and optional, and it was never that. But whatever it is that I was, that there is no good word for, I am no longer that thing.

How do we talk about the loss of a thing for which there is no word? The lack of a word implies that it was never anything. It was never real. But here I am in my kitchen and the height of a child is marked on the doorframe. Here I am in my living room and I am still finding Nerf darts behind the couch. There it is, evidence of my love. My pain. I find it. I see it. There's something that was once here. And now, it's not.

The next time Brynn comes, before we go to the clinic, I ask her if she could help me carry a mattress up two flights of stairs to my newly created guest room.

"I tried to do it myself," I say. "I did the bed myself but when I tried to do the mattress it fell on me and I felt ridiculous for thinking I could do it alone."

When I had failed to carry the queen-size pillowtop mattress by myself, when it had fallen on me at the base of the stairs in my basement, I'd just sort of lain there for a while. I lay in my basement under the mattress thinking how much I hated that there was anything at all in this world I was forced to accept I might need a second person to do.

"Will it be bad for your follicles if you carry a mattress before this appointment?" I asked.

"Dude, no," Brynn said

At the top of the stairs in my house is the room I painted cantaloupe orange after Peter moved out. This was the first thing I did. It used to be the bedroom of a cool little girl, Lydia's room, and it was ruining me, this room. It was breaking my heart. So I made it into a guest room. I told myself that people I loved would exist in this space again.

You're allowed to stay in my guest room only if you call it by its real name, which, because it glows sunsetty orange and is full of Florida rattan furniture and desert plants, is the Georgia O'Keeffe Womb Room. This is a rule.

Brynn and I are huffing a little, sweating, after having laid down this heavy, unwieldy mattress on the bed frame. And I thank her for helping me and then I say, "I hate that some things are so much easier with two people," and then I clap my mouth shut, realizing what a bad thing this is to say on our way to the clinic.

But Brynn tells me that the other day she was on the phone to a friend and she was sort of choked up about doing this alone. And then she looked out the window and she saw our

friend E., who had been helping in her garden. She saw beautiful E. there, tilling the soil. Shoveling compost. And then her
phone lit up and it was me, asking about coming along for the
next fertility appointment. And she said she started laughing.
Because there she was, saying she had no help, but here were
these women.

Why does it feel like, even among ourselves, we do not
count?

Why was I a woman with Marcus first instead of with those
girls singing Whitney Houston songs? How can we be surrounded by friends of many genders and still have people look
at us and think that because we are unpartnered, we are alone?

Sometimes even we forget.

In the Georgia O'Keeffe Womb Room, Sharpie in hand,
like a tiny vandal tagging up, I write on my own wall: WE WERE
HERE. There are a couple of names under the tag now. Because
when people stay at my house, they sign the wall. And, like
this, maybe I can remember. Like this, maybe we won't forget
to count ourselves.

At the appointment that day, Brynn is wearing a vintage Adi-
das sweater in blue and the nurse compliments it and I say it
reminds me of old pictures of my dad from the seventies, and
Brynn says she basically *is* everyone's dad from the seventies,
and this clinic room, to me, seems like such a perfect place to
claim that power.

They measure Brynn's follicles again. They have grown, but
not quite enough yet. She must do this two-hour drive again
before they're ready for the trigger shot. About a day or so
after that, she will come back again, for the insemination. The

nurse, in her BELIEVE shirt and turban headband, clicks her pink-tipped nails on the counter and looks from Brynn in the stirrups to me. She considers, reconsiders. Then she turns to me and says, "Do we have a plan for the sperm?"

My eyes go huge, and I turn to Brynn, and Brynn says, so calmly I know she is trying very hard not to laugh, "You guys are holding sperm for me from the cryobank." The nurse nods, and walks out.

"A plan," I say, and I am trying to laugh quietly. "I'm sorry I don't have a plan for sperm?" Brynn is pulling on her jeans and laughing.

"A plan," she says, shaking her head.

———

Whether I was full of self-protective shit or not, once I detached ideas of parenthood from ideas of sex and love, things shifted. When I stopped thinking about the people I kissed as being part of some sort of pathway to shared parent-hood, I found I was interested in different people. I became open to seeing polyamorous people. I saw women more frequently. And the monogamous cis-men I was interested in were different, too.

In an act of precisely the sort of performative sexual abandon I always think is going to make me feel free and seldom does because I always wind up dating the person instead of walking away, I attempted to have sex with a relative stranger I met on the internet in a fancy hotel and then never see him again.

Adam and I succeeded at the first part of this. We met up at the charming bar in the lobby of the fancy hotel where I was staying. He was incredibly handsome. We drank cocktails and talked about books and our families and the ocean. He cupped the back of my neck, and when my face lit up he pulled me to him and kissed me ferociously on the velvet lobby couch. Soon I had invited him upstairs.

We had sex that I loved more than most sex. A tumbling, kinetic sort of fucking with so much saying yes in it. He bit my shoulders and I squeezed his chest and we tossed each other around. And it's not that I hadn't had sex somewhat like this before, but there was something about being *only myself* in bed, not as a person who might someday want to date this person or marry this person or have children with this person, but just myself, right then, that made everything particularly free and good.

All the other parts and versions of myself I thought I had to someday be? They were not invited into that bed. I'm really not sure I had realized how many other selves of mine were doing ride-alongs in my life—asking questions, making judgments, running simulations on hypothetical futures—until they were suddenly no longer in the room.

Adam squeezed my tits, and then asked if this was okay, heard yes, and did it again and harder, and asked if *this* was okay, heard yes again, and squeezed me again, and this was pleasure.

In the morning there were little blooms in lilac and moss dappled across the tops of my tits. He studied me in the hotel mirror. "Was that me?" Adam said.

And I said yes.

"Was that okay? I'll be gentler," he said.

"No," I said. "Please don't."

A day later, at home, I studied those lovely dapples in the mirror and the thing I actually thought was this: *Maybe if I am only myself, and not always/also the future mother of the children I might have with a person, then this thing that brought me pleasure can be a part of our dynamic. Maybe I am allowed to like this.*

There was no reason, no reason at all, to limit the things my body wanted to be or do because I conceived of them as mutually exclusive with some role I thought it needed to someday fulfill.

Because I am lousy at one-off sexual abandon, I soon found myself visiting Adam again. He invited me to stay with him in New York, and we rode a scooter to the Met. We wore goofy helmets and drove through the park, and it was spring, and even rushing along as fast as we were, we could smell the lilacs.

As we waited outside the museum, we watched the fountain jump in patterns too complicated to keep track of.

Inside, in the ancient Egyptian art wing, we found a small statue of a couple behind glass. A woman with her arm around the waist of a much taller man, he with his long arm draped over her shoulder, his hand resting perfectly on her tit. They both looked proud and comfortable.

"I like this," Adam said.

"Me, too," I said.

And he leaned in next to me, and I put my arm around his waist, like the ancient people in the statue. He put his arm over my shoulder and placed his hand on my tit, gently, bringing me in close.

He read the little placard.

"It's called a 'reciprocal embrace,'" he said.

"Yes," I said.

The day we go for Brynn to be inseminated, the nurses are extra nice. One wishes Brynn good luck. Another crosses her fingers on the way out the door. The nurse who will do the insemination is already our favorite for being a woman without a filter. She has glow-in-the-dark rubber sperms clipped to her ID badge. She apologizes for the existence of the speculum. Tells us her son is engineering-minded and could probably invent a better solution to the speculum and she'd put him to the task if he weren't seven years old. She tells Brynn that there are thirteen million sperm in the vial she's about to use to inseminate her and Brynn confirms this is in fact the correct vial of sperm she'd like to be inseminated with.

After the insemination, she tells Brynn to lie still for about ten minutes. Then she asks Brynn if she wants to keep the vial.

"Yes?" Brynn says.

"I forgot to keep all my kids' stuff," the nurse says, "and now they ask where it is." She leaves.

"No one asked me that the last times," Brynn says, still lying on the table. "About the vial."

"You could turn it into a Christmas ornament," I say. "Hang it on the tree every year and reminisce."

Brynn laughs. "Or I could keep it in a drawer somewhere and take it out when they want to do anything and say, 'Why don't you ask your father about that?'"

I am wheezing I am laughing so hard.

If you are waiting for me to tell you how the story of my going to the fertility clinic comes together with the story of the man who drove me through the park in lilac season with the story of whether or not I want to keep my tits, you are missing the point.

I will not bring these threads together for you.

I will not bring them together for myself.

It took *so much work* for me to separate them. And I won't put them back together for the sake of being narratively satisfying. Because to disentangle the threads of the story of love and lovers, and living, and parenthood, and myself, lets me makes space for each to get what it needs.

If you are feeling unsatisfied that I am not tying these threads together for you, because I am insisting on treating each thing on its own, because I am not resolving things, ask yourself: Who told you these things went together? What stories were you told, and not told, about the shape of love, the shape of yourself, the shape of a happy life?

Listen, I'm not even going to tell you whether or not Brynn got pregnant that day we went to the clinic.

What were you told had to happen in a story for it to feel complete?

I'm not going to tell you because I don't want you to pay attention to that. What I want you to pay attention to is this: in the parking lot that day, after the insemination, I said, "Maybe I should take a picture of you?" Brynn laughed. She took the empty sperm vial from my purse and I took a picture of her standing in the parking lot, in front of a blooming shrub, squinting into the sun and smiling in a laughing way, holding out the vial.

Later, when I texted her the picture, I wrote: EVIDENCE OF STOPS ALONG THE WAY!

And Brynn wrote: A THING HAPPENED!

This trying, wondering, choosing, *is the thing*.

I'm trying to tell you to look at this photo of Brynn I am showing you. Don't think about what it might mean later. Think about what this photo means all on its own.

———

I am making peace with my tits. I am finding ways for lovers to touch and squeeze them that make me pleased they are still here. I am marking my body with tattoos and putting little gold rings in my nose and golden beads in my ears because they please me, and I do not care what some imaginary someone might think of them. And maybe someday I will be a pregnant person, in this body, or a mother, in this body or not. And maybe someday I will get surgery and my body will look a new way, with scars, and those scars will be evidence of my work to shape my own happiness in this body, which is mine. In shaping this life. Which is mine. And if and when I meet more new and good people who can accept the shape of my body, the shape of my life, recognize that they please me, and feel happy for me, they are the ones I will welcome, welcome, welcome, into some sort of reciprocal embrace.

Siberian Watermelon

Here is a memory my father tells me:

It's 1960-something. He is in high school geometry. His teacher approaches the chalkboard and draws a circle. He has drawn hundreds of circles in his lifetime and does this without care. After he's drawn it, though, he steps back from the board and stares. The class, my father, they see it, too.

"That's a *perfect* circle," someone says.

The class applauds.

And at the end of the session, they don't erase it. They leave it on the board for the rest of the school year. A dusty patch of unclean slate surrounding the circle.

That's it. The whole memory, as my father tells it.

Here's how a fiction writer like me might ruin that story. On a day something awful has happened to our protagonist, his Little League team lost a big game, say, and ruined a winning streak, he sneaks into the room and wipes the circle away.

Or how about this: the teacher who made the circle dies tragically in, I don't know, a car accident, or maybe he kills himself. And then, when a substitute arrives to teach his class, she tries to erase the perfect circle. The students rush to preserve it, a legacy. Or maybe they don't. Maybe they watch her wipe it away, the circle gone without a trace.

My father would hate these stories. In fact, if either of these versions of events had actually happened, I bet he never even would have told me about it.

The actual circle story isn't even a story, really; it's just a detail, a moment. Which is why my father tells it. Because while *I'm* always fishing around for drama, for a shapely narrative, he prefers this perfect little stand-alone circle of a non-story. And that's so, so, *him*.

I am obsessed with Charles Baxter's essay "Regarding Happiness." A fellow creative writing teacher, Baxter writes: "[T]he students in class complain that the texts they have been assigned to read are 'depressing.' The stories are 'morbid.' Their endings are 'sad.' Sometimes the students become more aggressive in their pursuit of good cheer. 'Why,' they ask, 'can't we read some novels and stories about happiness?'"

I relate to this anecdote. I teach a lot of different kinds of authors and writing in my own undergraduate workshops. I thought my readings were diverse in most of the important ways. But then one day a student made a handout for her story presentation and at the top of it was a version of the crying Selena Gomez meme she'd made to say:

TFW PROF. HAUSER ASSIGNS ANOTHER
STORY ABOUT DEATH

She wasn't wrong.

So Baxter gives the people what they want. He assigns them Hemingway's "Big Two-Hearted River," in which, as Baxter tells us, "Nick Adams tramps his way to a river, where he fishes for trout and for eleven pages is guardedly happy and then blissful." The effect on Baxter's students is underwhelming. They say, "There's no story." Or: "Where's the plot?" Or: "Nothing happens."

His response: "Didn't you ask for a story about happiness? Well, here it is."

I'm pretty sure my father's circle story is about happiness.

And for most of my life I would have been like Baxter's students, and found it dull, without action. But I've started to think that, if I could become a person who loves the circle story, who loves Nick Adams's fishing, if I could make my life a little more like these stories, even, I might be happier. I'm starting to think that living a dramatic, story-worthy life and happiness are, at worst, mutually exclusive, and, at best, giving each other a run for their money.

I was a teenager when I first read Emerson, and I had to look up a lot of the words he used, but it was *naturlangsamkeit* that almost killed me:

> Respect the *naturlangsamkeit* which hardens the ruby in
> a million years, and works in duration, in which Alps and
> Andes come and go as rainbows. The good spirit of our
> life has no heaven which is the price of rashness. Love,
> which is the essence of God, is not for levity, for the
> total worth of man. Let us not have this childish luxury
> in our regards, but the austerest worth; let us approach
> our friend with an audacious trust in the truth of his

heart, in the breadth, impossible to be overturned, of his foundations.

"The slowness of natural development" was what I came by as a definition, when I looked it up. Or, more literally: "nature-slowness." And immediately I thought: *Dad*.

My father is a gardener. Not professionally, but spiritually. I say this not to tell you that he keeps a garden, or that he does the work of growing plants and food—I mean this as a matter of identity. He *is* a gardener. My favorite photograph of my father: he is in dirty jeans returning from the garden. Uplifted in his fists are two enormous bunches of harvested carrots. They are elegant roots, festooned with luxurious, frilly, plumage.

I cannot tell you how many times I have toured my father's garden over the years. He will offer you a tour no matter what time of year it is. It would not occur to him that, say, a blank bed of black soil is not something to see. Because seeds have been planted. This is the site of future green beans, future tomatillos, future beets, and, especially, future tomatoes with fantastic names like Mr. Stripey, and Black Krim, and Mortgage Lifter.

These gardens of my father's, he plans them out. There is no freestyling. He draws them on graph paper, in pencil. *Only* ever graph paper, only ever mechanical pencil. (Incidentally, for as long as I can remember, my sister and I have asked our father whether there's anything in particular he might like for his birthday or Christmas, and without fail, he always responds, with a mix of earnestness and cheek, that he could use "a few more mechanical pencils.")

I also keep a garden. I have a generationally diluted aptitude and patience for it. But gardening, for me, is as much about enjoying feeling close to my father, about thinking about him when he is far away, about trying to think more *like* him, as it is about gardening itself.

Here, in my late thirties, I want to learn his nature-slowness. This, for me, is a change. It is the opposite of the kinds of drama that used to make me feel reassuringly alive. But I think I'm finally getting it. This kind of living isn't the absence of story or of life. It's just a story happening so slowly you can't really see it taking place. It's something that is plodding along, changing, and growing at such a rate that most people lose interest in it. But I think it's there. I think it's possible. And if such happiness exists, I believe it is a slow-growing thing. I think that sustained, lived-in happiness, to the naked eye, might look a lot like stillness.

The first time I heard the circle story I thought of it like this:

One day someone randomly drew a really good circle.

But now I'd rather think of it like this:

You can spend your whole life drawing blackboard circles and then, one day, after all those hours have been logged, there is one moment of perfection that you've been slowly building toward this whole time. And everyone notices. And everyone says: *It is good.* And it's okay that it's only a moment because that one circle contains in it all the past circles, too. That moment was always already happening, even if it didn't feel like it at the time.

It is not only students who find us writers so depressing.

Our parents also find us inexplicably morbid.

My father has said to me, more than once, that he wishes I would write something lovely and funny. "You're very lovely and funny in real life," he says, "but that's not the sort of thing you write!"

In "Regarding Happiness," it is Baxter's mother who introduces the question of happiness and storytelling:

"'I just have this one question,' she said, digging for a cigarette in a mostly empty pack. . . . 'My question is, when are you going to write a happy poem?'

"Thirty-seven years later, I cannot remember what I replied, but I hope I didn't say what probably occurred to me: 'Well, okay, when I'm happy, *then* I'll write a happy poem.'"

What I hope I did not tell my father was: *When I have enough distance to laugh at the world we seem to be living in, then I'll write something lovely and funny.* What I hope I did not say to him was: *But I am writing about love. And that's not what a love story is.*

I don't know, he might have said back, if I'd replied, already going back to doing the Sunday *Times* crossword, in pen. *It just seems like you could try.*

What to make of these parental wishes? I think it has less to do with art than it does with what they fear might be true of us. The way our expectations for what a story, what a life, should be makes us seem strange, or sad, or far-distant from the children we once were. Or, perhaps, far-distant from the generation that raised us.

This summer I planted something called a Siberian watermelon. I live so far north that my growing season is too short to grow regular watermelons without a greenhouse, and so I ordered some seeds to grow these round little melons with orangey-coral insides. A fruit meant for short summers, presumably developed for the growing of watermelons in Siberia, either practically or metaphorically. If I'm honest, I also ordered the seeds for their name. There is something so *lovely* about the name. Impossible, frivolous sweetness in the same breath as the difficult reality of weather and the world.

This was summer 2020, my watermelon summer, our pandemic summer, and I had not been able to see my father in months. With so much time at home, I'd decided this was the year I would do my garden properly. I started out, as he would have, with graph paper. A drawing. I stood in the ruins of last year's garden, the tomato cages still up, dead plants crookedly testifying to my lack of care, a thing my father would never do. But never mind, never mind. I drew the existing beds. Then I drew the new beds I wanted to build. Then I remembered that one of last year's beds had been a failure because it was too close to the house, so I made plans to migrate it. Then I remembered that last year's tomatoes had done better in the beds that were double tall. I sketched out a new arrangement of beds. Calculated how much lumber I'd need for the new one. How much dirt to top up the old beds and fill the fresh ones. I tried to learn from all the years of mistakes that had come before, even as I was sure I was making new ones.

My graph-paper-and-pencil drawing looked a lot like my father's orderly sketches of perennial beds and vegetable troughs. But then, my mother's genes flaring within me, I stuck on little neon stickers to signify which plants would go in which beds, color-coded, rainbowy. I texted a picture of my map and plans to my father.

He replied: I HAVE A LEGACY!

Why is my father's request that I write something lovely and funny so anathema to the sort of writing I think I'm doing? Why can't happiness be worth some page time even if it's not dramatically compelling? Sometimes I tell myself that this is just how storytelling works. How love does. But then I remember the Sutherland Dunthorne Luck Index.

Ross Sutherland is a poet and playwright and an all-around gorgeous madman. He has this podcast called *Imaginary Advice* and the "Sutherland Dunthorne Luck Index" is my favorite episode. There's a running gag among his friend group that whenever something good happens to his friend fellow writer Joe Dunthorne, something bad happens to Ross. And so they devise a test to determine whether this is true. They go to a casino together. And sure enough, Joe wins some money and Ross loses all of his money. Theory proved! But then they talk about what happened in the casino. Ross asks Joe why he cashed out when he did, and Joe says it was because he'd won some money. He cashed out not because he was financially prudent but because he'd achieved a sort of narrative completeness: man goes to casino, plays cards, wins money, the end. Ross, on the other hand, had been up and down throughout the night, too, but he didn't stop playing. Not because he loved gambling but because, he sort of realizes as he's talking about this, the story of the night couldn't quite seem *over* to him until he'd lost all his money.

It had nothing to do with luck. It had to do with what kind of story expectations they were carrying around inside them. For Joe, the story he was in didn't feel over until something good had happened. For Ross, only losing everything could feel like the end.

The story rules are coming from inside the house.

And the house always wins.

For me, a love story isn't a love story unless there's huge feeling and drama. Unless there's a kind of active narrative through-line of good and bad fortune. Undramatic love isn't as flashy as grand romances and tragic, star-crossed some-things, and I have been choosing this dramatic, storified kind of love my whole life. I have been courting it, lingering in it overlong, even when it makes me unhappy. And I think that's my version of the Sutherland Dunthorne Luck Index. It has less to do with love and more to do with what I think love acts like.

And the thing is, this is so impossibly, terribly dumb, because the love of my father has been there, literally, my whole life. This love that isn't anything like the dramatic shapes I'd talked myself into thinking love requires. Isn't anything like the sorts of things I normally write about.

The very good and plainspoken fact of my father's love should have taught me this lesson long before now, but it didn't. Perhaps because we don't write stories about this kind of love. We seldom even write stories about good fathers. No drama. No need. What's there to tell?

This: my father has always loved me in ways I felt and knew and could rely on, and if that doesn't sound *radical* to you, doesn't seem worth writing about, you're wrong.

To have a person, any person, in this life, who offers you that kind of love is a goddamn miracle. It's more than most of us get.

I've decided that this is also a kind of love story. Maybe even the best one a person can hope for.

. . .

My dryer has been on the fritz lately. Or rather, my dryer has been on an inevitable march toward convalescence and an untimely demise and I have done nothing to stop it. As the interior fins have all rattled themselves off, the dryer became less a machine that dries clothes and more some hot womb in which damp clothes slip about for a time. The point is that somewhere along the way, my finless dryer gained the ability to produce *perfect lint balls*. I mean, I opened the dryer door, and a perfectly round, evenly gray ball popped out, felted but smooth, the size of a Ping-Pong ball.

I was obsessed with this lint ball.

So obsessed that I wanted to tell someone about it but then it occurred to me that probably no one wanted to hear about my perfect lint ball. *Telling someone about your lint balls* sounds like a euphemism for telling someone the most excruciatingly boring details of your life. But it was *so perfect*. It made me *so pleased*. And then I realized I knew someone who would appreciate its glory. I snapped a picture and sent it to my father.

THAT IS A PERFECT LINT BALL! he wrote.

ISN'T IT???

WHAT ARE YOU GOING TO DO WITH IT?

SAVE IT FOREVER, I wrote.

I sowed my Siberian watermelon seeds the last week of May. This was an optimistically early choice for the cruel, Narnian climate in which I live.

I sent my father a picture of the blank soil.

THIS WILL BE WATERMELONS, I said.

When the first curling tendril emerged from the ground,

I screamed and sent my father a picture. When the first buds were visible, I sent another. When the flowers opened, another. When a small nub of a thing that would someday be a watermelon appeared at the bud's center, another. Eventually, a watermelon the size of a shooting marble weighed down the leafy vine.

I must have sent my father dozens of photos of that little watermelon during our pandemic summer. They probably all looked the same, but they weren't. Something was always happening, too nature-slow for the narrative lens, but worthy of attention and celebration all the same. And my father understood this. Every time I sent him a watermelon picture he'd write back something lovely like GOOD WORK THERE, BUD.

It is winter again as I write to you, and maybe it's a good moment for embracing narratives that creep along less quickly than we'd like. My appreciation has grown for the slow and steady, for the small ever-present good, for the kind of love that is not easily tumbled by the elements, for the *boring*, even. These are the kind of stories and ways of being that are getting me through. These conversations with my father. These Siberian watermelons. The documentation of a small, sweet thing almost invisibly growing into an ever more perfect circle, into the possibility of a fruit we all could eat.

ACKNOWLEDGMENTS

This is the unlikeliest of books. I meant to go on inventing people and islands and ducks in fictional perpetuity and never write about myself at all. And I don't think I ever would have if quite a lot of people hadn't talked me into it. And if quite a lot more people, after I had done it a little, hadn't screamed, in a very lovely way, that I should do it a lot.

Some of those people may even have been you, dear reader. So thank *you* first. Because the reason I decided writing a book like this was a thing I wanted to do after all was that so many people seemed to want to talk about hard, messy, truthy, real-life shit after they read "The Crane Wife." And not even with me—with each other? And I sort of live for that. It made me feel like this book could be a tin can telephone to readers. That if I said some true things into a soup can over here at my house, there might be someone really waiting to hear them, echoing in their empty tin of peaches, on the other end of a trembling line.

To everyone who wrote me letters or happily yelped nice things about these early essays when they were first published: I wish I could have written back to every one of you and know that I was busily writing this book to you instead. And hi! I see you! And I read your letter. Thank you for your letter. I'm so grateful.

The process of creating this book was more collaborative than I could have dreamed. I am in awe of the hivemind of powerful, empathetic, funny women who made this book with me:

Lee Boudreaux: you are my favorite phone call to pick up because we are always laughing or screaming in the best possible way and truly no one else gets my shouty caps and exclams like you do. I am so grateful for your editorial brilliance and sheer elemental energy. Thank you for always approaching this book with curiosity—for treating it like a living, growing thing we might train up some lovely heretofore unimagined trellis together.

Isabel Wall: I cannot believe this book gets to swim across the sea to the U.K. From the moment we first spoke about the manuscript I knew I would be so lucky to have your mind and heart at work on this project with us. Your insights, your grace, your deep thinking about this work (and sometimes, my life!) has made it an infinitely better book. I am so glad to know you. Thanks upon thanks.

Meredith Kaffel Simonoff: I can hardly even turn to you on the page here without welling up with joy and gratitude for our friendship and the years we have spent working together. It feels a bit like the moment when Dorothy turns to the Scarecrow as she's about to board the balloon in Oz, which makes me cry every time because, like, *you most of all, friend. You most of all.* Karass-member. Champion of all humans you light your passionate heart upon. I am so lucky we are in cahoots and I admire the hell out of you. Thank you for helping me find a voice and the space to speak as myself. I am changed for it.

Good god there are too many other beloveds to list! I am the sort of person who would get the hook at the Oscars. But to be long-winded in one's gratitudes is to be a very lucky person indeed and I am such a one and so long-winded I must be:

I am so grateful to Bill Thomas for making Doubleday a place I am proud to call home.

Cara Reilly you are an absolute star and this book would not exist without you. I think we should start a cult with Courtney Barnett and the ghost of Katharine Hepburn.

Todd Doughty, you're an absolute dynamo and I'm so grateful

for your finesse and powers. (Also thanks to you and Emma Joss for telling me that the boat went last.)

Much gratitude to Elena Hershey, Lindsay Mandel, Rosie Safaty, Poppy North, and Alexia Thomaidis for shining their bright lights into the world so this book could find its way.

Gratitude to absolutely everyone at Doubleday and Viking UK and DeFiore and the Gernert Company who has helped to bring this project together.

Nadja Spiegelman and Emily Nemens and *The Paris Review:* you are the reason this book took flight.

Many of these essays were shaped by brilliant editors at their original outlets including Nadja Spiegelman, Celia Blue Johnson, Melissa Denes, and Jess Zimmerman. Emma Komlos-Hrobsky and Rob Spillman: thank you not only for editing and publishing "Blood," but also for getting me the press pass for the DARPA Robotics Trials. I'm sorry the essay took me eight years to write . . . I suppose I've missed my deadline.

I'm terrifically grateful to Colgate University for being such a wonderful home to me as a writer and teacher. Especially my writing colleagues: Peter Balakian, Jennifer Brice, and Greg Ames, whose work I admire so much. Special thanks as well to Constance Harsh, who has guided me through these past years with grace, and Brian Casey, who loves books.

I must say a particular thank you to Jennifer Brice: I feel certain I accidentally absorbed a master class on nonfiction by teaching the honors students alongside you—thank you for the steadying gift of your friendship, for being such a model of all things I hope to be, and for teaching me how to write this book along the way.

Brooke Ehrlich, queen B! Gentle warrior, maker of magic, absolute comrade: I am so grateful to you. Xo—Harriet

Monica Garwood and Emily Mahon and Charlotte Daniels: thank you for Sweaterboi and for sending this book out into the world looking better than I could have dreamed in its multiple fancy jackets.

Niki Keating: I am pretty sure the first snowy night I stumbled into your office zipped to my chin in defensive Carhartt gear I was mumbling about whether or not *therapy would change my art because did you know David Lynch doesn't believe in therapy because he thinks it changes a person's art and*—good god. My time with you *has* changed my art, and for the better. It opened the door to this book. Thank you, thank you.

Thank you to the Corporation of Yaddo and all the artists and folks who work for Yaddo I met during my weeks there who offered love and inspiration and baby carrots. This book became a book in the Breast Room.

Thank you to the Sewanee Writers' Conference for your support and for making the domain the place I always feel most myself as a writer. Thank you for bringing artists together in such an authentic and meaningful way.

Thank you to the Pocoapoco residency, and the city of Oaxaca, and everyone who banded together there in March 2020. Thank you for slowing me down and showing me love in a difficult time for us all. Also for the crickets, which were delicious. And the mezcal, which was necessary.

Thank you, Jeff and Lindsay and Jan and Warren and Earthwatch and everyone at the Aransas National Wildlife Refuge and the cranes and at least twenty pigs. I could never have imagined the time we spent together would have such an effect on my life to come, but it was always clear it was such a gift to have it precisely when I did.

Thank you to every author and artist whose work has helped me survive this life, but especially all the living artists whose work I talk about in these pages. Especially: Brian Christian, Ross Sutherland, and Charles Baxter. "Uncoupling" is indebted to Marie Howe's poem "Practicing." "The Two-Thousand-Pound Bee" is indebted to Melissa Febos's *Abandon Me.* Thank you Paige Lewis for lending your poetry to this book.

Thank you as ever to the Brooklyn College MFA program and

the Trout. Thank you as ever to the Florida State University PhD program, especially Mark Winegardner. Thank you, Janice Garvey, always, for *we few we merry few*. Thank you, Marie-Helene Bertino for being a surf babe. Thank you, Ndinda Kioko for our naked writers' residency. Thank you, Laura Mucha for a summer of research and humor. Thank you, Olivia Milch for becoming obsessed with birds. Thank you, Bishop for The Exchange. Thank you, Maria Dascălu for telling me about the Zeigarnik Effect. Thank you, Darcy and Heather and Kat and Bea and Briana and Morgan for wisdom about queer beginnings. Thank you, Jessie for the jazz. Thank you, Tonia Davis and Alex Pitz for believing in cranes. Thank you, Eric Simonoff and Kelly Farber for being dearest ones. Thank you, Cora, friend of my heart, for everything always. Thank you, Brynn for helping me create the Georgia O'Keeffe Womb Room and more. Thank you, Matthew for the lilac wine. Thank you, Andy and Joe for telling me about your childhood dream houses. Thank you, Jon Hickey and Edgar Paleo for talking to me about distortion pedals and fuzz even though three pages on the history of fuzz were ultimately deemed extraneous to this book. Thank you, James for four years so good they didn't need to be in this book at all. Thank you, Erik and Sheela for oysters and nostalgia. Thank you, Judy Jacklin for your memoir. Thank you, DARPA roboticists. Thank you, Special Agent Dana Scully. Thank you, Sullivan Street Fantasticks. Thank you, ghost of John Belushi. Thank you, ghost of Shirley Jackson. Thank you, ghost of Katharine Hepburn. Thank you, ghost of Daphne du Maurier.

The last time I wrote a book someone pointed out that it was very rude that I did not thank my dog, Moriarty, and *I* pointed out that he was illiterate. Even so, I am grateful for his fuzzy animal soul, so often found sighing with deep ennui as I spend yet another day at my desk instead of hiking the woods with him. I suppose I should also thank Mori for being on social media so that I don't have to be.

Thanks to all my chickens—dear students: your passion and reinventing and questioning of the world gives me the energy to keep doing the same.

Thanks especially to the chickens of The Write-In, who worked alongside me as I created this book. Special shout-out to the online pandemic Write-In squad who brought a little light to some pretty dark evenings.

Liv and Meg: thank you for letting me plagiarize your wedding for this book. And for showing me a love story it was easy to believe in.

Thank you to all the young humans who talked to me about their dream houses! You all helped to write this book. Thank you: Simon and Nora and Claire and Beata and Eli and Nina and Andy and Sabine and Juniper.

Thank you to all my families:

Thank you to my *amigas sin fronteras*: Marta Pérez-Carbonell and Monica Mercado and Laura Moure Cecchini, for love and for houseplants and for fury.

Thank you to the SUVs on 12b, for humor and solidarity and snacks and endless matching Carhartt overall firepits.

Thank you, Emily Alford and Charlie Beckerman and Olivia Wolfgang-Smith, The Firefeet, for being inspiring writer friends/my therapists/my astrologers and for creating the funniest and wisest writing I read every week, available only on my phone.

Teddy and Ro: You're too young to read this book. Put it down right now. I love you much.

Tom Hauser, Boo Hauser, Leslie Caputo, Pat Caputo, and Randall Joyce are all convinced everyone is going to think our family is a bunch of nuthatches when they read this book. Well, we are. And I love you all a lot. Thanks for living interesting fucking lives. Thanks for letting me write about us. Thanks for all the care, and listening, and storytelling, and moxie.

I am sending love across the mountains, via crackling walkie talkie, to the roving spirits of Ed and Maureen Joyce.

AUTHOR'S NOTE

This book is a work of personal nonfiction. These essays reflect my life, as I remember it, and the stories I've made of that life to understand how to keep living in it. In the interest of storytelling I've taken some of the liberties of the essay form: collapsing minor timelines, turning multiple conversations into one, stylizing the dialogue of, for example, kind nurses who certainly never said the word *tits,* and even imagining up the direct dialogue of characters like my great-grandfather for whose misadventures I was not present, owing to the fact I was not yet born.

I have changed the names of some people who appear in this book, especially those who are not part of my life these days. All of the relationships I talk about are here as part of larger stories I felt I wanted to tell—ones more to do with my own trouble navigating the world than any particular partnership. These are not full histories of these relationships. They're not intended to be. Much that was good and much more that was not has been left on the cutting room floor, but nothing has been invented.

Most of all, this is a book about the ways each of us shape our lives, and our understanding of them, through stories. I respect that there are likely many quantum-entangled alternate and complementary and divergent versions of the stories I tell. As many different versions as there are people in the book, probably. And those stories are just as real as these. They probably have fewer birds and robots in them too.

CONTENTS

& CONTENT WARNINGS

———◆———